D1518145

Linguistic Anthropology of Education

Linguistic Anthropology of Education

Edited by Stanton Wortham
and Betsy Rymes

Westport, Connecticut
London

Library of Congress Cataloging-in-Publication Data

Linguistic anthropology of education / edited by Stanton Wortham
  and Betsy Rymes.
      p. cm.
   Includes bibliographical references and index.
   ISBN 0-89789-823-0 (alk. paper)
    1. Language and education. 2. Anthropological linguistics. I. Wortham,
  Stanton Emerson Fisher, 1963- II. Rymes, Betsy.
  P40.8.L55 2003
  306.44'089—dc21   2002067941

British Library Cataloguing in Publication Data is available.

Library of Congress Catalog Card Number: 2002067941
ISBN: 0-89789-823-0

First published in 2003

Praeger Publishers, 88 Post Road West, Westport, CT 06881
An imprint of Greenwood Publishing Group, Inc.
www.praeger.com

Printed in the United States of America

The paper used in this book complies with the
Permanent Paper Standard issued by the National
Information Standards Organization (Z39.48-1984).

10 9 8 7 6 5 4 3 2 1

Contents

Linguistic Anthropology of Education

An Introduction

Stanton Wortham

In "Resituating the Place of Educational Discourse in Anthropology," Bradley Levinson (1999) argues that cultural anthropology could benefit from research on education and that research on education could benefit from anthropology as well. He describes how contemporary cultural anthropologists, following a "cultural studies" focus on media, have not attended sufficiently to the role schools play in cultural production and reproduction. He makes a strong case that topics of central interest to cultural anthropologists—like globalization, post-coloniality, and the cultural production of identity—could be illuminated by research on educational contexts and processes.

"Globalization," for instance, refers to the increasingly global political economy; to the increasingly global movement of people, ideas, and objects; and to the increasingly common disjuncture between individuals' places of residence and their places of cultural identification (Appadurai, 1996). Levinson points out that schools are important sites of both clashes and congruence between global and local. The educational institution itself often brings culturally alien objects and practices from elsewhere in the world, and imported curricula embody globalized ideas that students and teachers incorporate and struggle with. If contemporary cultural anthropologists expanded their focus beyond media and included educational institutions more centrally in their ethnographic work, they would discover data that speak to central concerns like globalization.

In addition to what educational research can bring anthropology, Levinson also argues that anthropology can help educational research. Anthropologists have always been attuned to education that takes place in families, in apprenticeships, in rituals and other out-of-school contexts. Because school-based education always works alongside and is in important ways derived from these "informal" educational processes, an anthropological perspective can provide important data to help us understand schools.

This volume begins to do with linguistic anthropology what Levinson envisions for cultural anthropology. Contemporary work in linguistic anthropology can both benefit from and contribute to educational research. Educational institutions play a central role in processes important to linguistic as well as cultural anthropologists. A society's beliefs about language—as a symbol of nationalism, a marker of difference, or a tool of assimilation—are often reproduced and challenged through educational institutions. Linguistic anthropologists have also become centrally concerned with ideologies of language, with people's beliefs about how different ways of speaking both identify and create sociocultural categories (Schieffelin, Woolard, & Kroskrity, 1998). Educational institutions are not the only place language ideologies get created and implemented, but they are surely an important site.

Research on education can also benefit from linguistic anthropology. The learning and socialization that occur through education are mediated primarily through language. Linguistic anthropologists have studied not only how particular ways of speaking become vehicles for sociocultural categorization, but also how close attention to naturally occurring speech can provide insight into central processes such as learning and socialization. The chapters in this volume illustrate how contemporary linguistic anthropology has developed important concepts that can illuminate a wide range of educational phenomena.

AN EARLIER GENERATION

Contemporary linguistic anthropology of education shares Levinson's project of enriching educational research by using concepts from (linguistic) anthropology and vice versa. Given the centrality of language as both object and medium of culture, adding linguistic anthropology should provide important support for Levinson's project as well. However, although cultural anthropology and related disciplines did produce a few important studies of schooling and culture in the 1970s and 1980s (e.g., Bourdieu & Passeron, 1977; Willis, 1981), few cultural anthropologists have been centrally concerned with formal education. In linguistic anthropology, on the other hand, there has been an extensive body of work done on educational practices and institutions—primarily by Dell Hymes, John Gumperz, and their colleagues (e.g., Cazden, John & Hymes, 1972; Gumperz, 1982; Heath, 1983; Hymes, 1996; Michaels, 1981; Philips, 1983). This earlier work has laid the foundation for a contemporary linguistic anthropology of education.

Hymes and colleagues drew on several concepts from linguistic anthropology in their work on education. In this introduction I review seven of these concepts, divided into two groups. The first three—communicative competence, taking the native's point of view, and the connection between micro and macro—were extensively elaborated by Hymes and colleagues. The remaining four concepts—indexicality, creativity, regimentation, and poetic structure—were also present in earlier work, but they have been elaborated more fully in contemporary linguistic anthropology. This section discusses the first three concepts, and the remainder of the introduction addresses the last four.

First, Hymes and his colleagues maintained linguists' emphasis on precise analyses of various linguistic structures, but they applied these to study language *in use*. As defined by Hymes (1972), Duranti (1997), and others, linguistic anthropology takes advantage of linguists' discoveries about phonology and grammar, but it studies how grammatical categories are used in communicative practices. Linguistic anthropology of education studies speakers as social actors, not as repositories of linguistic competence. So Hymes (1972) and his colleagues were interested in communicative competence, the ability to use language appropriately in cultural context. As I argue later, the concept of communicative competence does have a central problem, but contemporary linguistic anthropologists of education nonetheless follow Hymes in studying the social presuppositions and consequences of language in use.

Second, linguistic anthropologists of education in the 1970s and 1980s also maintained the central anthropological emphasis on understanding the native's point of view. Unlike contemporaneous work that also studied linguistic action (e.g., Searle, 1969), Heath (1983), Philips (1983), and others did extensive ethnographic work and described how linguistic patterns were understood by the people they studied. Contemporary linguistic anthropology follows this principle—refusing to accept outsider models of people's categories, and instead insisting on evidence that people themselves explicitly or implicitly recognize the categories that we use to describe their communicative behavior.

Third, Hymes and colleagues also connected particular instances of language use to larger social patterns. They did not analyze particular texts for their own sake, but rather to understand larger processes that might be occurring through the language use. The best known instance is the "difference" or "mismatch" hypothesis, which tries to explain schools' role in social reproduction as a result of mismatched majority and minority cultural styles of speaking that clash in the classroom (e.g., Michaels, 1981; Philips, 1983). According to this theory, ethnic and class differences in access to resources are unintentionally reproduced by schools, when majority teachers misrecognize minority styles of speaking as intellectual deficits. At the same time as they gave accounts such as the "mismatch" one, which connected culturally embedded speech to larger social processes, early linguistic anthropologists of education also paid close attention to the details of particular interactions. Instead of ignoring particular contexts and treating instances as mechanical replications of larger patterns, they began to describe the interplay between larger social processes and the particular contexts in which they are enacted and sometimes transformed.

These three concepts—studying linguistic patterns in use, searching for the native's point of view, and trying to connect micro- and macro-level processes—remain central to contemporary linguistic anthropology of education. In addition to applying these three concepts from linguistic anthropology to educational research, Hymes, Gumperz, and their colleagues also began to use several other concepts that have become central to contemporary linguistic anthropology of education. I describe these concepts in detail in the next sections, under the terms indexicality, creativity, regimentation, and poetic structure. In the last decade, contemporary linguistic anthropology has extended these concepts in ways not available to Hymes, Gumperz, and their colleagues (cf., e.g., Hill & Irvine, 1992; Lucy, 1993; Silverstein & Urban, 1996).

This volume illustrates how contemporary linguistic anthropology of education can now return productively to the strategy begun thirty years ago by the earlier generation, with respect to several concepts that were not yet fully articulated then. We can use productive concepts from contemporary linguistic anthropology—concepts that have not yet penetrated educational research—both to enrich our work on educational processes and to illustrate how research on education illuminates issues of central concern to linguistic and cultural anthropology. The next sections describe these concepts, and the other chapters in this volume illustrate how they can be applied productively to educational research.

A CLASSROOM EXAMPLE

To introduce the concepts of indexicality, creativity, regimentation, and poetic structure, it will help to have an example. This section introduces an example drawn from a two-year study of high school English and history classes. Space limitations prevent a full analysis of these data here, but I have provided more detail elsewhere (Wortham, 1994, 1996, 1997). This case centers around a classroom "participant example." A participant example describes some actual or hypothetical event that includes at least one person also participating in the classroom conversation.

All speech refers to and characterizes something, and all speech takes place in and contributes to some interaction. The linguistic forms actually uttered communicate information about both what I will call the "narrated event" and the "narrating event" (following and slightly modifying Jakobson, 1971). Speech about participant examples describes a particular type of narrated event: some actual or hypothetical event that includes at least one individual who is also participating in the narrating event. Those with a role in the example have *two* interactionally relevant identities: as a teacher or student in the classroom conversation (narrating), and as a character in the event described as the example (narrated).

This participant example occurred in a ninth grade history class. The class has read Cicero's letter to Atticus, in which Cicero ponders what he should do about the tyranny of Caesar and the plot to overthrow him. Should he tell Caesar? Should he join the plotters? Or should he just keep quiet? In this respect, the text describes a three-part role structure in Rome: Caesar the tyrant, those plotting against him, and Cicero stuck between the two. The teacher, Mr. Smith, presents his participant example to illustrate Cicero's dilemma. (See the Appendix, page 27, for transcription conventions).

```
        T/S: Maurice let's give a good example, you'll love this.
             suppose this dictator, me. there was a plot going on.
150     and you found out about it. and you knew it was gonna-
             it's existing (3.0) among the people you knew. would
             you tell me. (5.0)
             MRC: you said they know about it.
             T/S: the plotters, against me. they're planning to push me
155     down the stairs. [   and you know about it
             STS:              [hnhhahahaha
             T/S: now we all know Maurice and I have ha(hh)d
             arguments all year. would you tell me about it.
             MRC: well- I might but uh what if they- what if they found
160     out that I told you then they want to kill me. (5.0) so I'm
             putting myself in trouble to save you, and I'm not going to
             do it.
             STS: hnh hahahaha
```

The example describes a role structure analogous to that in Rome: Mr. Smith the hypothetical tyrant, the conspirators plotting to push him down the stairs, and Maurice the potential informer stuck between the two.

Figure 1-1 represents the classroom discussion at this point. The embedded rectangles represent the two realms described as narrated events: the situation in Rome, with the tyrant, the plotters, and the potential informer; and the example, with three analogous groups. The outer rectangle represents the narrating classroom interaction among teachers and students. Mr. Smith has already presupposed his "argumentative" relationship with Maurice (see line 157, and the discussion below), and the line between them represents this. The other students are not yet occupying any salient interactional positions other than the standard classroom role of students.

Speech about participant examples often has important implications for interactional positioning in the narrating event. While discussing participants' characters in an example, speakers inevitably attribute certain social attributes to those (narrated) characters. Participant examples can have rich interactional implications because characteristics attributed to participants' characters in the example often have implications for those participants' own interactional positions in the narrating event.

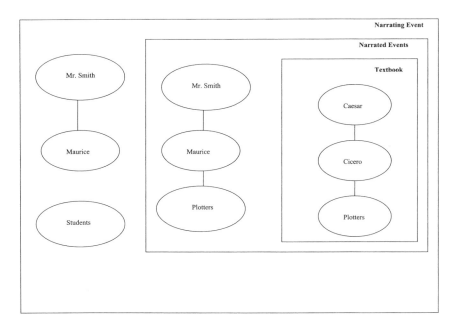

Figure 1-1. Introducing the participant example.

For instance, by asking whether Maurice would (hypothetically) side with him, against the student plotters, Mr. Smith may be raising an interactional question: is Maurice on the teacher's side or not? This could be an important interactional question in this classroom, because of Maurice's liminal position. Classroom conversation among these students in both their English and their history class has been dominated all year by the girls. None of the other boys volunteers information in class. They only speak when called on, and then tersely. Being male in this context seems to require silence. The teachers have tried both to entice and to force the boys into participating, but almost all of them have resisted. Maurice is the one exception. He has intelligent things to say, and he often participates in class. But he also sits in the back with the rest of the boys, and he clearly wants their respect as well. So Maurice faces the delicate task of maintaining his status as a "real" male while joining the girls and teachers in classroom discussion. In this context, when Mr. Smith asks Maurice whether he would side with him, the teacher, against the student "conspirators," the discussion might have implications for Maurice's own in-between position, which is analogous in some ways to Cicero's.

We cannot conclude at this early point in the discussion that Maurice's own interactional position is in fact relevant. But the possibility has been opened up, such that later discussion can presuppose and strengthen the parallel between Maurice's hypothetical position as a potential informer and his actual position as a boy caught between a desire to do well in school and his peers' injunctions against this.

Immediately after the example gets introduced, Mr. Smith does mark a potential connection between the example and his own (narrating) relationship with Maurice. At line 157, Mr. Smith says "now we all know Maurice and I have ha(hh)d arguments all year" (the (hh) indicates laughter breaking into the words while speaking). Before the example, everyone in the class knows that Mr. Smith and Maurice have had a strained relationship. Mr. Smith holds students to a relatively rigid code of conduct, and Maurice has resisted this all year. Most other students acquiesce, withdraw sullenly, or misbehave in a teasing way. But Maurice's resistance seems more of a genuine struggle for power.

As shown in line 157, and also in his "you'll love this" at line 148, Mr. Smith recognizes his power struggle with Maurice. He mentions it at this point because he *also* recognizes that the (narrated) example may have implications for their actual relationship. It gives Maurice the opportunity, within the example, to express his anger at Mr. Smith-the-teacher. Maurice takes this opportunity, in places, by imagining that he would leave Mr. Smith-the-hypothetical-tyrant to be killed.

I argue that, in discussion of this example, Maurice's own interactional position—caught between the teachers and the resistant boys—becomes increasingly salient and awkward. As it becomes increasingly presupposed that Maurice's hypothetical decision about whether to side with Mr. Smith has implications for Maurice's own interactional position in the classroom, the discussion becomes increasingly uncomfortable for Maurice. We begin to see this in the following segment:

```
        T/S: well that was my next question, do you think Caesar was
              a tyrant.[              do you think Cicero thought=
185     ST?:              [I don't think so.
        T/S: =Caesar was a tyrant.
        ST?: no
        MRC: yes
        T/S: then what's his problem. if the man- you just told me
190     point blank [ that we could be pushed down stairs=
        MRC:       [so.
        T/S: =and you wouldn't feel a thing about it. what's his big
        deal, if he believes Caesar is a tyrant, so what.
        MRC: well- he- if u:h he [ 4 syll ] that they're making
195     some kind of plot against him, but he doesn't want to get involved.
        He doesn't know if he should get involved, he could get himself in
        more trouble. since he's already [ 3 syll ]=
        T/S: well if Caesar's a tyrant why shouldn't you get
        involved. tyrants are generally dictatorial nasty people,
200     that prevent peo:ple from being at their ease.
```

When Mr. Smith says "you just told me point blank that we could be pushed down stairs and you wouldn't feel a thing about it" (lines 189–192), both the volume and tempo of his speech increase. He seems angry. Even though they are speaking about the example, Mr. Smith-the-teacher treats Maurice's choice not to tell him as a betrayal. (Mr. Smith uses "we" here, because the other teacher in the classroom, Mrs. Bailey, has by now been included with him as another hypothetical tyrant, within the example).

This starts to put the same sort of pressure on Maurice himself that was applied to Cicero and to Maurice in his hypothetical role as a potential informer. Note that Maurice's characterization of Cicero's hesitation (lines 194–198) could apply to Maurice-the-student's own situation. He can tell that his answer does not please Mr. Smith-the-teacher, but he does not know what to do about it.

Indexicality

Although the analysis of this example is necessarily truncated here (cf. Wortham, 1994, 1995, for more detail), it can help introduce the second set of concepts central to contemporary linguistic anthropology of education. The central issue in contemporary linguistic anthropology is: how do linguistic signs come to have meaning in cultural and interactional context?

To answer this question, it helps to use a distinction made by Peirce, between "indexes" and "symbols." A sign represents its object indexically if the sign and the object co-occur, such that the sign points to the object (Peirce, 1897/1955). The linguistic form *I* provides an example, as it refers by pointing to the individual uttering the form itself in the narrating event. A sign represents its object symbolically if that type of sign is connected to a type of object, such that a token of that type of sign represents that type of object. The verb *go*, for instance, refers to an event where the subject moves away from some presupposed place.

Despite extraordinary efforts to describe natural language use as primarily symbolic (by Saussure, 1916; Chomsky, 1965; and many others), it has turned out that much of everyday speech gets its meaning indexically (e.g., Garfinkel, 1967; Hanks, 1990; Silverstein, 1976). Both *I* and *go*, for instance, contribute to what gets denoted by an utterance only if speaker and hearer presuppose important knowledge about the context—namely, who is speaking at the moment, in the case of *I*, and where the presupposed point is, away from which the subject is/should/might be moving, in the case of *go*. In a more complex case like the preceding classroom example, we need extensive contextual information to understand what the speech contributed both to denotational and interactional meanings (i.e., both to narrated and narrating events). For instance, to understand Cicero's predicament, we need to understand the source of tyrants' power and the often secretive nature of conspiracies. And we need to understand Maurice's position as a male student caught between the resistant boys and the teachers before we can see how the example presupposes and intensifies this awkward position.

Given that linguistic signs are indexical as well as symbolic (i.e., that the meanings of verbal signs always depend in part on how those signs presuppose aspects of the context as relevant) analysts of language have faced a choice. Some have chosen to abstract away from contextualized speech and to study the purely symbolic aspects of language. Chomsky (1965), for instance, does this by studying "deep structure" instead of empirically occurring speech. This strategy has yielded many important insights into grammatical categories, because some aspects of human language do seem to operate independent of context.

But this strategy leaves open the question of how such decontextualized categories operate when they are actually used. Real speech has meaning through simultaneous indexical and symbolic processes. In other words, decontextualized meanings compose part of what actual speech communicates, but context-dependent, indexical meanings are also always essential to interpreting an utterance. The discipline of linguistic anthropology has been one important site for studying how symbolic and indexical processes work together to produce meaning in cultural context. As mentioned previously, linguistic anthropology studies language in use, not linguistic structure for its own sake. Because they take advantage of linguists' discoveries about (symbolic) grammatical categories but examine how these categories are used in communicative practices, linguistic anthropologists are particularly well placed to study intersections between symbolic and indexical processes.

For instance, linguistic anthropologists of education would borrow grammatical analyses of personal pronouns—"participant and nonparticipant deictics," if one wants to borrow the jargon as well—to study cases like the preceding one. We know that in English a singular referent can be referred to with the deictics *I, you, he, she* or *it*. We know that each of these presupposes a different model of the narrating event, identifying the referent as playing different roles in that event. *You* presupposes that the referent is the addressee, while *he* and *she* presuppose that the referent is not participating in the narrating event. As the classroom discussion of Maurice's (hypothetical and not-so-hypothetical) predicament continues, pronouns do an important job. We can see this in the following excerpt.

As described previously, Maurice-the-student has begun to occupy Maurice-the-potential informer's role, as it is described in the narrated event: he is getting caught between someone in power (the teacher) and others who oppose the teacher. In the narrating event itself, the other (oppositional) group includes male students who typically sit in the back of the classroom and refuse to participate. We have here an emerging parallel between the narrated and narrating events. Cicero was caught between those in power and those opposing the powerful. In the hypothetical example, Maurice was caught between the teachers and the students who opposed them. And in the narrating event, Maurice is getting caught between the teachers and the unresponsive male students.

In the excerpts presented above, however, Mr. Smith may simply have been play-acting to involve the students. And Maurice himself may not really have been at risk interactionally. But Maurice's problems become more serious, and the parallel between narrated and narrating events becomes more robust, in the following segment—when several girls volunteer to tell the teachers about the plot. (T/B is Mrs. Bailey, the other teacher leading the discussion.)

```
        T/S:    gee you sound terribly confused Maurice. sort of like
                Cicero here.
        T/B:    what w- if you knew that they actually- you know
                there's a group of kids that are actually going to do: this
225             dastardly deed. and you know that there's going to be
                some reaction. what might you do th- and you kn- you
                know basically wh:ile you might not be-, enamored totally
                of Mr. Smith or myself you- basically: don't wish that we
                were crippled for life or whatever, what might
230             you do that day. you know that's going to come- that
                this is all going to happen on Wednesday. what are you
                going to do that day.
        CAN:    I would try to warn you.
        STS:    right. I would ((* overlapping [ comments *))
235     T/B:                                [ he's- he's not- he's not
                going to warn us though.
        T/S:    no.
        T/B:    what- what are you going to do that day Maurice. (1.0)
        MRC:    stay away. [ 2 syll ]
240     T/B:    what are you going to do?
        MRC:    I'm going to stay away so I won't be- be:=
        T/B:    so you're not going to come to school on Wednesday.
        MRC:    °no°
        CAN:    that way he's a coward.
245     ST?:    what would you do.
        MRC:    what would you do.
        T/S:    a coward.
        CAN:    yeah 'cause he's scared.
```

At lines 233–4, Candace and then other girls affiliate with the teachers,
within the example. In the narrated event, this adds another interactional group—loyal subjects. In the narrating event, when Candace and
then Mr. Smith call Maurice a coward (lines 244ff.), she begins to speak
as Candace-the-student and not just as a hypothetical Roman. Her
energetic tone here indicates that she is not only elaborating the example, but also picking on Maurice himself in the narrating classroom
interaction. This establishes another group in the narrating event—the
girls—who position themselves with respect to Maurice and the teachers. Like their characters in the example, in the classroom the girls
affiliate with the teachers and exclude Maurice.

   Gender plays an important interactional role here, as in many ninth
grade classrooms. Girls and boys generally occupy separate, often
antagonistic groups. Girls typically have more latitude to affiliate with
teachers without damaging their standing with other students. Boys act
more oppositionally toward teachers, and risk losing face if they do not.
Thus the girls have intensified Maurice's interactional predicament in

the narrating event. He might like to affiliate with Mr. Smith-the-ty-rant—and thus, implicitly, with Mr. Smith-the-teacher—since he may have aroused Mr. Smith-the-teacher's anger by distancing himself. But to do so, he would have to affiliate with both the teachers and the girls. This would damage his standing with the other boys.

Figure 1-2 represents the classroom discussion at this point. Candace's comment has inserted herself and other girls into the (nar-rated) participant example. Now Mr. Smith-the-tyrant has loyal sub-jects who would warn him of the plot. In the (narrating) classroom interaction, Candace and the girls have analogously inserted them-selves between the teacher and Maurice. This puts more pressure on Maurice to choose between the resistant boys and the girls aligned with the teacher.

Like Maurice-the-potential informer, and like Cicero, Maurice him-self gets excluded by the other groups as he thinks about what to do. We can see this exclusion in a pattern of pronoun usage. For most of the remaining discussion, other speakers exclude Maurice from the conver-sation, referring to him as *he*, whereas before they had referred to him as *you*. This shift from *you* to *he* establishes a different organization for the narrating interaction. Maurice himself started out participating with the teachers in discussing the example. But immediately after

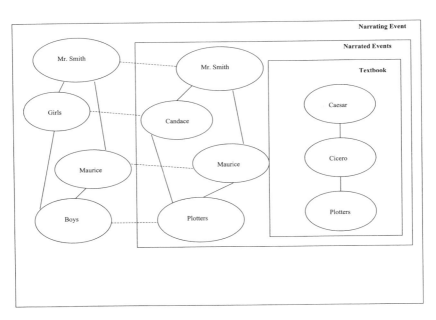

Figure 1-2. the participant example late in the discussion.

Candace has said that she, unlike Maurice, would warn the teachers about the plot, Mrs. Bailey and some of the girls start to exclude Maurice—talking about him as *he*. (They could have continued to refer to him as *you*, as they do while discussing Mr. Smith and Candace as characters in the hypothetical example.) This switch to *he* sends an interactional message: Maurice no longer belongs to the group that includes the teachers and female students in the narrating interaction. In both the narrated and narrating events, Maurice is caught on the outside.

To understand what this switch from *you* to *he* means, we need to have more than just a grammatical account of the pronouns. We also need to know why people like the female students might be excluding someone like Maurice and why this might be something Maurice cares about. All this information is signaled indexically. Thus a linguistic anthropological analysis draws on accounts of language as symbolic, but it supplements these accounts with analyses of how language also gets meaning from particular aspects of the context.

Creativity

The earlier generation of linguistic anthropologists also made this point, arguing that cultural context was essential to the meaning of particular utterances. Hymes (1972) developed the concept of communicative competence to expand the Chomskyan focus on grammatical competence, arguing that language always gets used in cultural context and that systematic aspects of speech are tuned to cultural contexts. This was important in maintaining linguistic anthropology as a viable field in the early days of the formalist revolution in linguistics. But the concept of communicative competence had another consequence.

Based on the analogy with grammatical competence, the concept of communicative competence presupposes that cultural groups have relatively stable styles of speaking—which are identified by characteristic phonological, grammatical, and pragmatic cues. Competent hearers identify members of their own linguistic community and make sense of utterances by attending to cues that are used in appropriate contexts. Michaels (1981), for instance, describes how some African-American narrators do not explicitly mark the transitions between events in a story or state the overall point of the story. When hearing a narrative told in this more "topic associating" style, African-American narrators from those communities will recognize it as competently produced and, all other things being equal, will identify the narrator as a member of their linguistic community. Hearers from linguistic communities with other conventions, however, may have trouble understanding the utterance and will often interpret the absence of explicit transitions and thesis statements as evidence that the narrator is not a member of their group. In school, as Michaels showed, this can lead mainstream Anglo teachers to the mistaken conclusion that some African-American students are not only different but also deficient.

The concept of communicative competence, then, presupposes a style of speaking shared among a cultural group and a set of rules that stipulate which linguistic cues (phonological, grammatical, pragmatic) are appropriate in which contexts. Despite the power of this perspective, it cannot fully explain how people use and interpret language. Two types of argument have been made against communicative competence theories. The first relies on what Prague School linguists call "foregrounding" (Havránek, 1932/1955). Rules of communicative competence say that, given the appropriate presupposed contextual features, a given type of utterance will count as appropriate for a member of a particular cultural group. But any such regularity can be deliberately disregarded to generate an interactional effect. Speakers regularly utter forms in inappropriate contexts and achieve definite effects. One can use overly colloquial speech in a formal setting, for instance, in a bid to achieve solidarity with someone or to make an ironic comment on its pomposity.

Thus the analogy between interactionally effective and grammatical utterances breaks down, and ultimately it is the analogy with Chomsky (1965) that drives communicative competence theories. Violating a grammatical rule generates an incorrect structural type, but speakers often act contrary to pragmatic regularities and generate interactional effects. The competence theorist could propose a new rule for every effective "inappropriate" use. But such an explanatory strategy gets awkward quickly, and it seems unlikely that people carry around rules covering all possible foregrounded usages. Furthermore, any theory of linguistic action that depends heavily on rules must be incomplete, because no matter how many rules are proposed the last one can always be deliberately disregarded to achieve an interactional effect.

Contemporary critics of competence theories have reiterated the arguments made by the Prague School, and they have extended them (e.g., Goffman, 1976; Levinson, 1981). Linguistic forms can be uttered in appropriate contexts but yield unexpected results. Some aspect of a context unforeseen by the rule can always be made salient so as to negate or to transform the expected effect of an utterance—as when hearers catch the irony of a comment only by noting some anomalous aspect of the context. A new rule can be written to explain each exception, but this gets awkward quickly and can never be sufficient. An indefinite number of potentially relevant aspects of the context can be made salient in any given case. Because communicative competence theories describe only relatively generic contextual factors, they cannot explain the subtle ways that particular contextual features can become relevant to and change the interactional functions of utterances in practice.

These critics of competence theories present a different picture of verbal interaction. Instead of following rules to make their utterances both grammatical and appropriate to particular cultural contexts, speakers deploy cues that could have multiple meanings and hearers must infer which of several possible messages the speakers are communicating. To be fair to Hymes (1972) and some of his colleagues, they did recognize that rules of communicative competence are sometimes inadequate to capture creative manipulations of cultural rules. They often described such manipulations in terms of "keying" (see also Goffman, 1974). But, with their continued emphasis on communicative competence, they did not develop adequate conceptualizations of how keying gets accomplished in practice. Contemporary work in linguistic anthropology has analyzed this process more fully.

A central shift in perspective has been to consider language use as creative, and not merely as reflecting social structure. Many sociolinguistic analyses (e.g., Labov, 1972) have studied how particular linguistic patterns correlate with presupposed social categories. As with communicative competence, such regularities undoubtedly exist and play an important role in social life. But speech does more than presuppose stable social groups and types of individual identities. In addition, speech can itself create novel social and interactional patterns. As described by Duranti (1997), Silverstein (1976, 1998), and others, contemporary linguistic anthropology studies how language use can constitute aspects of culture and identity. The most important work in this direction focuses on the concept of creative or entailing indexicality.

Competence theories fail because of the indeterminacy of relevant context. Other features of the context can always become salient, so as to transform the appropriateness or the meaning of an utterance. Because the meaning of any utterance can be refigured by making different contextual features relevant, the analytic question becomes: how do certain contextual features become salient, such that an utterance comes to have identifiable interactional functions? Something more flexible than communicative competence mediates between the cues in an utterance and people's conscious or non-conscious construal of its meaning. The concept of "contextualization cues" (Gumperz, 1982, 1992) or indexicality (Garfinkel & Sacks, 1970; Silverstein, 1976) captures this mediating step. A contextualization cue or index indicates how its context should be construed, by pointing to a particular aspect of context. Hearers attend to sometimes conflicting cues in utterances, on that basis select aspects of the context as relevant, *then* apply their knowledge of cultural regularities to determine what an utterance means.

So the relationship between an utterance and its meaning is mediated by participants' construal of the context. This process of "mediation" (Wortham, 2001) or "contextualization" (Silverstein, 1992) is crucial to preserving Hymes' insight into the important of cultural context while overcoming the limitations of a "competence" theory. Note that, on this sort of account, two questions must be answered: (1) How do the linguistic and non-linguistic cues that compose an utterance make certain aspects of the context salient? (2) How does a set of cues and salient contextual features establish an utterance's meaning?

In response to the first question, linguistic anthropologists like Gumperz (1982) and Silverstein (1976) have answered: verbal cues signal indexically, to point out and sometimes create aspects of the context. Silverstein (1976) distinguishes between two types of indexical relationship that a sign can have with its object. First, the sign can indexically "presuppose" its object. In this type of case it points to an element of the context that exists *independent* of the occurrence of the sign itself. Second, the sign can indexically create or, in later terminology (e.g., Silverstein, 1993), "entail" its object. In this type of case the sign points to an element of the context that exists as a *result* of the particular use of the sign itself.

Particular signs do not essentially presuppose or entail, although some forms lend themselves more to one type of relationship than the other. *We* and *he*, for example, generally have determinate indexical presuppositions. In the example, by the time Candace says "that way he's a <u>cow</u>ard" about Maurice, it has been established that Maurice is on the other side from the teachers and the female students, closer to the plotters and the boys who sit in the back of the room. Candace's use of *he* refers to Maurice as a member of this group that is excluded from the narrating interaction, and it points to a *presupposed* aspect of the context. Speakers have by this point already come to presuppose that both within the example and in the classroom itself Maurice has chosen not to align himself with the teachers.

We and *he* can also have indexical entailments, however. The teacher's "he's not <u>going</u> to warn us though," at line 235, is the first use of *he* to refer to Maurice in the classroom discussion. This *he* points to an aspect of the context that results in part from this particular use of the sign. The use of <u>we</u> in this particular utterance begins to position Maurice as an outsider in the interaction. An adequate account of language use in cultural context must capture both presupposing and entailing indexicality—both how speech involves expectable patterns and how it can have unexpected effects.

Regimentation

Whether a sign actually accomplishes indexical entailments for subsequent interaction depends on how subsequent utterances recontextualize it. This involves the process of "entextualization" (Silverstein, 1992) or "emergence" (Garfinkel & Sacks, 1970; Wortham, 2001). When a speaker uses an entailing indexical, the element of the context potentially created will either be presupposed by following utterances or not. When the teacher said "he's not going to warn us though," hearers concerned to understand whom *he* referred to would have to search the context for a singular, masculine referent that was not at the moment a speaker or addressee in the narrating classroom conversation. The denoted content of the utterance also provides information: the referent of he was in a position to warn Mr. Smith and some others, but he chose not to. This makes Maurice the most plausible referent. Given that Maurice had just been referred to as *you*, by Mr. Smith and others, however, the switch to *he* carries more than denotational information. It also communicates that Maurice may be getting excluded from the narrating event. Whether or not this potential entailment takes place depends on whether subsequent utterances presuppose it. When Candace and then others also begin to refer to Maurice as *he*, the potential entailment "solidifies" and Maurice's new interactional position can be taken for granted as a fact about the narrating classroom interaction.

This concept of *emergence* was developed in ethnomethodology (Garfinkel, 1967; Garfinkel & Sacks, 1970) and conversation analysis (Schegloff & Sacks, 1973) to describe how subsequent utterances can transform the functions of prior ones. The conversation analysts argue that other participants' responses to an utterance can change its meaning. Without knowing what responses followed an utterance, participants and analysts often cannot know whether an utterance was appropriate or what identity the speaker was adopting. An utterance has particular interactional functions, ultimately, because of the effect it *comes* to have in the interaction. Indexical cues in an utterance establish its functions only as *subsequent* utterances indicate that those cues have been taken in a certain way. On this account, in order to interpret or react to an utterance, participants and analysts must attend not only to the moment of utterance, but also to some later moment when subsequent context has helped the meaning of the utterance solidify. At the moment of utterance the relevant context has often not yet emerged.

(Sometimes, of course, meanings do not solidify and utterances remain ambiguous, despite subsequent context.)

The concept of emergence is central to answering the second question raised in the last section: How does a set of cues and salient contextual features establish an utterance's meaning? By answering that speakers' own subsequent reactions are central (i.e., whether speakers themselves come to presuppose a potentially entailing indexical determines whether that entailment happens) contemporary linguistic anthropologists are following a traditional anthropological emphasis on the participants' own point of view. In some cases, of course, participants do not consciously represent the categories that they use to organize their thought and action, but they do systematically react to them (Garfinkel & Sacks, 1970; Silverstein, 1981). Instead of imposing outsider categories, linguistic anthropology induces analytic categories that participants either articulate or presuppose in their action, and it insists on evidence that participants themselves are presupposing categories central to the analysis.

The concepts of contextualization and entextualization, or mediation and emergence, however, do not in themselves explain how relevant context gets limited and an utterance's interactional functions get established in practice. These concepts give a more precise formulation of how particular utterances point to elements of the context and make certain types of events salient. The denotational and interactional meanings that emerge in a conversation *are* shaped by the indexical cues in the utterances. But the relevant indexical values also depend on the type of event presupposed as going on at the moment of utterance. In other words, the account of utterance meaning described thus far is too linear. In understanding or reacting coherently to speech, participants and analysts cannot move sequentially from verbal and nonverbal cues, to construals of the context, to established meaning. To identify relevant indexical cues, and to construe relevant context, participants and analysts already need some presuppositions about what is going on.

Any utterance could index various aspects of the context. So the indexicals in any utterance cannot themselves determine interactional events. If they did, then analysts could develop rules that connect types of indexes to types of context. This would yield a somewhat more sophisticated theory of communicative competence. In fact, participants and analysts can make multiple construals of the indexical values of almost any utterance. This circularity makes it difficult to explain the connection between an utterance and its meaning. The values of particular indexes in an utterance highlight certain aspects of the context—and thus indicate that a particular type of event is likely to be going on—but at the same time prior conceptions about what type of event is occurring influence the values of the indexes.

For example, the *he* in "he's not <u>going</u> to warn us though" might presuppose various things about Maurice's identity. Grammatical information tells us that the shift from calling Maurice *you* to calling him *he* excludes him from the speech event. But hearers must search the context for reasons why he is being treated this way. This switch to *he* might index various things: perhaps Maurice has been teasing the teachers and they are just teasing back; perhaps Maurice is known for being nervous and diffident, such that he wouldn't get involved; or, as I have argued, perhaps Maurice is torn between the resistant boys and the cooperative girls, and the teacher's utterance casts him as siding with the boys in this instance. Because this latter set of identities and interactional issues has already been made salient in the classroom discussion, hearers are more likely to interpret the indexical as presupposing Maurice's in-between position. Contemporary linguistic anthropologists say that the larger set of identities and issues, or the frame, "regiments" or constrains the values of the indexical cues.

So a particular type of entextualization, or a coherent understanding of the conversation as being some recognizable type of event, emerges through construal of relevant indexical cues. But the identification and interpretation of relevant indexical cues depend on a presupposed understanding of what is going on. There is thus a back-and-forth or dialectic interpretive process required to understand speech. This process involves *two types* of cultural and linguistic knowledge: participants must know what particular cues index, and participants must be familiar with types of denoted content and enacted events. For example, participants must know that "coward" often indexically presupposes that the person thus characterized is unmasculine. Participants must also be familiar with the cultural text or script that involves adolescent girls teasing an adolescent boy. Silverstein (1993, 1998) and other contemporary linguistic anthropologists refer to this dialectic process as the "regimentation" of indexical cues by available cultural types of events. When speakers and hearers presuppose that a particular type of event is going on, the expectable script for that type of event comes to regiment many indexical cues—in other words, those indexicals are construed so that they come to support the emerging pattern of what is understood to be going on.

This presupposed pattern or cultural type of text or script has been called a "metadiscourse" (Urban, 1996). Social categories exist empirically in practice, as people enact characteristic events and adopt types of positions within those events. Silverstein (1993) and Urban (1996) describe this process in terms of the metadiscourses that come to regiment particular events of language use. Members of any society explicitly and implicitly recognize complex sets of types of events. When confronted with empirical evidence of an ongoing event, these members will generally come to understand the event as coherent when the indexical signs that compose the event come increasingly to presuppose that a particular type of event is going on (Silverstein, 1992). Metadiscourses are the explicit and implicit framings available in a given society for understanding social events as coherent. Social life can only be coherent insofar as metadiscourses are available for understanding the types of events that typically exist and the types of people who characteristically participate in them. Another term often used to describe this process, as illustrated in several chapters in this book, is "language ideology." In understanding speech, people rely on ideologies about how particular kinds of speakers typically use particular kinds of language to participate in recognizable types of events.

Metadiscourses or language ideologies, then, are publicly circulating devices for interpreting or regimenting their object discourses—the patterned indexical signs that compose discourse. All coherent discursive interactions get inscribed or "entextualized" as particular types of denotational and interactional messages (Silverstein, 1993; Silverstein & Urban, 1996). That is, participants understand or orient to the interaction as if it were a particular metadiscursive type. As particular metadiscourses get invoked across speech events, they circulate more widely. The circulation of metadiscourses explains the "contextually-situated, interactional establishment, maintenance, and renewal (transformation) of social relations in societies" (Silverstein, 1993, p. 35). The social events, relationships, and identities characteristic of a society are made recognizable by the metadiscourses that typify them (Urban, 1996).

In Maurice's case, the relevant metadiscourses involve his position as a black male student caught between resistant peers and the expectations of mainstream institutions. As the interaction develops, Mr. Smith comes to speak about Maurice's interactional position in the past tense, as if it has already been settled.

> T/S: you told <u>us</u> you wouldn't tell us <u>any</u>thing.
> ST?: haha
> ST?: °<u>I</u> wouldn't.°
> T/S: you'd rather see our mangled <u>bo</u>dies at the bottom of
> 365   the staircase.
> MRC: I: told you I wouldn't be coming to <u>school</u> that day.
> T/S: does that mean you're not part of the plot.
> ST?: yeah
> MRC: I'd <u>still</u> be part of it. I- [if I
> 370   T/B: [if you- if you <u>know</u> about it=
> T/S: if you <u>know</u> about it that's: an ac<u>com</u>plice. you <u>knew</u>

about it. you could have <u>stopped</u> it. all you had to do is say-
it shouldn't be done, it's wrong.

By this point, Mr. Smith has given up trying to entice Maurice to join
his group. He accuses Maurice of wishing for the teachers' violent
demise. At lines 364–5, his colorful comment might be taken as a joke.
But Maurice's tone at line 366 is quite earnest. In his comment at line
372, Mr. Smith's tone is angry again. And, by using the word "accomplice" to refer to Maurice-the-potential informer, Mr. Smith casts
Maurice's character in the example as morally questionable.

Within the example, Maurice has made his decision, and this has
consequences in the narrating event. After this segment, teachers and
students consistently refer to Maurice as <u>he</u> for about six minutes.
Maurice himself has been excluded from the teachers' and the girls'
group, in the narrating event. He can still be a member of the boys'
group, but the other boys almost never participate in class. So in joining
that group he gives up participating in classroom activity.

Maurice thus gets interactionally positioned by the example in ways
that could influence his identity development and his position in larger
social orders. Maurice's responses in this discussion may have implications for his identity as a "good" or "bad" student and as a "real"
male. This one example, in itself, will of course not determine Maurice's
identity or the social location of African-American male students in
general. But, through the example, the students do re-enact something
about many students like Maurice: African-American males who want
to engage with school sometimes face a balancing act in many urban
U.S. classrooms, as they are caught between the often-opposed roles of
"good" student and "real" male. If Maurice consistently positions himself as opposed to the teachers and the girls, he may no longer qualify
as a "good" student. And if Maurice consistently positions himself on
the same side as the teachers in classroom discussions, he may no longer
qualify as a "real" male.

Poetic Structure

However rich the metadiscourses available for framing or regimenting an interaction as a particular type, we still face the analytic question:
How is the circular relation between indexical cues and potential
metadiscursive entextualizations or framings ever overcome in practice, such that a particular meaning emerges? This is a problem of
"chunking." Given a stream of speech and indefinite potentially relevant context, how do speakers and analysts know which chunks cohere
and have implications for establishing some recognizable meaning?
Jakobson (1960) and Silverstein (1992) suggest that a particular type of

implicit *structure* (a "poetic" structure) emerges, solidifies, and thus establishes a relevant context and a more plausible set of interpretations for a series of utterances.

Poetic structure involves patterns of indexical cues that come collectively to presuppose each other, such that they "lock" together in a mutually presupposed set. Just a few indexical cues may be interpreted in multiple ways, and they often cannot overcome the indeterminacy of relevant context. But a pattern of indexical cues that not only presuppose relevant context but also presuppose each other can solidify and (provisionally) limit the context relevant to interpreting a set of utterances. Such poetic structure is *contingent* on particulars of the event. It is also *emergent*—speakers create essential parts of it over the course of an interaction, and no one could reliably predict the details of the structure that eventually emerges. (Hymes [1981] also drew on Jakobson's concept of poetic structure to analyze culturally situated language use, but he focused more on the poetics of verbal art and less on the process of regimentation in everyday discourse.)

In the example of Maurice, the poetic structure includes the consistent use of *you* to refer to Maurice early and the consistent use of *he* late in the classroom discussion. Mr. Smith's use of terms like "accomplice" later in the discussion also consistently characterize Maurice's hypothetical character—and, by implication, perhaps his real self—as on the wrong side of a moral issue. In this example, however, there are some indexicals that do not easily fit into this poetic structure. Sometimes, like at line 364 when he says "you'd rather see our mangled bodies at the bottom of the staircase," Mr. Smith seems to be teasing. Some cues would fit more easily with this alternative metadiscursive framing of the event as teasing. Most everyday interactions contain some ambiguity like this. Poetic structure is rarely so consistent and dense that no alternative framings can be imagined, except in ritual events (cf. Parmentier, 1997). Nonetheless, in most cases a poetic structure solidifies enough such that participants and analysts have a sense of what is going on.

Methodologically, the importance of poetic structure means that exemplary work in the linguistic anthropology of education systematically analyzes *patterns of indexical cues* across particular segments of language use, instead of relying on isolated instances selected from the data. This contrasts with much classic and contemporary work in discourse analysis—which unsystematically extracts segments of discourse that support an analytic point. Owing to space limitations, the preceding example does not meet this methodological standard. See Silverstein (1985), Wortham (1994, 2001), and several of the chapters in this volume for more adequate illustrations.

Contemporary linguistic anthropology, then, has described how linguistic signs come to have meaning in cultural and interactional context. In addition to drawing on and modifying central concepts from an earlier generation—centrally, "communicative competence," taking the native's point of view, and the connection between micro and macro—the contemporary approach has elaborated four other concepts: indexicality, creativity, regimentation, and poetic structure. Indexical cues in utterances presuppose relevant context, and the concept of indexicality captures how the meaning of speech depends on context. Indexes not only presuppose established social identities and other aspects of context, but they can also create or entail new identities and arrangements that may come to be presupposed. A set of indexical cues in an interaction gets regimented, as a circulating metadiscourse or frame comes to organize the social positions being enacted in the interaction. This organization happens as a poetic structure of indexical cues solidifies, such that a particular relevant context can be consistently presupposed.

THE CHAPTERS

This volume contains seven core chapters—in addition to this introduction and a concluding commentary—each of which applies a contemporary linguistic anthropological approach to educational data. Each of the chapters adopts the general approach sketched in this introduction, but each emphasizes some concepts more then others. Some chapters also argue that this general approach should be supplemented with concepts from other traditions (e.g., the chapters by Collins and He). Thus the foregoing sketch of contemporary linguistic anthropology of education should not be taken as definitive. Instead of a canonical account, we offer a set of tools for looking at educational phenomena in new ways. We hope that the cases in this book can both enrich educational research and illustrate how educational institutions can be important research sites for anthropologists and other social scientists.

Indexicality and Regimentation

The first four chapters illustrate how the concepts of indexicality and regimentation can illuminate talk in schools. Each of the authors also argues that linguistic anthropological analyses of particular events can and should help us study more broadly contextualized social relationships, such as those surrounding persistent inequities related to class, race, linguistic diversity, and new social relationships engendered by popular culture, communications technology, and the "information age" in general.

In Chapter 2, "Language, Identity and Learning in the Era of 'Expert-Guided' Systems," James Collins describes a university-based literacy tutoring program for middle school students with reading difficulties. Collins addresses three critical questions for a viable and contemporary Linguistic Anthropology of Education. (1) Does the widely proclaimed "information age" require a change in pedagogical relationships, towards greater self-awareness—heightened reflexivity—on the part of students and teachers? (2) Does a change in pedagogical relations lead to greater diversity in the linguistic resources drawn upon in schooled literacy lessons? That is, is there a heightened intertextuality or "discourse hybridity" relevant for today's students? (3) If there is a need in today's schools for heightened reflexivity and an understanding of discourse diversity, are these concepts essential or incidental to notions of language, identity, and learning? Collins shows how a linguistic anthropological perspective provides useful tools to investigate these questions, but he also shows that these tools must be applied within careful ethnographic studies and in dialogue with social theory.

In Chapter 3, "Communicative Practice, Cultural Production, and Situated Learning: Constructing and Contesting Identities of Expertise in a Heterogeneous Learning Context," Kevin O'Connor focuses on a contemporary brand of intertextuality—a collaborative educational project taking place in part through a geographically distributed learning context—in order to explore the cultural production of the "educated person." The chapter shows how a linguistic anthropological approach can illuminate processes of cultural production by examining the interplay between indexical presupposition and indexical entailment in interactions among participants in a multi-institution undergraduate engineering project. Two microanalyses reveal how students align themselves with differing views of what it means to be an "expert." In self-introductions by participants at Tech, a relatively lower-status school, this process results in the validation of the working class identity of one student, as subsequent participants indexically align themselves with him and construct a local understanding of expertise consistent with his identity. In contrast, in a later project meeting involving Tech students and students from the Institute, a higher-status school, Institute students draw upon available but unofficial contextual features in a way that promotes their own view of expertise—in a way that not only contrasts with but also denigrates the identities of Tech students.

Agnes He's chapter, "Linguistic Anthropology and Language Education: A Comparative Look at Language Socialization," examines the relationship between a theory of language socialization and the linguistic anthropology of education. She argues that, while contemporary concepts such as indexicality and creativity from linguistic anthropology have not yet directly influenced mainstream educational research and practice, language socialization, which rests on a theory of indexicality, has already made an important impact on language education in particular. To illustrate this point, she describes research she had done in Chinese heritage language classes. The chapter first reviews critically and comparatively the notions of indexicality and creativity, as expounded in language socialization. She uses language education as both a site and a set of practices to demonstrate that language socialization's notions of indexicality and creativity can be enriched by the conversation analytic concepts of intersubjectivity and emergence. Her analyses illustrate how both theoretical issues and everyday practices in language education can be reconceptualized with an intersubjective, emergent account of language socialization—an account complementary to the contemporary linguistic anthropology of education.

Betsy Rymes' chapter, "Relating Word to World: Indexicality During Literacy Events," uses the concept of indexicality to examine literacy events in two very different classroom settings. She shows how aspects of particular teacher-student interactions limit teachers' and students' implicit conceptions of what literacy can or should be. She does this by examining two classroom contexts in which highly different curricula are in place. In one of these literacy contexts, the teacher follows a carefully scripted phonics program, while in the other the teacher freely selects children's literature trade books as well as themes and activities to accompany these books. Both of these teachers were seeking the best practices to help struggling readers who were already falling far behind their peers. However, these students' experience of the reading process is not necessarily related to the methodology teachers follow. Instead, Rymes argues, it may be that children's success as readers is crucially affected by the stance these teachers take in interactions as students use words of a text to index worlds outside that text. This chapter illustrates how analytical tools from linguistic anthropology can provide the first step to reforming the kinds of interactions that go on in classrooms and the way that literacy is constructed through those interactions.

Ideology and Linguistic Diversity

While Chapters 1 through 4 closely examine school language use to understand educational, social, and theoretical problems, Chapters 5 through 7 draw on linguistic anthropology—and in particular on the concept of language ideology—to investigate issues of linguistic diversity. The authors describe indigenous language revitalization in Corsica, perceived dialectal variation in Costa Rica, and children's language ideologies in a dual immersion elementary magnet school in the Southeastern United States, respectively.

In Chapter 6, " 'Imagined Competence': Classroom Evaluation, Collective Identity and Linguistic Authenticity in a Corsican Bilingual Classroom," Alexandra Jaffe looks closely at Corsican language literacy work in one of the classes in a Corsican/French bilingual school. She explores the interplay between the macro level of language ideologies and politics, and the micro level of classroom interaction, by focusing on minority language linguistic competence—both "real" and "imagined"—and how it is related to issues of individual and collective cultural identity and authenticity. She approaches these issues through close analysis of a familiar participation structure—initiation, response, evaluation—as it is used by one of the teachers in this school. She relates evaluative practice surrounding Corsican at the micro-interactional level to the overall patterning of literacy practices in the classroom in both Corsican and French. Jaffe shows how schools like this one face a key challenge: teaching a language that many of the schoolchildren do not know while at the same time authenticating their legitimate cultural claims to "own" that language.

In her chapter, " 'Ellos Se Comen Las Eses/Heces': The Perceived Language Difference of Matambú," Karen Stocker also examines the intersection of language ideologies and particular interactions. Her analyses illuminate not "imagined competence," but what might be called "imagined difference"—a case of the perceived language difference of Matambugueños, the residents of an indigenous reservation in Northwestern Costa Rica. She maintains that this perceived language difference is the result of the commonly held correlation between ethnic identity and language use, in a place where there is no clear ethnic distinction between Matambugueños and non-Matambugueños, but where the desire to create difference is great. As outsiders seek to define those residing within an arbitrarily defined reservation as distinct from them, they hear linguistic difference where it does not exist. The perception that Matambugueños speak a stigmatized dialect, different from that spoken by outsiders to the reservation, serves to place Matambugueños in a lower social status. As Stocker illustrates, the issue of perceived language difference is, perhaps, most noticeable in the school setting in which Matambugueños and non-Matambugueños occupy the same social terrain on a daily basis. She analyzes indexical and ideological processes through which the use of a particular dialect is perceived to identify a given group of speakers as intellectually inferior. She shows how a language ideology which privileges standard language and values its speakers is taught, directly, in the classroom, and how teachers use this to rationalize their treatment of students from the reservation. She also provides examples of linguistic creativity and the poetic function of language, as indigenous students draw attention to—and parody—circulating language ideologies.

In Chapter 8, "Voices of the Children: Language and Literacy Ideologies in a Dual Language Immersion Program," Norma González and Elizabeth Arnot-Hopffer examine the construction and negotiation of language ideologies in a dual language immersion program in which many of the English dominant students are Latino. They illustrate how the process of biliteracy development shapes and is shaped by language ideologies circulating within the school and the larger ideologically charged political context within which the school is situated. By bringing together theories of language ideology, the study of children's perspectives, and longitudinal study of biliteracy development within a dual language program, they affirm the social and historical essence of childhood and, simultaneously, illustrate the connection between children's formation of language ideologies and their biliteracy development. As their research illustrates, children never learn language in a vacuum. Students are inevitably learning, through two languages, the language ideologies circulating around each—the students' immersion in ideological context is inseparable from their development as critically bilingual/biliterate students.

In the concluding chapter, "Linguistic Anthropology of Education in Context," Nancy Hornberger, an educational and anthropological linguist who has worked in multiple research contexts spanning the fields addressed by the authors in this volume, reflects on the chapters and the prospects for a contemporary linguistic anthropology of education.

APPENDIX: TRANSCRIPTION CONVENTIONS

'-'   abrupt breaks or stops (if several, stammering)

'?'   rising intonation

'.'   falling intonation

'_'   (underline) stress

(1.0)   silences, timed to the nearest second

'['   indicates simultaneous talk by two speakers, with one
            utterance represented on top of the other and the moment of
            overlap marked by left brackets

'='   interruption or next utterance following immediately, or continuous talk represented on separate lines because of need to represent overlapping comment on intervening line

'[…]'   transcriber comment

':'   elongated vowel

'°…°'   segment quieter than surrounding talk

','   pause or breath without marked intonation

'(hh)'   laughter breaking into words while speaking

REFERENCES

Appadurai, A. (1996). *Modernity at Large: Cultural Dimensions of Globalization.* Minneapolis: University of Minnesota Press.

Bourdieu, P., & Passeron, J. (1977). *Reproduction in Education, Society and Culture* (trans. by R. Nice). Thousand Oaks, CA: Sage.

Cazden, John V., & Hymes, D. H. (Eds.). (1972). *Functions of Language in the Classroom.* New York: Teachers College Press.

Chomsky, N. (1965). *Aspects of the Theory of Syntax.* Cambridge, MA: MIT Press.

Duranti, A. (1997). *Linguistic Anthropology.* New York: Cambridge University Press.

Garfinkel, H. (1967). *Studies in Ethnomethodology.* New York: Polity Press.

Garfinkel, H., & Sacks, H. (1970). On the formal structure of practical actions. In J. McKinney & A. Tiryakian (Eds.), *Theoretical Sociology* (pp. 337–366). New York: Appleton Century Crofts.

Goffman, E. (1974). *Frame Analysis.* New York: Harper and Row.

Goffman, E. (1976). Replies and responses. *Language in Society, 5,* 257–313.

Gumperz, J. (1982). *Discourse Strategies.* New York: Cambridge University Press.

Gumperz, J. (1992). Contextualization revisited. In P. Auer & A. DiLuzio (Eds.), *The Contextualization of Language* (pp. 39–53). Philadelphia: John Benjamins.

Hanks, W. (1990). *Referential Practice.* Chicago: University of Chicago Press.

Havránek, B. (1932/1955). The functional differentiation of the standard language (P. Garvin, translator). In P. Garvin (Ed.), *A Prague School Reader* (pp. 1–18). Washington: Washington Linguistics Club.

Heath, S. B. (1983). *Ways with Words: Language, Life, and Work in Communities and Classrooms.* Cambridge, New York: Cambridge University Press.

Hill, J. H., & Irvine, J. T. (Eds.). (1992). *Responsibility and Evidence in Oral Discourse.* New York: Cambridge University.

Hymes, D. H. (1972). On communicative competence. In J. Pride & J. Holmes (Eds.), *Sociolinguistics* (pp. 269–293). New York: Penguin Books.

Hymes, D. H. (1981). *"In Vain I Tried to Tell You."* Philadelphia: University of Pennsylvania.

Hymes, D. H. (1996). *Ethnography, Linguistics, Narrative Inequality: Toward an Understanding of Voice.* London, Washington: Taylor & Francis.

Jakobson, R. (1960). Closing statement: linguistics and poetics. In T. Sebeok (Ed.), *Style in Language.* Cambridge: MIT Press.

Jakobson, R. (1971). Shifters, verbal categories and the Russian verb. In R. Jakobson, *Selected Writings* (Vol. 2). The Hague: Mouton. (Original published 1957.)

Labov, W. (1972). The transformation of experience in narrative syntax. In W. Labov, *Language in the Inner City* (pp. 354–396). Philadelphia: University of Pennsylvania Press.

Levinson, S. (1981). The essential inadequacies of speech act models of dialogue. In H. Parret, M. Sbisà, & J. Verschueren (Eds.), *Possibilities and Limitations of Pragmatics* (pp. 473–492). Amsterdam: John Benjamins.

Levinson, B. (1999). Resituating the place of educational discourse in anthropology. *American Anthropologist, 101*, 594–604.

Lucy, J. (Ed.). (1993). *Reflexive Language*. New York: Cambridge University Press.

Michaels, S. (1981). Starting time. *Language in Society, 10*, 423–442.

Parmentier, R. (1997). The pragmatic semiotics of cultures. *Semiotica, 116*, 1–115.

Peirce, C. (1897/1955). Logic as semiotic. In J. Buchler (Ed.), *Philosophical Writings of Peirce* (pp. 98–119). New York: Dover.

Philips, S.U. (1983). *The Invisible Culture*. New York: Longman.

Saussure, F. de (1916). *Cours de Linguistique Générale*. Paris: Payot.

Schegloff, E., & Sacks, H. (1973). Opening up closings. *Semiotica, 8*, 289–327.

Schieffelin, B., Woolard, K., & Kroskrity, P. V. (1998). *Language Ideologies: Practice and Theory*. New York: Oxford University Press.

Searle, J. (1969). *Speech Acts*. New York: Cambridge University Press.

Silverstein, M. (1976). Shifters, linguistic categories, and cultural description. In K. Basso & H. Selby (Eds.), *Meaning in Anthropology*. Albuquerque: University of New Mexico Press.

Silverstein, M. (1981). The limits of awareness. Sociolinguistic working paper number 84. Southwest Educational Development Laboratory, Austin, TX.

Silverstein, M. (1985). On the pragmatic "poetry" of prose. In D. Schiffrin (Ed.), *Meaning, Form and Use in Context*. Washington: Georgetown University Press.

Silverstein, M. (1992). The indeterminacy of contextualization: When is enough enough? In A. DiLuzio & P. Auer (Eds.), *The Contextualization of Language* (pp. 55–75). Amsterdam: John Benjamins.

Silverstein, M. (1993). Metapragmatic discourse and metapragmatic function. In J. Lucy (Ed.), *Reflexive Language*. New York: Cambridge University Press.

Silverstein, M. (1998). The improvisational performance of "culture" in real-time discursive practice. In K. Sawyer (Ed.), *Improvisation*. Norwood, NJ: Ablex.

Silverstein, M., & Urban, G. (Eds.). (1996). *Natural Histories of Discourse*. Chicago: University of Chicago.

Urban, G. (1996). *Metaphysical Community*. Austin: University of Texas Press.

Willis, P. E. (1981). *Learning to Labor: How Working Class Kids Get Working Class Jobs*. New York: Columbia University Press.

Wortham, S. (1994). *Acting Out Participant Examples in the Classroom*. Philadelphia: John Benjamins.

Wortham, S. (1995). Experiencing the great books. *Mind, Culture & Activity, 2*, 67–80.

Wortham, S. (1996). Mapping participant deictics: A technique for discovering speakers' footing. *Journal of Pragmatics, 25*, 331–348.

Wortham, S. (1997). Denotationally cued interactional events: A special case. *Semiotica, 114*, 295–317.

Wortham, S. (2001). *Narratives in Action*. New York: Teachers College Press.

2

Language, Identity, and Learning in the Era of "Expert-Guided" Systems

James Collins

By the end of the 2000 presidential election cycle, few people in the United States remained unaware that the state of literacy in America was a problem toward which political and economic resources would be devoted so that, in the words of the candidates, "no child is left behind." It turns out that many students are "left behind"; that is, they are not manifesting the literacy skills, aptitudes, or competencies officially deemed appropriate for a person of their age or place in the educational system (Jochnowitz, 2001; Schemo, 2001). This is the case with primary school students who are not reading, writing, or testing as well as their cohort on district-wide, statewide, or national surveys (Brownstein, 1999). It should not surprise us that differences in literacy attainments often increase over time, such that those who are having problems with literacy in early school years have bigger problems when they reach middle or high school (Jencks & Phillips, 1998).

In policy and research debates about literacy and schooling, this exacerbation of literacy problems as students progress through school has not received much research attention. Until recently literacy problems were either the domain of primary education or of remedial adult education. Although the Carnegie Council on Adolescent Development expressed its view a decade ago that "a volatile mismatch exists between the organization and curriculum of middle grade schools and the intellectual and emotional needs of young adolescents" (Carnegie Council, 1989, p. 8), only in recent years has a specific focus been given to adolescents and literacy, marked by the emergence of specialized journals and research interest groups. For example, only in 1997 did the National Council on Teachers of English move to create a special section on middle school interests. In the same year the *Journal of Adult Literacy* became the *Journal of Adolescent and Adult Literacy*. In short, little attention has heretofore been directed at middle school students' literacy learning, and even less has been focused on middle school students who are struggling with becoming literate. Although there are various potential sources of difficulties for students at this level of development and schooling—difficulties at the level of word analysis, difficulties arising from the shift in the nature of texts to be read or from the uses of texts in the middle school's increasingly compartmentalized curriculum, difficulties resulting from conflicts between academic achievement and class-, ethnic-, or gender-based identities—there is not a substantial body of research suggesting what the major areas of difficulty are for struggling readers or writers in middle school.

Notwithstanding the relative scarcity of research into adolescent literacy, the causes of literacy shortcomings among primary and secondary school students have been the object of an increasingly acrimonious debate between adherents of rival visions of literacy. This debate pits advocates of a "phonics-based" curriculum against those who advocate a "whole language" approach to learning (Adams, 1993; Coles, 1998; Lemann, 1997). Although phonics adherents place their faith in a teacher-proof curriculum, and whole language proponents trust more in the efficacy of teachers' insights and situated responses, both camps believe that they have science, or at least systematic scholarship, in support of their pedagogies (Coles, 2000).

In this widely debated but loosely defined problem area, salient issues include the balance of school versus student knowledge and the balance of school-sanctioned versus everyday language in literacy learning. One issue in the ongoing debates concerns the ways in which pedagogies and teaching practices should draw upon and regulate students' everyday knowledge. A related issue is the question of whether literacy primarily consists of "cracking a code" (a linguistic code to which expert teaching might provide privileged access) or entering into "a communicative practice" (for which practice "conversation" and "dialogue" are often cited as guiding metaphors).

Within this debate, I would like to suggest there is a useful role for a linguistic anthropology of education with multiple commitments to linguistics, ethnography, and social theory. At this stage in the argument, let me phrase the concern with linguistics and ethnography as a need for discourse analysis, understanding discourse to involve domains of everyday as well as institutionally situated practical action, in which language use is a salient mode of such action. As with other kinds of qualitative inquiry, the level and detail of discursive analysis cannot be determined in advance of establishing a research problem and some theoretical commitments. In further developing a sense of problem and theoretical engagement, I will draw upon concepts from both linguistic anthropology and critical discourse analysis. Taken together, these concepts allow us to explore how the issues raised above—of teacher/student relations, of language and literacy learning—are rooted in patterns of language use and also reflect pervasive social dynamics.

In the next chapter, I explore several questions that have pedagogical significance, linguistic dimensions, and contemporary sociological features. First, are there increasing needs for reflexive awareness in learning activities as teachers' expertise shifts vis-à-vis students' knowledge and identities; that is, does a widely proclaimed "information age" require a change in pedagogical relationships, towards greater self-awareness on the part of students and teachers? Second, is there a heightened intertextuality, or discourse "hybridity," accompanying such shifts; that is, does a change in pedagogical relation lead to greater diversity in the linguistic resources drawn upon in schooled literacy lessons? Third, if there is evidence of heightened reflexivity and discourse diversity, what are the implications for how we think about language, identity, and learning; that is, are concepts such as reflexivity and hybridity essential or incidental to notions of language, identity, and learning? These questions are explored through a case analysis of a university-based literacy tutoring program for middle school students with reading difficulties. In addressing these three questions, I also develop a viewpoint on what a linguistic anthropology of education might be and suggest how it should develop. In particular, I argue that linguistic anthropology offers well-suited tools for approaching such questions, but only if they are grounded in ethnography and framed vis-à-vis social theory.

A THEORETICAL FRAMEWORK

Let me now address the theoretical relevance of two lines of inquiry both for addressing the preceding questions and for exploring how a linguistic anthropology of education might orient itself in the current intellectual world. The first line of inquiry, unsurprisingly, is composed of the concepts and arguments found within contemporary linguistic anthropology (LA). In accordance with other chapters in this volume, I assume that we must distinguish between *referential* aspects of language, that is, that speech or writing "says something" via recognized lexicon and grammar, and the *indexical* or pragmatic aspects of language, that is, that speech or writing "does something" through complex contextual cues that both reflect and affect ongoing social action. That language is used to say something is a familiar enough starting point, but it is only a starting point, for meaning is inherently contextual or situated. To say that meaning is "inherently contextual" is to say that it is necessarily beyond or more than the purely literal, the "simply said." That beyondness or excess of meaning we talk about by saying that meaning "depends on context," but establishing what aspects of context are relevant can present its own formidable complexities in actual analysis.

The concept of indexicality tries to enrich and anchor the insight that meaning "depends on context" in several ways. One way is to note that all languages have categories that are inherently context-dependent. Pronouns, such as "I," "We," and "You" are examples: their meaning depends on the situation of speaking or writing. As we will see in the following analyses, they can provide vital clues to how meaning is being constructed. And there is a rich literature on such "deictic"/indexical categories (Hanks, 1996; see also Rymes, this volume). Another way of approaching the issue of context is to draw a general distinction between modes of indexicality, distinguishing between (1) reflected or presupposed indexicality—that linguistic forms mean what they mean because of learned association between those forms and situated relationships, identities, actions, and so forth—and (2) performative or creative indexicality—that the use of linguistic forms can be and is part of the ongoing creation, negotiation, and contestation of context, in which an evoked relation, identity, or activity can become the basis for subsequent relating, identifying, or acting (Ochs, 1992; Silverstein, 1976). As Wortham argues in the introduction to this volume, indexical creativity is an emergent (i.e., contingent and non-deterministic) phenomenon. Hence its importance, for it provides tangible evidence of human agency. Hence also, however, its complexity: whether discourse participants or analysts, we often do not know what is "relevant context" until some shared sense of what is going on has been agreed upon or imposed.

Perhaps a brief example can help clarify these matters. The profiles analyzed later involve literacy tutors working with students. As we will see in one of the profiles, when a tutor asks questions of a student she is tutoring, she often receives "I dunno" as the answer. At the level of literal meaning, this is simple enough to understand: "I dunno" in response to a question means "I do not know the answer to the question." In this case, however, subsequent responses by the tutor and the student, including the tutor's pointblank rejection of "I dunno" as an appropriate answer, suggest that there is more at stake than a simple profession of ignorance. But what is at stake, and how might we know it?

Understanding what is at stake, as participants or analysts, requires attending to the pattern of responses—of tutor to student and student to tutor. This patterning can be seen as *poetic structure*, that is, "patterns of indexical cues that come collectively to presuppose each other such that they 'lock' together in a mutually presupposed set" (Wortham, Introduction, p. 32). As we will see, discerning such a structure will require analysis of multiple cues: other answers given by the student, the tutors' varied responses to "I dunno," and the tutors' and students' use of reported speech. As Wortham (Introduction) and others have argued, poetic structure provides one strand of evidence of indexical or pragmatic *regimentation*, of establishing or imposing a frame of understanding of what a stretch of discourse is about (Collins, 2001; Gumperz, 1996; Haviland, 1996).

The idea of pragmatic regimentation or metadiscursive framing—that is, establishing a general guide for interpreting an unfolding communication—has been richly explored in *Natural Histories of Discourse* (Silverstein & Urban, 1996). This volume is a substantial collection of work contributing to current linguistic anthropological inquiry, though it is not typically associated with language-oriented education research. Pertinent to our concerns, however, it is a set of advanced explorations of textuality that argue you cannot study texts as separable from and somehow reflecting other entities, such as culture, power, or identity. Instead, analysts must study *entextualization*, the continuous interplay of text, context, and evaluation from which emerge what we think of as texts. From the study of this interplay or process, rather than of text artifacts in isolation, we gain insight into how linguistic practices construct, as well as reflect, aspects of "culture," "power," or "identity." Drawing upon the concept of *entextualization*, I argue that simultaneous analytic attention to denotational language, indexical-interactive patterns, and metadiscursive framing is necessary if we wish to understand language, literacy, and identity—not as decontextualized, autonomous, or essential, but rather as situated processes that both (re)present and (re)construct more abstract features of the social order.

Having introduced a set of concepts drawn from or consistent with those framing most of the contributions to this volume, let me now introduce a second set of theoretical concerns. I do this because, in my opinion, a linguistic anthropology of education needs to look outside of its own disciplinary matrix. A motive for looking outside the confines of anthropology are suggested by Wortham in the introduction to this volume. There he argues that (1) "trying to connect micro and macro-level processes" is central to linguistic anthropology of education (p. 5) but (2) "cultural anthropologists have never been centrally concerned with formal education" (p. 3). In my understanding of the discipline of anthropology, it is social or cultural anthropologists who have been most steadfast in trying to understand and develop theories of micro/macro connections. Assuming that Wortham is correct in (1) and (2), then we face this question: How are we to understand the relation between school and society? Put another way, whether we see ourselves as linguistic anthropologists who study education, or as education researchers who believe that a systematic study of language use can be fruitful, where do we look to understand our contemporary social conditions and the place of learning and schooling in such conditions?

I further suggest that the classic writings on the ethnography of communication (E of C) (Gumperz & Hymes, 1986), which provided an orientation and inspiration for much qualitative sociolinguistic research in education (e.g., Cook-Gumperz, 1986; Heath, 1983; Philips, 1982), would need considerable retooling before being of much help in understanding the nature of identity and inequality in the so-called information society (Castells, 1996) that seems to be our current condition. Three quick points are pertinent here. First, core concepts of this tradition, such as "speech community," look quite different in an era of transnational capital, global media, and postmodern identity dynamics (Rampton, 1998). Second, many key social institutions, such as family, school, and work, which were taken as stable and predictable within the E of C tradition, have undergone radical change in the last thirty years (Group, 1996; Heath, 2000). Third, processes such as emergence were either absent from or underdeveloped in E of C concepts such as "communicative competence" (a point made by Wortham, in the Introduction, as well as by Gumperz, 1982).

Although recent work by linguistic anthropologists has moved beyond earlier frameworks, taking up questions such as nationalism, state-endorsed hegemonic culture, and, most generally, how "member's language ideologies mediate between social structure and forms of talk" (Kroskrity, 1998, p. 12), little of this recent work has directly addressed questions of education or, for that matter, whether we live in a distinctly "late" or "post" modern era. More pointedly, although the concepts discussed here—indexicality, creativity, poetic structure, and metadiscursive framing—contribute to a viable social-cum-linguistic constructivism, they do not, in and of themselves, provide a clear image of what society is like: how it is organized, what its primary institutions are, or whether it is changing or static. This involves two problems or shortcomings, which I can only list here. First, there is an agnosticism about macro-sociological structure, or, what is effectively the same, an assumption that such structure need not be analyzed unless directly evident in language use. Second, there is an aloofness from, or implicitness about, normative questions, and this leads to the impression that scholarship is somehow its own reward, or that social criticism is at best an ad hoc and occasional concern.

There is, however, a line of inquiry that is robustly sociological, if not anthropological, and persistently oriented to language analysis as well as normative social critique. I refer here to critical discourse analysis (CDA), represented focally though not exclusively by various publications of Fairclough and collaborators (Chouliaraki & Fairclough, 1999; Fairclough, 1995). This tradition has taken education as a major area of focus, but it is not regarded as ethnographic or anthropological in its orientation to language. As contrasted with the constructivist orientation of linguistic anthropology, CDA argues a more socially determinist position—in particular, that you can study texts in (relative) isolation as simultaneously reflecting local, institutional, and societal domains. Critics have argued that CDA analyses often work with decontextualized language samples (Verscheuren, 2001) and that its institutional analyses are schematic at best (Blommaert, 2001); however, there are promising developments by new workers in this framework. Rogers (2000), for example, presents an ethnographically grounded study of family literacy practices, which consistently applies CDA research categories, and Tusting (2000) presents a similarly grounded exploration of textual practices and religious identity formation. The determinist/constructivist contrast is a significant area of disagreement, however. Essentially, it reflects from marxian commitments on the part of CDA and philosophical pragmatist commitments in LA. In addition to this philosophical difference, as Blommaert et al. (2001) have discussed in a special journal issue exploring links between LA and CDA, both traditions tend to ignore each other's work. However, as I have argued as part of that discussion (Collins, 2001), there are significant areas of agreement and overlap, notwithstanding the differences. For example, there is a shared commitment in both lines of inquiry to a tripartite schema of analysis involving language form per se (the denotational), interaction and situated interpretive practices (the indexical), and society-wide ideological processes (the metadiscursive).

The particular concept that I want to draw from CDA is that of the *technologization of discourse*. This awkward term builds on the idea, drawn from social theory about late modernity and global capitalism, that heightened reflexive awareness is a systemic need in contemporary society, a pervasive feature of organizational life as well as practical consciousness (Castells, 1999; Giddens, 1991; Habermas, 1987). Put most simply, such heightened reflexivity demands emerge from the lessening of traditional authority (e.g., religious or parental authority), widespread deregulatory dynamics in the economy and other formal institutions (e.g., the upward ratcheting of self-involvement in "health care"), and the need for "information" in basic production (e.g., the use of computers in the workplace). Needed reflexivity can be imposed top-down, by so-called expert guidance, or it can spring up from sources in the lifeworld, that is, in everyday life and interaction. The term *technologization of discourse* refers to a top-down strategy, involving a combination of the following:

> (i) research into the discursive practices of social institutions and organizations, (ii) redesign of those practices in accordance with particular strategies and objectives, usually those of managers and bureaucrats, and (iii) training of institutional personnel in these redesigned practices. (Fairclough, 1995, p. 91)

However, as Chouliaraki and Fairclough acknowledge in a recent survey of theories of late modernity, there is always a counter-pressure, a resistance to or appropriation of imposed strategies and practices (1999, pp. 93–94). It is here, I would suggest, that the encounter between LA and CDA can perhaps be most fruitful. LA insists on analyzing connected stretches of discourse and allows for more power-neutral (or at least nondominant) metadiscursive framing. This should enable us to discern those situations in which "technologization of discourse," although perhaps a pervasive tendency toward regimenting discourse, is only one strategy among many. The contested nature of the discursive field, which LA concepts allow us to analyze with some precision, comes out sharply in the case I develop below. This case examines a situation in which the redesign of teacher discourse is aimed at producing a less authoritarian style of instruction-as-conversation, and this design-shift in expected discourse makes novel reflexivity demands on both tutors and students.

Before immersing ourselves in the details of this case, let us recall that questions about heightened reflexivity and hybridity in pedagogic exchanges will be addressed by analyzing indexical dimensions of language, including pronoun use, poetic structure, and metadiscursive framing. The analysis of these processes is intended as an exploration of the notion of entextualization, a testing of the CDA concept of technologization of discourse, and a descriptive/analytic contribution to a linguistic anthropology of education.

CASE: THE UNIVERSITY LITERACY LAB

The material presented in this section is drawn from a set of case studies that focus on middle school struggling readers being tutored in a university practicum. Such practica are a standard part of the clinical training of reading specialists. In this practicum the teachers tutored individual students while being taught themselves by university instructors and peers, through teaching conferences grounded in peer observation and discussion of ongoing and previously video-taped tutoring sessions. What was distinctive about the university literacy lab in which the practicum occurred was its commitment to a student-centered pedagogy. What this entailed was encouraging reflexive self-awareness on the part of the students in tutoring sessions while also, through the practicum, encouraging the teacher/tutors to reflect upon and change their teaching practices. More specifically, the literacy pedagogy used in the tutorials was a neo-Vygotskian approach that required students learn to be better readers by developing "self-extending systems of learning" (Lyons, Pinnell, & Defrod, 1993). That is, they were to become better readers by becoming more aware of their own reading practices and of their role as agents in the act of reading or writing. This emphasis seems worthwhile enough, on the face of it, but, as we shall see, there is evidence that it poses difficulties for the students and tutors—on the one hand, because the requirement to be reflexive itself can be unfamiliar and in conflict with a student's or a tutor's view of what reading is; on the other, because reflexivity invites agency, which can exceed the usual bounds of the teacher-student encounter, blurring the line between engagement and disruption. At the heart of the tutorial encounter we analyze there was thus a reflexive pedagogical duality: how did tutors learn to reflect on the practice of teaching while encouraging students to reflect on the act of reading, all without over-burdening the practice or the act with commentary?

As noted earlier, the case reported in this chapter was one of a set of case studies of students, tutors, and families.[1] The overall project developed primarily through collective research meetings—involving research professors, graduate research assistants, tutors, and practicum instructors—in which we reviewed a range of materials and studied videotapes of tutorial sessions. The primary focus of the case reported here was tutor/student interactions during the tutorials, which occurred twice weekly over the course of three months. There were also initial and concluding assessments of students by tutors, as well as a concluding performance by students for parents and tutors. The overall practicum project included a host of material concerning students, their teachers, and the instructional processes; and the differing case studies drew on audio- and video-tapes of tutoring sessions, student essays, student self-assessments and tutor assessments, journals between tutors and students' parents, and students' reading diaries and writing samples.

Our initial and provisional research question about the tutorial encounter had to do with the interplay of learning, pedagogy, and identity; but it also raised the issue of a diffuse yet undeniable intertextuality: how did students' reading performances relate to their understandings of themselves as readers, to the school's prior judgments, and to a tutor's initial assessments as well as ongoing interactional guidance during specific tutorials? In this regard it is pertinent that there was a general evaluation that preceded the tutorial encounters and influenced both the tutors' initial assessment and the students' sense of themselves as literate—that is, the students' literate identities. All of the students in the tutorials in the study period, the spring of 2000, were "struggling middle school readers," more specifically, they were adolescents who were failing to meet official school standards for reading and writing. The two boys profiled below had both been "sent to resource rooms" for special education assistance. In other words, they had been assigned to periods of remedial reading instruction that occurred outside of the regular classroom, presumably because they had scored more than two years below their grade level on standardized tests of their reading ability (the official criterion for such special placement). Both desired to escape such stigmatized extra assistance and were thus willing to attend three months of after-school tutorials. But the history of their falling behind and of the symbolic violence of failing in school seemed to have produced in them opposed yet familiar responses, either a passivity or a combativeness in the pedagogical encounter (Bourdieu & Champagne, 2000). In the case at hand, however, such summary generalizations—"passiveness," "combativeness"— will need to be unpacked as we examine how positioning of self and other occurs while engaging with text and talk about text. What we will see is that apparent lack of engagement or confrontation depend on how a tutorial encounter is framed, or, more precisely, on how a dynamic interplay of speaking, acting, and evaluating results in a certain entextualization of pedagogy, identity, and text.

PROFILES AND COMPARISONS

Overview

The student/tutor profiles that follow are interpretive summaries based on the following data sources. We examined the tutors' initial and final assessments of the middle school students they tutored, looking at the language used to describe students and also at specific evidence of changes in literacy practices. We also examined the students' ideas about reading and writing, as these were stated on written questionnaires about literacy activities, conducted as part of the tutorial sequence. Our research group developed a working sense of tutorials from (1) conversations with tutors and the practicum instructor, (2) viewing several complete tutorials, and (3) intensively studying smooth and difficult tutorial segments, as judged by participant tutors. We selected these last, contrastive, segments because we wanted to have a set of examples in which there was engagement and a shared sense of activity and in which the opposite held, in which there was apparent disengagement and uncertainty between tutor and student about one another's conversational intentions. We collectively viewed and discussed these segments in order to clarify the bases for our sense of interactional difficulties and our interpretations of what activities the students and tutors were negotiating as they dealt with each other in the tutorial context.

Billie (& Sarah)

The first tutor/student team we will discuss involved a young Euro-American adolescent, Billie, and his tutor, Sarah, a Euro-American woman. Billie was initially characterized by the practicum instructor as quiet and cooperative. The initial assessment of his reading and writing, by Sarah, commented on his pleasant disposition and interest in improving his learning, but also on his placement in the "resource room," his word-by-word reading style, in which he used his finger to guide his eyes, and on his need for a wider range of strategies for approaching texts. His own written or interview comments about reading focused on recognizing words and reading quickly and without too many mistakes. In viewing videotapes of several tutorial sessions, it was clear that Billie was quiet in this setting. Perhaps naturally shy, he seemed uncomfortable with reading and being asked about his reading, and he was unforthcoming except under the gentlest of questioning strategies.

What was striking when viewing segments showing interactional difficulty was a pattern of pursuit-and-avoidance. This was consistently signaled through eye gaze, gesture, and verbal response. While the tutor, Sarah, looked directly at Billie most of the time, Billie looked away, rarely making eye contact; if he were facing Sarah, Billie would look up and away instead of looking directly at his tutor. In terms of posture, a parallel display occurred: Sarah would orient her body and lean toward Billie frequently, while Billie would orient straight ahead, at a perpendicular angle to Sarah, and at times he simply leaned away. Sarah asked many direct questions about what Billie was reading and his reading strategies, and Billie gave minimal answers, with many "I don't knows" and "maybes" expressed in the faint voice and flat intonation of "if you say so" compliance.

The tutoring sessions flowed smoothly in places. For example, at the beginning of sessions Sarah and Billie sometimes exchanged little stories about their day or some event in their past. But difficulties seemed to occur when Sarah asked Billie about his strategies for reading. To illustrate the layering of referential talk and indexically signaled interactional positions, which together contribute to a situated framing of "reading," let us examine a transcript excerpt in detail. Before the excerpt in (1), Billie has just finished reading a passage aloud from a book, and Sarah is praising him for his performance. She then begins asking about previewing strategies, but she is in fact doing more than asking. In accordance with many reading pedagogies, and specifically with the pedagogy of the practicum, she is "modeling" strategies. She does so by providing Bakhtinian (Bakhtin, 1981) voices, momentary embodiments of a readerly identity for Billie to try out; these are presented as an imagined utterance that Billie might himself speak when embarking on a reading task. Billie, for his part, through his shrugs, nods, and brief responses, signals an awareness of the kind of routine they are engaged in, the pragmatic demands of this talk, at least at the level of responding to a teacher's questions. Twice he also gives voice, albeit briefly, to his view of reading, and, as the segment ends, he speaks to a different yet related aspect of himself as student.

(1) Billie and Sarah: Avoidance, Pragmatic Compliance, and Reported Speech[2]

1	S:	Did it help thinking about (xxx) first before you actually got to
2		reading it? You know..before you actually read the message?
3	B:	Yeah ((brief eye contact))
4	S:	Or do you think that when you came to that part it kind of fell
5		together for you anyway?
6	B:	(3) ((looking down)) I don't know. I'm trying if I have to read... I
7		bet I can do it...Like if I started to read ..if I came to it.. it might take
8		me a little bit but not as long as some words.
9	S:	So you think it was better looking at it ahead of time so you can
10		have a more fluent read=
11	B:	=((looks up, makes brief eye contact, nods head))=
12	S:	=Do you ever think about doing that when you're alone reading?
13		Like say you know how we do the introduction?=
14	B:	=((makes brief eye contact, nods head))=
15	S:	=You know how we say *'there might be words in here'*? Do you ever
16		try doing that ahead of time? Like say.. *'Well.. I want to read this page..*
17		*But maybe I want to look for words that might.. you know.. I might trip up*
18		*on or might be confusing to me.'* Do you ever think of doing anything
19		like that?
20	B:	((shrugs shoulders)) (2) I dunno ((looks away))
21	S:	Is that something you might want to think about?
22	B:	Yeah.. Maybe ((brief eye contact))=
23	S:	=Does it help when we do an introduction like that? Does it
24		become.. you know... what? Tell me about that.
25	B:	It helps.. Like when ((looks down at book in lap)).. So it doesn't
26		take me a long time. Like.. Or if I get stuck.. ((begins moving book
27		around))=
28	S:	Uh huh. So.. you know it's okay to do that. It's okay to look in a

29   section that you're going to read to say.. *'Um.. Let's see what words*
30   *might give me a little bit of trouble'.* Maybe try to get to them first... ((B
31   flips through book, looks down)) You know.. just not spending a
32   whole lot of time.. But looking what words and maybe reading a
33   sentence and so when maybe when you went to read the whole
34   passage... So.. but I don't know.. Just another thing I was thinking
35   about for yourself.
36 B: ((nods head slightly, looks at book))
37 S: (4) But that was really nice, fluent reading. Very nice (2) What..
38   What did you think about it?
39 B: Good. ((looks at ceiling, leans back and away in chair))
40 S: Just good? You don't feel much like talking today.. Do you?
41 B: ((smiles, shakes head))
42 S: ((laughing)) Uh.. why?
43 B: I dunno. I'm tired.
44 S: Yeah? Kind of tired? Too many questions?
45 B: Well.. no. I like went to bed late at night because I had to put a
46   project for math together. ((looks away))
47 S: What was the project.. you know.. about? What did you do?
48 B: ((Looks back at S)) We had to take like ten shapes.. Anything.. And
49   then you could do anything but you had to have ten shapes.
50   ((straightens self in chair)) And then I made them into a statue. It
51   took all night because I forgot to tell my Mom.

Throughout this excerpt, Sarah asks questions aimed at whether Billie previews a text before he reads it, and Billie responds with nonverbal assent or very brief replies. In characterizing this set of exchanges, we might say that Sarah consistently enacts a metadiscursive frame of reading as "thinking and talking about what you are reading." There is evidence, however, that Billie has a different frame or model of reading in mind. Thus, in lines 5–6, after a long three-second pause, he gives voice to a view of reading as a struggle in which he can improve his speed, as he says "I'm trying . . . I bet I can do it . . . it might take me a little bit but not as long as some words." This view of reading, as fluent decoding, is a well-documented trap that struggling readers fall into: they take a symptom of skilled reading, speed, as the substance (Adams, 1993; Edelsky, 1996). Note that in line 21, in response to Sarah's questions about previewing a text, Billie again expresses this assumption when he replies "It [previewing] helps . . . so it [reading] doesn't take me a long time."

Sarah, for her part, is simultaneously questioning Billie about strategies and providing imagined utterances for Billie and herself. In particular, in lines 12–15 Sarah provides a set of virtual, as/if voices and speaking positions for Billie. These are worth considering in detail, for they exhibit considerable interactional complexity, in which a layering

of voices and speaking-subject positions constitute potential orientations to a text-that-might-be-read. In line 15 Sarah's "You know how we
say *'there might be words in here'*?" establishes a joint speaking perspective: "You know" is a performative index evoking a common or shared
viewpoint; in "How we say" the "we" encompasses both Sarah and
Billie; and "'there might be words in here'" literally puts words in their
virtual, collective mouths. "Do you ever try doing that . . ." provides
advice, phrased as a question, about when such talk to self-and-a-text
might be appropriate. "Like say," in line 16 continues the potential
dialogue: "*'Well, I want to read this page, but maybe I want to look for words
that might, you know, I might trip up on or might be confusing to me.'* " In
this imaginary monologue with oneself, about a text one intends to
read, the "I" is Billie who might say "Well, I want to read this page."
But it is a virtual or possible Billie that Sarah's represented dialogue
invites. The actual Billie, when asked "Do you ever think of doing
anything like that?" shrugs his shoulders in line 20, and waits a long
two seconds, before replying "I dunno" and looking away.

When Sarah presses this noncommital gestural and verbal response,
asking "Is that something you might want to think about" she is met
with "Yeah maybe" in line 22. She begins with a further specific question on line 23, "Does it help when we do an introduction like that?"
Then she changes the focus of her question with "Does it become,"
slowing down her speed and delivery and inserting another "you
know," before ending the question with an open-ended "what?" and
following with the elicitation directive "Tell me about that." This garners from Billie more than the usual nod, shrug, or two words. Instead
he responds with another statement of his difficulties with reading,
phrased as a lack of speed or as stasis (on lines 25-26): "It helps, like
when, so it doesn't take me a long time. Like, or if I get stuck."

The cycle, if I may call it that, is repeated. Sarah acknowledges his
reply with an "Uh huh" in line 28. This is followed with a "So" and a
pause ". . .," which frequently suggests a reorientation of topic in conversation exchanges (Schiffrin, 1994), after which Sarah begins to reas-
sure Billie that previewing is appropriate: "you know it's okay to do
that." She then establishes the imaginary pedagogic scenario, that is,
the reading and self-interrogation that a reflective pedagogy encourages: "It's okay to look in a section that you're going to read to say..
'Um.. Let's see what words might give me a little bit of trouble'." In the actual
real-time of this interaction, however, Billie restricts himself to nodding,
looking away, or one-word responses.

I would suggest that there are two discursive or interactional planes
relevant to this encounter: (1) a "local" interactive plane in which Sarah
questions Billie about previewing a text and he replies, and (2) a "virtual" plane in which Billie speaks to himself about a text he intends to

read. The virtual plane is largely if not entirely Sarah's creation. She is enacting a model, providing utterances that enact a metadiscursive frame of reading-as-talking-and-thinking-about-text. She is suggesting, through questions and, more evocatively, through questions Billie might speak to himself, an ideal reader who would orient to a text as her teacherly self suggests.

Attention to pronouns provides a line of evidence linking one plane and another; or, in the theoretical terms introduced earlier, pronouns index participant positions, and their patterned use poetically structures or otherwise supports a regimentation of participant positioning. Thus in line 13, the "you" with which Sarah has heretofore (locally) addressed Billie becomes the "we" of a virtual space: "You know how **we** do the introduction," which referentially establishes a cognitive scene and interactionally prepares the "how **we** say . . ." in line 15. After this discursive joining of Sarah and Billie, Billie is then redifferentiated, not as "you" but rather as the "I" and "me" of "*I want to read this page . . . I want to look for words that might trip me up*" (lines 17, 18).

Billie, however, does not enter into this suggested frame. He appears reluctant to discuss strategies for reading, perhaps because reading is an activity he associates with "getting stuck" and "tak[ing] a long time" but not with questioning a text. The local interaction plane provides various evidence that Billie cannot or will not enter into the virtual interaction: he nods and shrugs, glances away, and gives one-word responses, but he does not take up Sarah's offered dialogue or otherwise ratify her usage. His general dis-ease with talking about reading is plainly evident in lines 37–41, here repeated:

> S: (4) But that was really nice, fluent reading. Very nice (2) What.. What did you think about it?
> B: Good. ((looks at ceiling, leans back and away in chair))
> S: Just good? You don't feel much like talking today.. Do you?
> B: ((smiles, shakes head))

Sarah, who is attempting to manage the local and virtual planes, not only provides the voices and speaking positions of an imaginary strategic reader, but also shifts gears, evoking sociability through "you know" and changing from precise to open-ended queries. In lines 34–35, her speech becomes noticeably slower, more filled with pauses, and she expresses considerable tentativeness: "So . . . but I don't know .. Just another thing I was thinking about for yourself." Indeed, the somewhat strained phrasing "another thing I was thinking about for yourself" expresses well the complexity of the enterprise which is temporarily being abandoned: suggesting a way of thinking for another through modeling how that other person might "think aloud" for himself in novel ways. At the end she also acknowledges the simple humanity of this struggling adolescent reader, alluding in line 44, with "too many questions," to the often relentless quality of schooled inquiry. She elicits in the final lines (48-51) the longest response from Billie during this segment, a response that brings into play another, ironic aspect of his student identity, for he inhabits a familiar world of school time pressures in which it is necessary to "take all night" on math projects but to not "take a long time" when reading.

In the exchanges between Sarah and Billie we have Sarah trying to present "reading" as a highly reflexive activity, in which one previews the act as part of entering into it, asking questions of the text and one's capacity before the text, as in *"I want to look for words that might trip me up."* She attempts this metadiscursive framing of reading by interweaving direct interaction, what I have called the local interaction plane, with imaginary dialogue, a virtual interaction plane, which offers a "readerly" voice for Billie to try out. Billie does not take up the framing or otherwise enter into the virtual dialogue. Faced with Sarah's diversity of pronouns and voices, he shrugs or looks away and expresses a different conception of reading, a less self-aware vision of reading as speed and fluency. This model or alternative framing of reading is consistent with what he otherwise says, for example, in a initial interview with Sarah. However, lest this seem simply a story of pedagogical disconnect, let me also note that there is evidence that by the end of the tutorial program, Sarah's programmatic insistence about strategies had apparently taken hold. In other, later tutorials, and in his final assessments, Billie reports using such strategies in regular schooling and in out-of-school reading activities. The point of the foregoing analysis was to explore the discursive underpinning and interactional challenges of novel reflexivity demands. This is shown from a different perspective in the next profile.

Karl (& Stacey)

The second student-tutor team consists of a young African-American adolescent, Karl, and his tutor, Stacey, a Euro-American woman. Karl was initially characterized by the practicum instructor as active and "really interesting." In Stacey's initial assessment of Karl, she wrote that he was apparently reading several years behind his grade level and that, although curious and interested in books, he read in a quick and heedless fashion, neither correcting his own errors nor attending to punctuation. In Karl's own responses to a literacy questionnaire he professed to like reading "better than writing," and he phrased the purposes of reading as "to find out what [a text] is about" and to learn "bigger words." In viewing videotapes of several tutorial sessions, it was clear that Karl was anything but quiet in the tutorial setting. Alert and quick to respond, even if only with "I dunno," he often seemed unwilling to follow Stacey's line of questioning and at times contested her claims or her choice of topic.

When viewing segments that had been selected as showing interactional difficulty, there seemed to be a pattern of confrontation (rather than the pursuit-and-avoidance found with Sarah and Billie). Stacey oriented to Karl often, turning her body toward him and reaching toward him with her hands when she spoke. Karl, for his part, usually oriented straight ahead, perpendicular to Stacey, and he often manipulated food or drink during the session. But unlike Billie, he did meet Stacey's eyes frequently, and he occasionally turned and oriented his body toward her. Once, dramatically, Karl pretended to pour drink from a soda bottle onto Stacey's head and body in response to, and pointed rejection of, her warning to him to be careful and not spill the drink. There was also a notable verbal pattern, found in several interaction sequences, in which Karl undercut Stacey's verbal "openings," either denying their importance ("I know, I have experienced X already"), or their factual accuracy ("X is Z, not Y"), or simply changing the subject (for example, once when Stacey asked something about reading, Karl announced he was going to the "Great Escape," a popular amusement park in the area).

At issue in the frequent negotiations between Stacey and Karl were different conceptions of reading. As with Sarah and Billie, this seemed to divide into a contrast between a metadiscursive framing of reading as talking about a text versus a model of reading as a more directly text-focused (and less interactive) decoding and reading aloud. Examining the indexically anchored interaction planes that compose the tutoring sessions will enable us to see that creating a shared referential orientation (that is, a sense of topic and relevant background knowledge) and evoking different aspects of participants' identities are central to the negotiation of what reading is "really about."

The next transcript excerpt (2) occurs near the beginning of a tutorial session. Karl and Stacey have been talking about music videos, a brief conversation about some shared, non-school item of interest being a common opening exchange in their and other tutorial sessions. Stacey then begins questioning Karl about the content of a book he has previously read. He denies knowing an answer to her first question, and then provides an answer, in a form that is pragmatically hard to incorporate into Stacey's plan of questioning. This pattern is repeated several times. In the latter part of the excerpt, Stacey and Karl begin to quote voices, or construct voices, from the text. In a characteristic move, Karl begins to link the voices to the world outside the text being read; in this case he links them to Stacey herself. As we will see, the different visions of what reading is are directly expressed near the end of the excerpt, after a somewhat tense engagement.

(2) Karl and Stacey: Confrontation, Pragmatic Undercutting, and Reported Speech

1	C:	But what happened last time? Let's think back (3)
2	K:	((eating, looks up))
3	S:	Do you remember what happened last time?
4	K:	Uh uh. ((plays with marker on desk))
5	S:	Let's look back in the book and see=
6	K:	=got in a fight ((muffled by food being chewed))
7	S:	Who got in a fight?
8	K:	Mongoose=
9	S:	=Why?
10	K:	I dunno=
11	S:	=Yes you do:.
12	K:	No I DO:N'T.
13	S:	Okay .. So.. before that what happened was Weasel wanted him to
14		go where? To steal the candy.. Right?.. and then Mongoose did what?
15	K:	((chewing candy)) yeah.. To go steal the candy
16	S:	And Mongoose did what?
17	K:	I dunno
18	S:	Okay.. Where did he go instead?
19	K:	Home.
20	S:	No. Where did Mongoose go instead? Remember? Where did
21		Mongoose go instead?
22	K:	((Checking the front of the book)) Library.
23	S:	Yeah.. And then remember Mongoose was saying- the library-
24		the librarian was like *'Oh, is this back? Are you finished with this?'*
25		And Mongoose said what?
26	K:	I dunno ((drinking from soda bottle))
27	S:	What did he say? Did he say he was finished with it? So.. he wasn't
28		finished with it so he took the book back.... Now.. Was Weasel mad?
29	K:	This is what he say.. He said *'WHEW!'*
30	S:	Did he say that?
31	K:	That's what he should- This is what he really was saying..
32		I dunno .. He said like *'Mmono'*
33	S:	I don't think he said that.. He said something- Okay.. So.. Weasel
34		was mad because of the fact that he kind of dissed him.. You know
35		what I mean?
36	K:	Like *'buwrt urrt'* ((hand in air as if stopping blow))=
37	S:	((laughing)) =And remember when we were talking about if your
38		friend like betrayed you.. You know=
39	K:	I dunno
40	S:	=Or if somebody
41	K:	PSYCHE!

```
42   S:   You would be=
43   K:   =you would be too
44   S:   I would be too.. I know
45   K:   (in a "girly" voice) 'I am coming over to your house to beat you up!'
46   S:   Huh?
47   K:   That is what you would say.
48   S:   I wouldn't say that.
49   K:   Can we get on with reading?
50   S:   Yes.. But we have to talk about it first.
51   K:   You always wanna talk about it when I wanna read..but when I
52        wanna read- when I don't wanna read you wanna read ((eats more
53        candy, looking at S))
54   S:   That's not true.
```

To get a sense of what I mean by "pragmatic undercutting," note that in line 4 Karl responds with a negative "uh uh" in response to the question "do you remember?" But then, in line 6, after Stacey has begun a different conversational move, he answers the question posed in 3 with a sentence fragment "got in a fight." The tutor clarifies this answer with a question "who," receiving the subsequent answer "Mongoose," but in line 9, when she asks "why," Karl replies quickly "I dunno." When she pointedly insists he does, he emphatically counters in line 12 "No I DO:N'T." Stacey tries another line of questions involving a second story character, Weasel, and in line 15 Karl offers a fragment "Yeah, to go steal the candy." But this is not an answer to the question just posed in line 14 about the character Mongoose; rather, it is a reiteration of the context of that question. When she repeats the question about Mongoose, she receives "I dunno" in line 17. In this exchange, Stacey and Karl are simultaneously pragmatically engaged and conversationally "off center." Karl does not simply refuse to interact with his tutor or retreat into silence. Instead, when asked a question, he often denies knowing the answer, then moments later provides an answer, but then rejects a further, clarifying question (lines 3-10); or, when Stacy has asked several questions in a row, he answers an earlier question, rather than the most recent, with an utterance "to go steal candy" that is not really an answer, and then he refuses to clarify (lines 13–17). There is some sort of ongoing delay and lack of fit between questions and answers, that I am calling "pragmatic undercutting." Whatever Karl's intentions might be, and they are likely diverse, the effect seems to be to keep Stacey uncertain. I take this to be the case given her responses and especially her frequent use of "So" or "OK" (13, 18, 27, 33), utterance forms which are frequently used to "repair" conversation that has gone awry (Schiffrin, 1994). It is also plausible that this interactional uncertainty contributes to Stacey's very traditional "check the facts" approach to pedagogy.

Let us now consider Stacey's use of pronouns and mental verbs as she attempts to establish a sort of "recalled text" for them to discuss. We can consider the use of the first person plural "us" in lines 1 and 5 ("Let's think back"; "Let's look back"), together with the question in line 3 "Do you remember what happened last time," as an effort to establish a referential space or "topic" for their joint consideration. The entire sequence might be roughly translated in mental and interactional terms as something like: "Let us both think back to the previous tutoring session and remember what was said and what we discussed about the text." But, as we have seen, this initial effort to orient current reading to previous understandings is undermined by Karl's responses.

In lines 20 and following, Stacey begins to introduce a new approach, abandoning the joint pronoun of "let's," again using the locution "remember," in lines 20 and 23, and now linking the injunction to recall things said in the text. Beginning around lines 23–24, Stacey and Karl begin to quote from the book, or, more specifically, to provide represented discourse that the book characters might have said. In line 23, Stacey opens "And then remember . . . the librarian was like *"Oh, is this back? Are you finished?"* Initially her question about what the character Mongoose said in response to the librarian's utterance garners from Karl another "I dunno." However, echoing the familiar pattern seen previously, the pragmatic undercutting or delay, when Stacey shifts to another question, Karl suddenly gives voice to the character Mongoose. In lines 29, 32, and 36, Karl seems to be reporting fragments of a dramatic exchange between two erstwhile friends, the characters Mongoose and Weasel, who have become angered with one another and might, in an imaginable world, come to blows: line 29 "This is what he say, he [Mongoose] said *'WHEW!'*," and in line 32 "He [Mongoose? Weasel?] said like *'mnonno'*," and in line 36 "[Mongoose said] Like *'burtwurt'* [while avoiding a likely blow]."

In an intervening line 33, Stacey has rejected Karl's quoting as insufficiently faithful to the text: "I don't think he [Weasel] said that." She begins to offer an alternative voice of the character Weasel but checks herself: "He [Weasel] said something-. . . So, OK. . . ." She then tries to evoke yet another realm of indexically presupposable "content" for their consideration, not the text per se, but aspects of a lifeworld that she and Karl have previously discussed. There follows a striking interactional dance in which Stacey and Karl both try to control the line of questioning and the evocable personae, which is reproduced below (lines 37–46, repeated):

S: ((laughing)) =And remember when we were talking about if your
      friend like betrayed you.. You know=
K: I dunno

S: =Or if somebody
K: PSYCHE!
S: You would be=
K: =you would be too
S: I would be too.. I know
K: (in a "girly" voice) *'I am coming over to your house to beat you up!'*
S: Huh?

In this exchange Stacey begins "And remember when we were talking about if your friend like betrayed you." Continuing across other lines, while Karl interjects, she seems to be trying to formulate an example to think with. Karl, however, refuses to join in this attempt to evoke a new shared context, replying "I dunno" to her non-interrogative "you know." This he follows with an emphatic "PSYCHE!," an idiom meaning something like "I fooled you," alluding directly to the playfulness of his prior "I dunno." Stacey, for her part, has continued formulating the new context as a likely emotional state of Karl's with "You [Karl] would be=." To this he immediately replies "=You [Stacey] would be too," and Stacey acknowledges "I would be too.. I know." This raises her own real self as a presupposable topic of talk, and Karl exploits this opening by "quoting" a virtual Stacey who, in a high-pitched and carefully standard-speaking voice, would threaten a disrespectful interlocutor with *"I am coming over to your house to beat you up."* It is with the rapidly spoken couplet "You[k] would be=/=You[s] would be too" that we can plainly see the indexically emergent properties of this stretch of discourse. Before this exchange, the lifeworld emotional state "When we were talking about if your [k] friend like betrayed you [k]" has been ostensibly about Karl. But Karl's rejoinder, "you would be too," and Stacey's acceptance, "I would be too.. I know"establishes either person as a presupposable referent of "you [k,s]."

With this commonality of a virtual lifeworld interactionally sanctioned, Karl then provides a mocking quotation of Stacey in such a world. To this Stacey replies with a non-ratifying "Huh?" Karl clarifies the virtual speaker of the utterance in line 48: "That's what you would say," and Stacey flatly rejects this utterance possibility: "I wouldn't say that." In giving voice to the book characters, and to each other, through represented speech, Karl and Stacey "enter into the book" (Willhelm, 1997). They become participants in an interactional text that includes their speaking positions and their quoted voices as well as the text-artifact being discussed.[3] This is when the tutoring session seems to "click," interaction becoming animated and smoothly timed, but it also leads into potentially dangerous territory. Karl has teased or mocked Stacey, and she rejects this. Then Karl bluntly asks in line 49, "Can we get on with reading?" This leads to a direct formulation of their alternative views of reading, Stacey's phrased as a "have to" obligation, Karl's as a clash of desired approaches (lines 49–51, repeated):

    K: Can we get on with reading?
    S: Yes.. But we have to talk about it first.
    K: You always wanna talk about it when I wanna read.

Karl and Stacey's exchanges resemble Billie and Sarah's in that virtual dialogue is employed in both as part of talking about a text to be read. Both boys are also reluctant to engage in this "talking about" reading. However, while Sarah is encouraging previewing as part of a strategy for reading, Stacey is insisting on reviewing. From one perspective, Stacey's pedagogy can be seen as quite traditional, simply a checking of students' understanding of literal content. I would suggest, however, that Stacey and Karl are nonetheless grappling with the challenges of reflexive pedagogy. This seems the case because of the numerous and intentional openings to Karl's lifeworld knowledge and experience included as part of the tutoring process. One of numerous examples can be seen in the excerpt just discussed, which begins with Stacey saying "You know how you would feel if. . . ." There is, however, a dynamic instability inherent in such efforts at student engagement. Students may simply enter into the virtual subjectivities on offer by replying with something like "Yes, I know how I would feel if. . . ." And presumably it is something like that orderly entering into virtual selves that Sarah sought of Billie and that Stacey sought of Karl. But students may also go beyond the proffered discursive position, seizing the moment for something more, as Karl does when he counters, "You would too. . . ." His response leads to a further discursive definition of teacher-as-equal, not authority, and, as equal, then as someone who can be mocked. Given Karl's propensity for egalitarian exchange, it is probably significant that both he and Stacey offer imaginary dialogue, as a way of animating the text being discussed and as a way of negotiating, of playing with possibilities, with what is "fair game" in the activity of reading.

DISCUSSION

In discussing both profiles, let me begin with the most obvious: teaching about and learning to read or write can involve multifaceted talk about and performances of text, as well as evaluations of said talk and performances. Such talk about and performances of text often involve Bakhtinian orientations to the voice of the other. As Bakhtin (1981) argued for a range of literary genres, appropriation of the voices of others, through various kinds of represented speech, is a pervasive device in socially attuned, indexically situated discourse (Lucy, 1993; Voloshinov, 1973). This may involve quoting one's direct interlocutors or a range of potential others, among them projections of characters in texts. Many possibilities can be seen in the represented discourse in Billie and Sarah's and Karl and Stacy's tutorial excerpts. However, such indexical maneuvers have emergent meanings; that is, they achieve their meanings depending on how context is construed, on how they are interactionally taken up. In excerpt (1), Sarah offers Billie a readerly identity that he might enter into through the speaker roles, the discursive positions, that she suggests. In excerpt (2), Stacey suggests that Karl "remember" what was said in a text by a character, offering a re-presented example of a character's utterance, as a way of orienting their discussion of the text. In both cases, however, these moves do not succeed. As noted, Billie is unwilling or unable to take up the voices that Sarah suggests, and Karl provides his own, other quotations, which are troublesome for Stacey's pedagogical strategy.

Something like poetic structure emerges in the effort to enforce or otherwise "regiment" given interpretations. In the cases already discussed, I have focused on one particular strand of evidence for such structure: the use of pronouns and their ratification, non-ratification, or indexical transformation in interaction sequences. In particular, the patterning of pronoun sequences in particular exchanges provides evidence of Sarah's linking of local and virtual interaction realms. Billie's shrugs and non-uptake, his inability or unwillingness to enter into the discursive "play," constitutes a non-ratification of Sarah's offering. This result is that the offering does not, at this time, become a shared representation of reading, readerly identities, and readerly voices. In the Stacey/Karl excerpt, Stacey's "You know how you would feel . . ." seeks to include the virtual/imaginable emotional world of locally present Karl as grounds for understanding the text being discussed. Her conversational move is transformed by Karl's "You would too . . .," which seeks to include the locally present Stacey into this virtual realm of presupposable feeling. This is a move that Stacey ratifies with her "I would too.. I know" and, henceforth, the indexically presupposable referent of "you" is either Karl or Stacey.

In the full excerpts just analyzed, there is evidence of considerable intertextuality or discursive hybridity. Along with familiar patterns of teachers questioning and students responding, voices are quoted of textual characters and interactants; quasi-therapeutic idioms are used (Sarah's "you know it's okay to do that"), as are vernacular phrases (Stacey's "dissed" and Karl's "PSYCHE!"); and Standard English voices are mockingly rendered. Recognizing and exploring this positional and discursive complexity bring out the dialogic messiness of these learning activities, while supporting the view of identities as complex amalgams. In the case at hand, they are minimally fashioned from prior institutional experiences as students and teachers; from lifeworld commonalities shared to create a bond (as when Sarah and Billie swap stories or Stacey and Karl discuss popular music); and from the possibilities and provocations of immediate, real-time interaction (and especially available voices).

Karl and Billie's institutionally defined identities as "problem readers" doubtlessly informed the interactional dynamics of their tutorials. It is quite likely that their resistance to a framing of reading as talk-about-the-text results from their familiarity with more constrained "drills and skills" approaches to literacy pedagogy, commonly used is remedial reading programs, in which fluent decoding is often emphasized over meaning-making (Spear-Swerling & Sternber, 1996).[4] However, each boy also engaged his tutor in ways that brought other aspects of who they were into play. In excerpt (1), an unforthcoming Billie presents his time-harried school life to a Sarah who will learn, over the course of the practicum, that taking time, extra time, is one of the keys to connecting with this young man, who is time-driven, so that he "stays up all night" on projects yet must not "take a long time" when reading. Combative Karl is at first glance hard to teach, and a plausible consequence of his frequent interactional challenges is to provoke from Stacey a defensive "check the facts" approach to discussing text. But the quickness with which he gives voice to characters in a text, and on this and other occasions enacts characters and scenes, continually reminds his tutor that he knows more than he initially professes, and that he expects more from reading than the formula that "you always begin with a review."

The analyses in this chapter have focused on difficult tutoring exchanges, in part because they seem to bring out clearly the difficulties of reflexivity. The concept of technologization of discourse sensitizes us to the myriad ways in which reflexivity is a strategic part of contemporary life. While appreciating the emphasis on top-down or expert-guided processes, in understanding cases such as the one just presented, as well as the more general politics of literacy, we need to remain alert to contrary tensions between top-down control and more bottom-up aspirations to self-awareness and self-guidance. Reading pedagogies are today hotly debated in political as well as academic realms. Many so-called explicit instruction programs (Adams, 1993) offer exemplary cases of the technologization of discourse: expert-designed and problem-oriented revamping of reading pedagogies in which teachers' roles, student responses, and available responses are all tightly "scripted" (Foorman, Francis, Fletcher, & Schatschneider, 1998; Lemann, 1997). In contrast, the tutorial program discussed previously opts for a more "bottom-up" reflexive orientation. Even without the rigors of explicit instruction programs, however, verbal interaction in classroom settings is typically highly regulated, with teachers controlling the direction and timing of talk (Mehan, 1979; Nystrand, Gamoran, Kachur, & Prendergast, 1997). In contrast, tutors such as those we have profiled are attempting something else: a more reciprocal, conversational exchange with those they are tutoring. Nonetheless, they maintain interactional control—Sarah through her persistence, Stacey through her reframing. Indeed, one of the conflicting demands the University Literacy Lab pedagogy makes on its practitioners is that they be simultaneously teachers and co-conversationalists in a world in which such a combination of roles in fact rarely occurs. The turn toward a more conversational style poses new demands for the students also. Billie is often baffled by queries that prod him toward a more self-conscious relation to his reading. His uncertainty is surely influenced both by his preoccupation with reading as fluent performance and by his apparent lack of familiarity with questions and approaches demanding heightened self-consciousness. Karl, for his part, presents ample evidence that when encouraged to be more engaged and self-monitoring, he will meet this programmatic reflexivity with flashes of insight that exceed the scope of lessons and with a vigorous testing of the student/teacher relation.

CONCLUSION

The pedagogical reflexivity preferred in the practicum and tutoring sessions was expressed through the trope of "teaching and learning as conversation." This approach was lauded in course books for the practicum (Lyons et al., 1993), and it is called for in other neo-vygotskian approaches to pedagogy. Pertinent to our concerns with discourse hybridity, such teaching-as-conversation is often proposed as a mode of coping, pedagogically, with the increasing sociocultural diversity of contemporary society (Cazden, 1988; Goldenberg, 1991). However, as Bernstein (1996) argues in an analysis of the prominence of education issues in contemporary politics, pedagogies are never simply about learning; they are simultaneously views of knowledge, modes of symbolic control, and schemes for identity. The trope of "teaching as conversation" may or may not match our prescriptions for the educational enterprise, but as linguistic anthropologists we are well aware, and can usefully demonstrate to others, that there are many kinds of conversation. What gets called conversation can include the tightly scripted exchanges of the "explicit instruction" currently favored by center-right politicians and their educational allies (Lemann, 1997); the reflexive yet nonetheless teacher-guided procedures of student-centered pedagogy, such as has been profiled previously; or the more open-ended dynamics of conversational exchanges embedded in everyday, non-institutionalized encounters (Schiffrin, 1994).

As the chapters in this volume argue, and as illustrated in the preceding analyses, the concepts and approaches of linguistic anthropology provide useful purchase on the interactional dynamics of situated meaning-making. But they can do more than this worthy but rather general task. Properly oriented, immersion in the systematic properties of situated language use can help us better understand the challenges faced by educational efforts in a society characterized by sharp inequalities and proliferating social differences—differences that can be both obstacles to and resources for learning and literate engagement. We live in an era in which "information" and self-guidance are increasingly central to fundamental economic, sociopolitical, and psychological processes (Bauman, 1997; Castells, 1999; Gee, Hull, & Lankshear, 1996; Giddens, 1991). Paradoxically, such "self-guidance" can be organized and imposed from the top down, or it can emerge from inchoate and "everyday" sources, or perhaps, as the preceding case suggests, from situated expert/non-expert negotiations of learning environments, identity potentials, and literacy practices.

Earlier linguistic anthropologists, also concerned with understanding language, learning, and social equity, rightly argued that we interpret discourse—and understand or misunderstand others—in terms of culture-based and situationally dynamic processes of which we are only partially aware (Gumperz, 1986; Hymes, 1996). I have argued that a linguistic anthropology of education needs to be aware of leading ideas drawn from social theoretic frameworks, such as those of postmodern reflexivity and elite-technical redesign of discourse. My argument does not entail that "empirical work," in this case close interactional and ethnographic description, merely confirms or disconfirms some "theoretical claim." In addition to its ethical concerns, our research should have as one of its goals theoretical engagement and reconstruction, in the sense discussed by Burawoy in *Ethnography Unbound* (1991): detailed, case-based work in dialogue with social theory. The more empirically grounded concepts of linguistic anthropology help us understand and characterize the emergent nature of all discourse. In the preceding analyses, for example, we see struggles for metadiscursive framing, for *entextualization*, not a simple technologizing of discourse. Such analytically principled demonstrations of emergence as well as system tendency are vital at a time when social theories are themselves concerned with non-deterministic models of interpretation and explanation and when a "linguistic turn" is widely acknowledged in social thought (Harvey, 1996). A linguistic anthropology of education that frankly engages with main currents in contemporary social theory can improve such theory while helping us better understand the efforts, obstacles, and mysteries of "teaching and learning" in the current era, a time of widely acknowledged social difference and ambivalent drives for control and autonomy in personal and social arrangements.

NOTES

The research reported here is part of a larger project, "Multiple Perspective Studies of Middle School Struggling Readers at a University Literacy Lab" conducted by a group of faculty and graduate students in the Department of Reading at the University at Albany/SUNY. Dr. Cheryl Dozier deserves major credit for pulling together the empirical materials for the analysis in this chapter, as well as the other "Multiple Perspective" studies. In developing the analysis and argument, I have benefitted from many sources: research discussions with colleagues and students in the Department of Reading at U Albany, among them Danielle Del Santo, Cheryl Dozier, Jennifer Grand, Susan Garnett, Peter Johnston, Mark Jury, and Becky Rogers; audience comments on early versions presented at the 99th Annual Meeting of the American Anthropological Association (November 2000, San Francisco, CA) and at the 22nd Ethnography in Education Research Forum (March 2001, Philadelphia, PA); and detailed comments on an earlier written version from Betsy Rymes and Stanton Wortham. All errors of fact or interpretation are my own.

1. The papers in the "Multiple Perspective" project examined four areas: (1) changes during the practicum in three middle school struggling readers (including two discussions in this chapter), (2) teachers' interactions with these students (the focus of this chapter), (3) interactions between university instructors and the tutors, and (4) the families' involvement (see Johnston et al., forthcoming). This chapter is the only one of the four studies to feature systematic analysis of language use in face-to-face interaction.

2. The transcript conventions are as follows: (xxx) signifies transcriber uncertainty; (( )) contains nonverbal descriptions of action, as in ((looks away)); two and three dots ".." and "..." indicate pauses of short but perceptible duration; (N) indicates a pause of N seconds duration; "=" marks utterances that continue with the same speaker, or quickly paired utterances between two speakers, or utterances and nonverbal acts which are interactionally continuous, as in a question which is followed by an immediate head nod or shrug. Full CAPS indicate emphatic stress on a word or syllable.

3. Very similar phenomena involving texts, participant identities, and the particular conditions of discourse are discussed in a book-length treatment by Wortham (1994); they are also the subject of several studies in Silverstein & Urban (1996).

4. Our project does not have direct evidence of how students in the tutorial program were previously taught. However, as noted earlier in the chapter, Billie referred in various places to his concern with reading "faster." As Stacey noted in her initial assessment, Karl usually read quickly and with little heed for word-recognition errors or punctuation. This reading style was observable in videotapes of him reading aloud early in the tutoring course. In short, the boys' expressed views and reading-aloud practices are consistent with a "drills and skills" pedagogy.

REFERENCES

Adams, M. (1993). *Beginning to Read: Thinking and Learning about Print*. Cambridge, MA: MIT Press.

Bakhtin, M. (1981). *The Dialogic Imagination*. Austin: University of Texas Press.

Bauman, Z. (1997). *Postmodernity and Its Discontents*. New York: Routledge.

Bernstein, B. (1996). *Pedagogy, Symbolic Control and Identity*. London: Taylor & Francis.

Blommaert, J. (2001). Context is/as critique. *Critique of Anthropology, 21*, 13–36.

Blommaert, J., Collins, J., Heller, M., Rampton, B., Slembrouck, S., & Verschueren, J. (2001). Introduction. *Critique of Anthropology, 21*, 5–12.

Bourdieu, P., & Champagne, P. (2000). Outcasts on the inside. In P. Bourdieu (Ed.), *The Weight of the World: Social Suffering in Contemporary Society* (pp. 421–27). Stanford, CA: Stanford University Press.

Brownstein, A. (November 6, 1999). Low scores add up to big job ahead. *Albany Times Union*, pp. A1, A5.

Burawoy, M. (1991). The extended case method. In M. Burawoy, A. Burton, A. Ferguson, K. Fox, J. Gamson, N. Gartrell et al. (Eds.), *Ethnography Unbound: Power and Resistance in the Modern Metropolis* (pp. 271–90). Berkeley: University of California Press.

Carnegie Council on Adolescent Development. (1989). *Turning Points: Preparing American Youth for the 21st Century: The Report of the Task Force on Education of Young Adolescents*. Washington: Carnegie Council of Adolescent Development.

Castells, M. (1996). *The Rise of the Network Society*. Oxford: Blackwell.

Castells, M. (1999). Flows, networks, and identities: A critical theory of the information society. In M. Castells, R. Flecha, P. Freire, H. Giroux, D. Macedo, & P. Willis (Eds.), *Critical Education in the Information Age* (pp. 37–64). New York: Rowman & Littlefield.

Cazden, C. (1988). *Classroom Discourse*. Cambridge, MA: Harvard University Press.

Chouliaraki, L., & Fairclough, N. (1999). *Discourse in Late Modernity*. Edinburgh: University of Edinburgh Press.

Coles, G. (1998). *Reading Lessons: The Debate over Literacy*. New York: Hill and Wang.

Coles, G. (2000). *Misreading Reading: The Bad Science That Hurts Children*. Portsmouth, NH: Heinemann.

Collins, J. (2001). Selling the market: Educational standards, discourse, and social inequality. *Critique of Anthropology, 21*, 143–163.

Cook-Gumperz, J. (1986). *The Social Construction of Literacy*. New York: Cambridge University Press.

Edelsky, C. (1996). *With Literacy and Justice for All: Rethinking the Social in Language and Education*. London: Taylor & Francis.

Fairclough, N. (1995). *Critical Discourse Analysis*. London: Longman.

Foorman, B., Francis, J., Fletcher, J., & Schatschneider, C. (1998). The role of instruction in learning to read: Preventing reading failure in at-risk children. *Journal of Educational Psychology, 90*, 37–55.

Gee, J., Hull, G., & Lankshear, C. (1996). *The New Work Order: Behind the Language of the New Capitalism*. St. Leonards, NSW: Allen & Unwin.

Giddens, A. (1991). *Modernity and Self-identity: Self and Society in the Late Modern Age*. Cambridge, U.K.: Polity Press.

Goldenberg, C. (1991). *Instructional Conversations and Their Classroom Applications*. Los Angeles: National Center for Research on Cultural Diversity and Second Language Learning.

Group, N. L. (1996). A pedagogy of multiliteracies: Designing social futures. *Harvard Educational Review, 66,* 60–92.

Gumperz, J. (1982). *Discourse Strategies.* New York: Cambridge University Press.

Gumperz, J. (1986). Interactional sociolinguistics in the study of schooling. In J. Cook-Gumperz (Ed.), *The Social Construction of Literacy* (pp. 45–68). New York: Cambridge University Press.

Gumperz, J. (1996). Introduction to part IV. In J. Gumperz & S. Levinson (Eds.), *Rethinking Linguistic Relativity* (pp. 359–373). New York: Cambridge University Press.

Gumperz, J., & Hymes, D. (Eds.). (1986). *Directions in Sociolinguistics* (2nd ed.). Oxford: Blackwell.

Habermas, J. (1987). *Lifeworld and System: A Critique of Functionalist Reason. The Theory of Communicative Action* (Vol. II). Boston: Beacon Press.

Hanks, W. F. (1996). *Language and Communicative Practices.* Boulder, CO: Westview Press.

Harvey, D. (1996). *Justice, Nature and the Geography of Difference.* Oxford: Oxford University Press.

Haviland, J. (1996). Text from talk in Tzotzil. In M. Silverstein & G. Urban (Eds.), *Natural Histories of Discourse* (pp. 45–78). Chicago: University of Chicago Press.

Heath, S. (1983). *Ways with Words: Language, Life, and Work in Communities and Classrooms.* New York: Cambridge University Press.

Heath, S. (2000). Discussant remarks, session on literacy studies and the ethnography of communication. Paper presented at the American Anthropological Association Annual Meeting, San Francisco.

Hymes, D. (1996). *Ethnography, Linguistics, Narrative Inequality: Towards an Understanding of Voice.* Bristol, PA: Taylor & Allen.

Jencks, C., & Phillips, M. (Eds.). (1998). *The Black-White Test Score Gap.* Washington: Brookings Institution Press.

Jochnowitz, J. (January 11, 2001). School aid overhaul ordered. *Albany Times Union,* pp. A1, A9.

Kroskrity, P. (Ed.). (1998). *Regimes of Language.* Santa Fe: School of American Research.

Lemann, N. (November, 1997). The reading wars. *The Atlantic Monthly, 282,* 128–134.

Lucy, J. (Ed.). (1993). *Reflexive Language: Reported Speech and Metapragmatics.* New York: Cambridge University Press.

Lyons, C., Pinnell, G., & Defrod, D. (1993). *Partners in Learning.* New York: Teachers College Press.

Mehan, H. (1979). *Learning Lessons.* Cambridge, MA: Harvard University Press.

Nystrand, M., Gamoran, A., Kachur, R., & Prendergast, C. (1997). *Opening Dialogue: Understanding the Dynamics of Language and Learning in the English Classroom.* New York: Teachers College Press.

Ochs, E. (1992). Indexicality and socialization. In J. Stigler, R. Shweder, & G. Herdt (Eds.), *Cultural Psychology: Essays on Comparative Human Development* (pp. 287–308). Cambridge: Cambridge University Press.

Philips, S. (1982). *The Invisible Culture: Communication in Classrom and Community on the Warm Springs Indian Reservation.* Highland Park, IL: Waveland Press.

Rampton, B. (1998). Speech community. In J. Verschueren, J. O. Ostman, J. Blommaert, & C. Bulcaen (Eds.), *Handbook of Pragmatics 1998 .* Amsterdam: John Benjamins.

Rogers, R. (2000). *Discourse and Literate Identities: A Critical and Ethnographic Study of Family Literacy in an Urban Community.* Albany: State University of New York Press.

Schemo, J. (January 11, 2001). Bush seems to ease his stance on school's accountability. *New York Times,* www.nytimes.com/2001/07/10/poli...C.html.

Schiffrin, D. (1994). *Approaches to Discourse.* Oxford: Blackwell.

Silverstein, M. (1976). Shifters, linguistic categories, and cultural description. In K. Basso & H. Selby (Eds.), *Meaning in Anthropology* (pp. 11–55). Albuquerque: University of New Mexico Press.

Silverstein, M., & Urban, G. (Eds.). (1996). *Natural Histories of Discourse.* Chicago: University of Chicago Press.

Spear-Swerling, L., & Sternber, R. (1996). *Off Track: When Poor Readers Become "Learning Disabled".* Boulder, CO: Westview Press.

Tusting, K. (2000). Written Intertextuality and the Construction of Catholic Identity in a Parish Community: An Ethnographic Study. Unpublished Ph.D. thesis, Lancaster University, U.K.

Verscheuren, J. (2001). Predicaments of criticism. *Critique of Anthropology, 21,* 59–81.

Voloshinov, V. N. (1973). *Marxism and the Philosophy of Language.* New York: Academic Press.

Willhelm, J. (1997). *You Gotta Be the Book.* New York: Teachers College Press.

3

Communicative Practice, Cultural Production, and Situated Learning

Constructing and Contesting Identities of Expertise in a Heterogeneous Learning Context

Kevin O'Connor

In this chapter, I consider some ways in which linguistic anthropology can contribute to understanding "the cultural production of the educated person" (Levinson & Holland, 1996), to use a phrase that nicely captures an important focus in recent anthropological approaches to education. Work on cultural production is part of a broader project in the social sciences over the past three decades, a project that explores how both persons and forms of social organization are constituted through social practice. Among the major aims of this work has been to challenge conceptions of culture as a stable and relatively unproblematic body of knowledge that is transmitted from one generation to the next. Instead, culture is seen as a dynamic process in which agents create meaning by drawing on cultural forms as they act in social and material contexts, and in so doing produce themselves as certain kinds of culturally located persons while at the same time reproducing and transforming the cultural formations in which they act.

Thus "cultural production" has a double meaning: it is concerned with how persons are produced as cultural beings, and with how this production of persons results in the (re)production of cultural formations. Recent anthropological approaches to education have been concerned with this process as it relates to learning and schooling. This work has focused on the interplay between social structure and human agency in sites in which "educated persons" are produced. In this view, becoming "educated"—or "uneducated," or even "uneducable"—however these might be locally understood, is an important way in which persons become produced within cultural groups, and thereby contribute to the production of the culture.

This chapter focuses on how local processes of interaction are related to broader, and often conflicting, conceptions of what it means to be educated. Specifically, I examine the negotiation of "identities of expertise" in one site designed to produce educated persons—a multi-institution undergraduate engineering project. This site is of interest for several reasons. First, the project was part of an attempt to challenge overtly what it means to be an expert in the discipline of engineering. It did this by attempting to elevate the status of traditionally devalued "practical" aspects of engineering activity. That is, practical, and not just theoretical, knowledge was taken as central to being educated. Second, and closely related, the consortium was challenging traditional views of how one becomes an expert by designing practical projects as privileged sites for learning, as opposed to teaching engineering science outside the context of "real world" activity.

This reconceptualization of the nature of expertise and the process by which it is attained drew heavily upon work by educational researchers and designers who have adopted and developed a view of cognition and learning that is itself grounded in theories of cultural production. This allows for an examination of the cultural production of identities of expertise, at a historical moment in which theories of cultural production are themselves used as a partial basis for defining what it means to be an "expert." The sponsoring consortium was also attempting to promote "boundary crossing" between historically separate institutions. In doing so, it had explicitly egalitarian objectives of providing participants from lower-status and less technologically well-equipped schools with access to the knowledge and the technological resources of higher status schools. However, this had another, unintended effect. It allowed for relationships to be negotiated among students who might otherwise never come into contact with one another, thus creating new possibilities for the construction of social identities. Thus, this project allows me to examine processes of "identification" and "contextualization"—that is, the mutual production of identities and contexts for activity—under conditions of overt conflict and transformation.

In analyzing this setting, I will draw on recent work in linguistic anthropology. Scholars in this field have been centrally concerned, as Duranti (1997) points out, with processes of cultural production, and have been developing sophisticated theoretical and methodological resources for understanding how language is involved in the construction of meaning and the production of persons and cultures. I will focus on how, in the detailed processes of moment-to-moment interaction, language is used to produce a world in which certain kinds of expertise are valued (or devalued) while at the same time speakers position themselves and others within those ways of understanding expertise.

The chapter is organized in the following way. First, I discuss recent theories of situated learning, which attempt to conceive of learning in terms of the kinds of processes of meaning-making that are central to theories of cultural production. I outline two general ways in which situated learning theories have been developed—which I call the "cognitive apprenticeship" approach and the "cultural production" approach—and argue that the second adopts a more adequate view of contextualization and identification, with consequences for how learning contexts should be examined. I then turn to a discussion of linguistic anthropological approaches to understanding contextualization, and outline a view of this process as involving a tension between "presupposing indexicality" and "entailing indexicality." Examination of the dynamic interplay between these two kinds of linguistic signs can usefully contribute to our understanding of the processes through which both cultures and persons are produced and transformed through activity, both within and across interactions. I then illustrate these points by examining communicative practices in two interactions that took place during the student project that was the site of my research.

SITUATED LEARNING

In this section, I discuss theories of situated learning in some detail. I identify what I see as two general directions in which these theories have been developed—"cognitive apprenticeships" and "cultural production"—and argue that while these positions are largely compatible and mutually informing, the second position more adequately accounts for learning as a cultural process. Specifically, I suggest that cognitive apprenticeships have tended to pay insufficient attention to some of the dynamics of contextualization and identification that are at the heart of processes of cultural production, and that this results in a somewhat limited and incomplete way of understanding the production of expertise. I argue that careful attention to these processes is an important strategy to adopt in understanding activity within learning contexts.

Theories of situated learning have been developed largely as an alternative to individualist, and especially cognitivist, approaches to understanding learning and schooling. Briefly, cognitivism understands learning as involving individuals' movement away from the concrete, situated, and presumably faulty and inefficient forms of thought that it takes to characterize everyday life, and toward the acquisition of abstract, general, and universally applicable conceptual knowledge. In this view, learning is best brought about by separating learners from the complexities of everyday experience and providing them with instruction designed to allow them to acquire explicit decontextualized concepts that can be transferred to and applied at other times and in other places. Theories of situated learning have challenged cognitivism on a number of grounds. Two of these are of particular importance for my purposes. First, research on everyday cognition shows that cognition is not best viewed as the application of explicit abstract knowledge, as cognitivism maintains. Rather, cognition is mediated by culturally evolved semiotic and material artifacts and realized in the routine activities of a "community of practice." In this view, concepts are implicit in the organization of everyday practice. Everyday cognition *is* concrete and situated; it is *not*, however, faulty and inefficient, but powerfully adapted to the forms of activity in which it occurs. Of course, if cognition is inherently situated in these ways, then learning clearly cannot be a matter of acquiring decontextualized knowledge. Thus the first challenge to cognitivism is that it proposes an inadequate view of the nature of cognition and learning. The second is a critique of cognitivist views on schooling. The cognitivist account of learning implies that the production of "educated persons" can be explained in terms of individual acquisition of knowledge. This implies in turn that "uneducated persons" can be accounted for in terms of *failure* to acquire knowledge. From the point of view of some work in situated learning, this account fails to appreciate the ways in which both "educated persons" and "uneducated persons" are involved in processes of cultural production.

These limitations of cognitivist accounts have led to efforts to reconceptualize learning so as to account for the situatedness of everyday practice. I describe two general directions in which this work has proceeded. The first, which can be called the "cognitive apprenticeship" approach, has been primarily concerned with improving instruction by designing learning contexts that take account of the practical basis of cognition. The second, which can be called the "cultural production" approach, has been primarily concerned not with the design of better learning contexts, but with formulating a general theory of learning, wherever it occurs and in whatever form, as an aspect of processes of cultural production.

It is useful to begin by briefly describing the important work of Lave and Wenger (1991), which has influenced virtually all subsequent approaches to situated learning. These authors, in challenging the cognitivist assumption that learning involves explicit transmission of abstract knowledge, examined successful practical apprenticeships in settings that involved little explicit teaching. Their specific focus was on how newcomers to a community move from "legitimate peripheral participation," in which they engage in the everyday practices of a community but with less than full responsibility for carrying them out, toward "full participation" in the community. In Lave and Wenger's account, learning takes place not through transmission of abstract knowledge, but through engagement in the "knowledgeable skills" that are realized in the everyday activities of a community; that is, people become good at the practices that they routinely participate in, gaining understanding of how to successfully engage under varying conditions by flexibly adapting their performance to the contingencies of particular occasions.

It is important to note, however, that the significance of Lave and Wenger's work goes beyond the claim that learning involves mastery of the "knowledgeable skills" of a community. This is because, as Lave and Wenger argue:

> Activities, tasks, functions, and understandings do not exist in isolation; they are part of broader systems of relations in which they have meaning. These systems of relations arise out of and are reproduced and developed within social communities, which are in part systems of relations among persons. The person is defined by as well as defines these relations. Learning thus implies becoming a different person with respect to the possibilities enabled by these systems of relations. To ignore this aspect of learning is to overlook the fact that learning involves the construction of identities. (Lave & Wenger, 1991, p. 53)

Thus, as one engages in the practices of a community, she is not simply becoming adept at carrying out those practices; she is also becoming identifiable as a certain kind of person within the community. It is important to note here that identities are not determined by "the possibilities enabled by [the] systems of relations" of a community; rather, participants actively identify themselves and others in terms of those possibilities, in the process both reproducing and transforming the community. Here we see clearly that situated learning is an aspect of the same processes that have concerned theorists of cultural production.

While all who adopt a situated learning framework agree with Lave and Wenger's central claims, there are subtle but important differences in how these claims have been developed within different approaches. The following two sections describe two central approaches.

Situated Learning and Cognitive Apprenticeships

Lave and Wenger's work on learning in practical apprenticeships has been an important inspiration for educational researchers and designers who have identified serious limitations in cognitivist approaches to schooling, and who have attempted to design contexts for learning in schools, sometimes called "cognitive apprenticeships" (Brown, Collins, & Duguid, 1989), which are based on the claims of situated learning. Proponents of cognitive apprenticeships have faulted cognitivist approaches to schooling for their tendency to produce "inert knowledge" (Collins, Brown, & Newman, 1989), that is, abstractions that learners are unable to apply in concrete situations. In contrast, this work has aimed to produce "usable, robust knowledge" by situating learners in "authentic" contexts (Brown et al., 1989). Rather than aiming for learning that results in the acquisition of decontextualized knowledge, this work has attempted to provide students with access to legitimate peripheral participation in valued social practices.

Cognitive apprenticeships retain some aspects of cognitivist approaches to school learning while at the same time transforming them in fundamental ways. Recognizing the social value of mastery of such "knowledge domains" as science and mathematics, they have continued to emphasize these and other traditional school subjects. But cognitive apprenticeships fundamentally diverge from cognitivism by arguing for the inherent social and material situatedness of learning. For example, Greeno et al. (1997) point out that a major goal of their work is to "create environments in which students can learn to participate in practices of productive inquiry and use of concepts and principles that are characteristic of subject matter disciplines" (Greeno et al., 1997, p. 99). Rather than being understood as a body of abstract knowledge, however, these disciplines are understood as communities of practice whose "concepts and principles" are implicit in a range of "knowledgeable skills." Researchers and educators working within this approach to situated learning explicitly model these knowledgeable skills and use these models to design learning contexts. In this way, through participation in practices modeled upon those in a particular target community or discipline, students serve as apprentices in the social practices associated with that community; this process is intended to result in "improved participation" in those practices and enculturation into the community (Brown et al., 1989; Greeno et al., 1997).

Proponents of cognitive apprenticeships have been quite successful both in designing new kinds of learning contexts in schools that overcome some of the major limitations of cognitivist approaches to educational practice, and, through their emphasis on learning as enculturation, in contributing to a broader theoretical movement that conceives of learning as primarily a cultural rather than an individual process. In recent years, cognitive apprenticeships have come to exert an increasingly prominent influence on educational practices and have become prevalent at all levels of schooling.

Situated Learning and Cultural Production

Besides its role in the development of cognitive apprenticeships, Lave and Wenger's work can also be situated within a broader project that aims to formulate a general conceptualization of learning as an aspect of cultural production. In this sense, "scenarios of apprenticeship learning are useful to 'think with' " (Lave, 1990, p. 311) in understanding how learning is related to processes of cultural production, no matter where or in what specific form learning takes place.

In understanding this aspect of situated learning, it is important to note that Lave and Wenger focused on communities of practice that they explicitly recognized as benign. That is, apprentices were willing entrants into communities of practice in which the development of positively valued identities was not only possible for and expected of all participants but in which activity was organized in such a way that newcomers in fact had ample support in developing these positively valued identities. This focus on benign communities was strategic. Lave and Wenger started with communities of practice that were arranged so as routinely to produce positive outcomes for virtually all participants and examined how learning was organized in these communities. The observed absence of explicit transmission of abstract knowledge, together with the successful learning of apprentices in these communities, provided important evidence against cognitivist accounts of how successful learning happens.

Lave and Wenger clearly recognized, however, that not all communities are benign, and this has important implications for developing a general theory of situated learning. It is important to be clear here that "learning," conceived as an aspect of cultural production, takes on a somewhat technical meaning, and one that differs in important ways from commonsense notions. Learning is not understood in this view as a special process that happens only some of the time and to some people; rather, as Lave puts it, it "is an integral aspect of activity in and with the world at all times. That learning occurs is not problematic" (1993, p. 8). In this view, learning is inherent in the processes of active meaning-making—of contextualization and identification—that are central in theories of cultural production, and all participants in practice are learning at all times.

Of course, if learning is an inherent part of activity, then it is clear that commonsense notions about "failure to learn" are in need of rethinking. Thus, Lave and others have proposed a view of "failure" as simply another form of learning; that is, "failure" is one way of "becoming a different person with respect to the possibilities enabled by [the] systems of relations" of a community. In this view, some communities are organized so as to allow for, or even *require*, that some participants "fail," or "successfully fail," to use Varenne and McDermott's apt phrasing (McDermott, 1993; Varenne & McDermott, 1998). Schools are one prominent example of this kind of community in Western culture, in that within schools, as Lave puts it, "not-learning and 'failure' identities are active normal social locations and processes" (1993, p. 16). For some participants in some communities, then, movement toward full participation in the community can involve actively positioning oneself and being positioned within negatively valued identities. In this way, commonsense notions of "learning" and "failure to learn" are conceived of in what could be called *symmetrical* terms, since both are accounted for as outcomes of the same kinds of process. Such a view clearly fits within the project of theories of cultural production to account for how both "educated persons" and "uneducated persons" are involved in cultural production (Levinson & Holland, 1996).

This symmetrical stance is useful as an analytic lens for showing not only how cognitivist assumptions about the production of educated persons in terms of *individual learning* are fundamentally flawed, but also how schooling practices based on cognitivism are implicated in *cultural production*. Cognitivism adopts an *asymmetrical* stance on the production of educated persons by assuming that this process is explained by the movement of some, but not all, persons away from faulty "everyday" forms of cognition toward "higher" forms of abstract rational thought. This view is asymmetrical in that it accounts for "learning" and "failure" in different ways. In this view, "failure to learn," as Lave points out, "is commonly assumed to result from the inability or refusal on the part of an individual to engage in something called 'learning' " (1993, p. 16). The result is that cognitivism holds individuals, and not processes of cultural production, responsible for their success or failure (cf. Lave, 1996). From the perspective of situated learning as an aspect of cultural production, however, both those who succeed and those who fail in school, like Lave and Wenger's apprentices, are simply becoming good at what they are given the opportunity to do on a routine basis—

that is, at engaging in the kinds of practices through which they become identified and identifiable, to themselves and others, within the cultural categories of "educated persons" or "uneducated persons."

This approach to situated learning, then, is not primarily concerned with improving contexts for learning, but rather with understanding how cultural production can result in persons being positioned within different kind of identities, some of which are positively valued and some of which are not.

SYMMETRY AND ASYMMETRY IN THE ANALYSIS OF LEARNING CONTEXTS

In my view, adopting a symmetrical stance on the analysis of learning contexts is crucial in adequately understanding learning as an aspect of cultural production. However, proponents of cognitive apprenticeships have sometimes paid insufficient attention to the dynamics of contextualization and identification that are central to cultural production theories, and this has led in turn to a view of activity in learning contexts that is in subtle but important ways *a*symmetrical. For example, Greeno et al. (1997) argue that, in their approach to situated learning, "difficulties that students have in learning to think and understand are interpreted as impediments to their participation in social practices" (p. 99). From a symmetrical stance, in which all participants are understood to be learning at all times, this might well be understood as the student being positioned by the "possibilities enabled by [the] systems of relations" of the learning context into a "not-learning" identity.

A major source of this asymmetry is a failure on the part of proponents of cognitive apprenticeships fully to appreciate Lave and Wenger's claim that learning "implies becoming a different person with respect to the possibilities enabled by [the] systems of relations" within a community of practice. To see how, it will be useful to return to the work of Lave and Wenger, and to examine in more detail some of the characteristics of the apprenticeships they discussed.

Lave and Wenger portrayed communities of practice in somewhat idealized and simplified ways (cf. Engeström & Cole, 1997; Nespor, 1994; O'Connor, 2001). For example, participants in Lave and Wenger's communities, both newcomers and oldtimers, were treated in terms of their community-based identities or roles; this has the effect of backgrounding tensions that might be introduced by participants' membership in multiple communities. In addition, while Lave and Wenger clearly recognized that innovation is an inherent aspect of social practice, they nevertheless treated their communities as characterized by relatively well-established and non-controversial forms of mastery, embodied in the practices of respected masters; and they assumed willing learners who accepted or at least did not resist prevailing community norms. In such a community, learning can be conceived of as a largely unidirectional process in which newcomers are guided toward full participation by recognized expert practitioners, and conflicts over the nature of expertise do not arise. Moreover, the cultural processes that direct certain kinds of people toward apprenticeships in certain kinds of communities of practice, and direct other kinds of people toward other kinds of communities, were not addressed, nor were differences among different communities in status or power.

These oversights most likely resulted from Lave and Wenger's strategic focus on benign communities of practice: in cases in which all participants are able to establish themselves successfully as valued members, tensions and conflicts within communities either do not arise or can be safely backgrounded. However, in communities that are not benign, schools, for example, attention to these conflictual processes is crucial in maintaining a symmetrical stance on learning, and failure to do so results in insufficient attention to important aspects of contextualization and identification. In this regard, it is important to note that Lave and Wenger were explicitly quite cautious about the possibility of using the apprenticeships they discussed as models for designing educational contexts to produce "successful learning" (Lave & Wenger, 1991, pp. 40–41). However, cognitive apprenticeships have by and large done just that and, in the process, have tended to assume that cognitive apprenticeships can be understood as benign, stable, bounded, and homogeneous.

As the cultural production approach to situated learning has become more clearly defined and developed in recent years, it has begun to move beyond Lave and Wenger's early portrayals of communities of practice as benign, stable, bounded, and homogeneous, and to pay increased attention to the heterogeneity of social practice, that is, to the ways in which activity is structured by the practices associated with multiple contexts and communities (e.g., Engeström & Cole, 1997; Lave, 1993, 1996; Nespor, 1994; Wenger, 1998; Wertsch, 1991, 1998). This work has begun to emphasize that participants in activity are never engaged simply and straightforwardly in a single practice or a single community. Lave (1993) for example, has argued that "local practices must inevitably take part in constituting each other, through their structural interconnections, their intertwined activities, their common participants, and more" (Lave, 1993, p. 22). According to this view, all activity takes place at the intersection of different communities, each with their own practices, norms, and values. Moreover, participants bring with them a history of participation in different contexts, and they will participate in still other contexts in the future. Actions performed and words spoken by a participant in the past, identities adopted by or ascribed to them, can be made relevant in the present interaction, and the present interaction can in turn be made relevant in the future. It is important to note, furthermore, that these various contexts are not necessarily easily embedded within one another, and this introduces potentially destabilizing elements into social practice. This makes close attention to the dynamics of contextualization and identification important.

This more complex understanding of context and identity has important implications for understanding activity in cognitive apprenticeships. From the point of view of cultural production theory, research on cognitive apprenticeships has tended to pay insufficient attention to the dynamics of contextualization and identification. Through its emphasis on highly stabilized "subject matter disciplines," cognitive apprenticeships have tended to implicitly assume the homogeneity of learning contexts, and to privilege "official" understandings of learning contexts through their use of particular models of practice as the basis for understanding the meaning of participation and for assessing learning or "improved participation." This strategy, however, backgrounds some of the subtle ways in which participants in activity draw on heterogeneous resources, both "official" and "unofficial," as they negotiate the meaning of the context, their ongoing activity, and their own emerging identities (O'Connor, 2001). As a result, cognitive apprenticeships themselves offer promising sites for examining "the relationships between local practices that contextualize the ways people act together, both in and across contexts" (Lave, 1993). Insofar as these learning environments involve an attempt to reproduce in schools conditions that will allow students to participate in the practices of some "target" context, such as scientific communities of practice, outside of schools, they are inherently heterogeneous contexts. Adopting a symmetrical stance on the analysis of these sites would require more careful consideration of the various ways in which participants orient themselves to these contexts and negotiate the meaning of their participation, and of the consequences of these processes for all participants.

LANGUAGE AND CONTEXTUALIZATION

Recent work in linguistic anthropology and related fields has devoted a great deal of attention to how participants in interaction use language to contextualize their activity (e.g., Bauman & Briggs, 1990; Duranti, 1997; Duranti & Goodwin, 1992; Gumperz, 1982; Hanks, 1996; Ochs, 1996; Silverstein, 1992). Contextualization is understood in this tradition as "an active process of negotiation in which participants reflexively examine the discourse as it is emerging, embedding assessments of its structure and significance in the speech itself" (Bauman & Briggs, 1990, p. 69). When speaking, participants constitute the interaction as being of a certain sort, while at the same time identifying themselves as persons of a certain sort. The contextualization process, then, is the process by which individuals take up positions, and position one another, with regard to the interaction and the broader communities in which they are participating. This view of contextualization has clear connections to the claims of situated learning theorists about the mutual constitution of persons and contexts. Work on linguistic contextualization has treated this process in considerable detail and offers useful theoretical and analytical resources for examining activity in learning contexts.

An important focus of this literature is on *indexicality*, or the ways in which linguistic meaning is related to context. One major aspect of indexicality involves the use of linguistic forms to point to aspects of context in a way that identifies those contexts as being of a certain sort. In this view, linguistic forms become associated with particular culturally recognized types of communicative event, or what have been called "metadiscourses" (Silverstein & Urban, 1996). Through habitual use, linguistic forms become associated with metadiscursive categories such as genres, social identities, types of speech act, and the like. As a result, the use of a particular linguistic form on a given occasion indexes, or points to, the kind of communicative event with which it is conventionally associated.

Silverstein (1992) has discussed this process, making an important distinction between *presupposing indexicals*, which index aspects of context that are presently understood by interactants to be "in play," or relevant for the purposes of the present interaction, and *entailing indexicals*, which index aspects of context not presently in play but having the potential to transform the currently presupposed context. Presupposing and entailing indexicals always exist in tension with one another in any stretch of discourse. Over the course of an interaction, participants establish the interaction as belonging to a particular metadiscourse, such as a classroom lecture or a project meeting. To do this, they might use various indexes of social identity (Ochs, 1996) to construct themselves within recognizable identities associated with that metadiscourse, such as professors and students, or bosses and employees. This metadiscourse comes to be presupposed by participants as the relevant context for subsequent interaction. At the same time, people have a history of participation in events associated within other metadiscourses, in which they act within other social identities. A given participant is not only, say, the project manager of a student project, but also is potentially identifiable as a student at a particular school, a resident of a particular geographical region, as well as many other potentially relevant social identities. These other identities, even though they might be backgrounded in a given interaction, are subject to being made relevant for interactional purposes, and can come to have entailments or consequences for the meaning of the interaction, sometimes transforming it in unexpected and unpredictable ways.

Wortham (1994) offers an analysis of the tension between presupposing and entailing indexicality that is relevant here. Wortham examines what he calls "participant examples" in high school classrooms. These are interactional events in which teachers and students, in the course of discussing a work of history, literature, or the like, *enact* the work, taking on the roles of the characters who are the subject of their discussion. During this enactment, the participant example serves as the relevant metadiscourse, providing the presupposed context for the interaction. At the same time, however, participants do not stop being, at least potentially, teachers and students, or white adults and African-American teenagers, and these other social identities are sometimes made relevant with consequences for the interaction. Wortham provides convincing evidence that aspects of the interactions among the *characters* in the participant example are sometimes "transferred" to the interactions among *teachers and students*, with implications that extend beyond the example and come to organize classroom relationships. In such cases, the "imaginary" or "pretend" identities and relationships indexed in the participant examples have consequences for the relationships of the teachers and students.

Wortham's work is relevant for the purposes of this chapter in that cognitive apprenticeships similarly involve participants' enactment of what can be seen as "pretend" roles or identities in addition to their continued occupation of enduring institutional identities, such as "teacher" and "student," or even "higher-status student" and "lower-status student." Cognitive apprenticeships tend to assume that individuals engaged in a project are occupying their "official" project roles, and are carrying out "official" project activity. That is, these approaches assume that the metadiscourse prescribed by the researcher or educator is guiding the interaction of the participants. However, this is a largely unexamined assumption, and one that Wortham's work should caution us to examine carefully. If it is possible for "unofficial" interactional events to proceed "submerged," as Wortham puts it, within an "official" event, it is necessary to examine ways in which participants in situated learning contexts might also draw upon unofficial metadiscourses, as well as how they coordinate whatever multiple events might be taking place. In the analyses that follow, I examine interactions among participants in a cognitive apprenticeship, paying particular attention to how participants negotiate tensions between official and unofficial identities.

A SITUATED LEARNING CONTEXT: THE MICRO
TRUCK PROJECT

The focus of this analysis is interactions among participants in a cognitive apprenticeship that was developed by the Production Consortium, a federally funded association of five universities attempting to "initiate a systematic reform of undergraduate manufacturing engineering education."[1] There were two major aspects of the Consortium's reform effort. The first was to challenge a traditional separation of design and manufacturing in both engineering education and engineering workplaces. This separation is related to a dominant model of engineering education, which values the "intellectual" work of engineering analysis and design over the "practical" work of manufacturing, and maintains that analysis and design can and should be taught outside of the complex conditions of "real world" manufacturing. Against this model, the Consortium aimed to "increase the understanding, and the standing, of manufacturing in the undergraduate curriculum," arguing that "manufacturing is a critical element in all engineering disciplines," and that "design and manufacturing are highly interdependent in the product realization process."

A second aspect of the Consortium's reform was the attempt to allow students to participate in "engineering workplaces of the future," in part by allowing them to work in "virtual organizations," which bring together different organizations on a temporary basis so that each can contribute its particular strengths or "core competencies" to the project as a whole. In addition, since the members of virtual organizations are often geographically separated, the Consortium provided students with various communication technologies, such as video teleconferencing, to allow students to "work with their peers at other universities as if they were in the same room."

A cornerstone of the Consortium's efforts was the use of geographically distributed "Product Realization Projects," which were intended to provide "an opportunity for engineering students at all levels to actually design and manufacture products." The Consortium's intention was that "this product realization experience will place the students' education in a new, relevant perspective," a goal that has clear links to the aims of cognitive apprenticeships of enculturating learners by situating them in "authentic" contexts (Brown et al., 1989, p. 32).

In this chapter, I analyze interactions among participants in the "Micro Truck Project," which involved twenty students from the five schools of the Consortium. The stated objective of the project was for these students to collaborate in modifying a small model truck to race in a competition. Before the start of the project, Consortium faculty divided the project into a number of subtasks, and these tasks were divided among student teams representing the various schools. For example, a team from "Tech" was assigned the subtask of project management and integration, and a team from the "Institute of Science" was assigned the subtask of producing the truck's electronic controls. The idea was that students at each school were or would become experts at their assigned task and bring these "core competencies" to the project as a whole. In addition, several "experts"—Tech students who had recently successfully competed in a National Micro Truck competition—were recruited by Tech's faculty advisor to serve as consultants to the entire five-school team.

These goals and the organizational structure of the Micro Truck Project reflect an "official" metadiscourse or model of the project, in that they are based on typifications of communicative events that take place in "real world" engineering workplaces. In particular, the Consortium was modeling a common practice in professional engineering in which members of project teams, with diverse specializations, work together to accomplish a common goal. The project based on this official model was understood as the official context of participation, within which students would learn by participating within their official roles, which were based on their specific forms of expertise.

There are different ways in which the analysis of such a project might be undertaken. Cognitive apprenticeships have tended to examine how participation is "guided" by the official model, and to explore the extent to which this results in "improved participation" in the product realization process. This strategy, however, privileges "official" interpretations of project activity. Analyses of situated learning interested in examining processes of cultural production, in contrast, would start by assuming that participants draw on multiple resources in constructing themselves and their activity. For example, in the interactions to be examined here, the Micro Truck Project might be taken to be the official context, and thus to provide roles or identities for participants in terms of their specialized "core competencies." However, these official identities are not the only identities that are potentially relevant. The Micro Truck Project is not *only* a geographically distributed engineering project that brings together multiple "organizations" to meet a common goal. For example, for the Tech project managers, it is also a project they are completing to fulfill a requirement for graduation. This might make certain "unofficial" identities, such as professor and student, potentially relevant. For "the experts," who have been offered a substantial budget by the Consortium to produce their own vehicle in exchange for serving as consultants, it is also a chance to compete in the next national competition. Thus other potential identities, such as "competitor," become potentially relevant. In addition, project participants continue to be potentially identifiable within enduring institutional roles, such as students at the Institute, a very high status university, or at Tech, a lower-status institution. And these various contexts and identities do not necessarily fit together easily. To the extent that these different contexts do fit together, it is through the active integrating work by participants in local interactions. In the analyses that follow, I pay close attention to these details of contextualization, and especially to the ways in which tensions between official and unofficial identities are coordinated as participants construct the project as a context for their activity.

The Micro Truck Project offers a useful site for adopting this analytic strategy, since the Production Consortium was overtly attempting to challenge traditional values about what it means to participate in engineering practices. How participants in this project orient to, for example, the Consortium's attempts at elevating the status of manufacturing, or at sharing information between institutions, has consequences for their participation in the project, their "home" institution, and their trajectories in the broader field of engineering. In my analyses, I show how participants, through their interactions in the "conversational borderlands" (Rymes, 2001) that characterize the Micro Truck Project, negotiate the multiple contexts of their activity, and in the process produce unanticipated kinds of social identities and relationships. The analyses examine the interplay between indexical presupposition and indexical entailment in interactions among participants in the project. As we will see, in "self-introductions" by participants at Tech, a relatively lower-status school, this process results in the validation of the working-class identity of one student, as subsequent participants indexically align themselves with him and construct a local understanding of expertise consistent with his identity. In contrast, in a later project meeting involving Tech students and students from the Institute, a higher-status school, Institute students draw upon available but unofficial contextual features in a way that promotes their own view of expertise, in contrast to and at the expense of the identities of Tech students.

Self-introductions and the Local Construction of Identity

In this section, I analyze the "self-introductions" of several participants in the first meeting of the Tech Micro Truck Project team. These introductions are of interest here for several reasons. First, self-introductions involve overt identity work on the part of participants, and thus they are useful in examining some of the dynamics of contextualization and identification that theorists of situated learning have argued are central to the cultural production of persons. Second, and related to this, self-introductions are not simply a matter of reporting some "given" identity; rather, self-introductions involve identifying oneself in terms of some perceived common purposes or interests of the group or groups of which one is a part. Thus, in identifying oneself to others, one must also make choices about what the relevant context is, and so identity and context emerge together in the act of a self-introduction. Third, while there might be an "official" context, participants might not be equally committed to that official context as the framework for their activity. In such cases, participants might draw on "unofficial" identities in ways that can come to have entailments for the emerging interaction.

I focus here on the self-introductions of three participants. Two of these, Joe Ryan and Katherine Steel, are seniors participating in the project in order to fulfill a Tech requirement for a Major Qualifying Project (MQP). The MQP is a major part of Tech's curriculum and is intended for students to display expertise at the level of a beginning professional engineer in their major field. The MQP is seen at Tech as the culmination of one's student career; students are drawing on the already substantial knowledge that they have built up through their participation in courses, other team projects, co-ops, and the like. The third participant, Bill Lewis, is also a senior at Tech, and had a few months earlier completed his own MQP as part of a team that had produced a vehicle to compete in the National Micro Truck Competition. On the basis of that experience, which resulted in a third-place finish nationally, Jack Sanders, the project's faculty advisor from Tech, has recruited Bill and his MQP teammates as "experts" to assist the entire five-school Consortium's team in producing their own truck.

The first student to introduce himself in this meeting is Joe Ryan. Joe is a mechanical engineering student in his late twenties who has recently returned to school after working for several years for the plant maintenance team at a food processing plant in the region. Jack Sanders, Tech's faculty advisor, recruited Joe for the Micro Truck Project largely because of his extensive hands-on experience with real-world engineering problems. Joe, for his part, was interested in this project because of its emphasis on "hands-on" manufacturing, as opposed to what he saw as the sterile and ungrounded theoretical work of engineering science and design. After being prompted by Jack to start, Joe begins to introduce himself in line 101:

	Jack	So. We'll get to you guys now, we'll just go ((gestures
100		counterclockwise)) (..) Joe?
	Joe:	Uh, My name's Joe Ryan, uh (.) mechanical engineering student,
		(.) I graduate in December of ninety six, I transferred last year, (.)
		courtesy of Major Foods closing my pla:nt,
	Jack:	((laughs))
105	Joe:	U:m (..) I just- that's about it.

                    (..)
        Jack: But you've been a<u>ro:und</u>.
        Joe: Yeah. I worked for Major Foods for about seven years in uh, the
                    juice division. And we made uh, Fruity Punch, and Sunshine
110   Orange Juice, in Kingsfield [state name]. And I had a choice-
                    choice to transfer to Houston Texas, Anaheim California, or
                    Ohio. And I decided to finish [my degree.
        Jack: [(inaud)
        Joe: ((slight laugh))
115   Jack: But you have degree:s~
        Joe: I have a bachelor's degree (.) in uh business, (.) associate's in
                    civil, (.) and I'm trying to finish my bachelor's in mechanical
                    so I can just (.) quit school altogether.
        Jack: ((laughs))
120   ((laughter))

Beginning in line 101, Joe first states his name and his position at Tech,
that is, mechanical engineering student. He goes on to mention his
graduation date and his recent transfer to Tech after the closing of the
plant he had worked at, before apparently finishing by saying "I just-
that's about it" in line 105. To this point, Joe has not yet identified
himself in terms of his official role in the project, and in line 107, Jack
responds to this by treating Joe's self-introduction as incomplete and
prompting him to say more by saying, "But you've been a<u>ro:und</u>." Here,
Jack is attempting to elicit more information from Joe about his background and experience, aspects of Joe's identity that Jack takes to be
quite relevant for his role in the project. Joe goes on here to state some
of his work experience with Major Foods. However, he does so in a way
that still does not integrate this experience into a project-relevant identity. In line 115, Jack responds by further prompting Joe to foreground
his relevant accomplishments: "But you have degre:es." Joe then provides information about those other degrees before completing his
introduction in lines 117-118, saying that he is "trying to finish my
bachelor's in mechanical so I can just (.) quit school altogether."
    Joe's introduction is of interest here for several reasons. First, he
introduces himself with a great deal of hesitancy and tentativeness. It
seems not to be entirely clear to him just what to say about himself that
would be relevant on the present occasion. This suggests quite clearly
that his identity is not simply a matter of stating some straightforward
facts about a "core identity" (cf. Packer & Goicoechea, 2000); instead,
he must orient himself to local standards of what identity is appropriate
in the present context. This task is, of course, made more difficult by the
fact that the "context" has many potential dimensions. For example, is
this a "real-world" project, as in the official model, or is it a project to
be completed for graduation? And how are potential conflicts between

project identity, school identity, relationships among peers, and the like to be reconciled?

A second interesting aspect of Joe's introduction is how he constructs an opposition between the theoretical world of school and the practical world of work, and places primary value on the practical side of this opposition. For example, in lines 101-102, Joe adopts an identity of "a laid-off worker who is trying to make the best of it by returning to school," thus presenting school as clearly not his first choice. In addition, in lines 116-118, Joe says that he is "trying to finish my bachelor's in mechanical so I can just (.) quit school altogether." Here, he playfully resists Jack's efforts to get him to frame his various degrees as project-relevant experience, instead framing his school experience from the apparent perspective of a worker. And Joe is indexing an identity not only as a worker, but as a particular kind of worker, that is, one involved in the practical, manufacturing side of production. He says that his transfer to Tech was "courtesy of Major Foods closing my pla:nt," not only stressing the word "plant"—the site for the manufacturing of products—but also identifying with it—"*my* plant." He goes on, in lines 109-110, to indicate that "we made uh, Fruity Punch, and Sunshine Orange Juice," with the use of "made" further indexing his identification with the practical side of the production process.

It is important to note that even though Joe has repeatedly resisted Jack's attempts to get him to "officialize" (Hanks, 1996, p. 244) his identity by relating his experience to his role in the project, Joe's self-introduction is nonetheless treated as successful. Jack, the faculty advisor and the primary representative of the official context, responds with laughter to Joe's account of his transfer to Tech in line 104. In addition, in lines 119-120, first Jack and then other participants in the meeting laugh at Joe's statement that he wants to "quit school altogether." Thus, Joe has constructed a successful identity for himself within the emerging norms of this interaction. And, as we will see, aspects of Joe's self-introduction are taken up and made relevant by other participants as they construct their own identities in their self-introductions.

When Joe has finished, two Consortium staff members introduce themselves, and then it's time for Katherine, Joe's partner on the MQP team, to take her turn:

	Jack:	Katherine.=
	Kath:	=Okay I'm Katherine Steel, I'm a mechanical engineering
190		student, I'm supposed to be graduating at the end of the
		summer term this year so (.) doing the MQP will be great.
		((slight laugh)) Get it over with as soon as possible.
	Jack:	Just back from co-op wi[:th~
	Kath:	[U::h Design Technologies? Then

195   ProCAD for six months? >I was< on the technical support li:ne so (.)
       I'm pretty familar [(.)=
       Jack: [Sh-
       Kath: =with that   [package.
       Jack: [she's our ProCAD (.) guru.
200   Kath: ((slight laugh))

In her initial turn, Katherine shows little of the uncertainty and
hesitation that we saw in Joe's introduction. Katherine seems much
more certain than Joe had been about what information about her
identity is relevant in introducing herself. It is important to note in this
regard that Katherine begins her introduction by using the same three
"slots" that Joe had used, and in the same order: name, major, graduation date. In this way, Katherine seems to be drawing on the structure
of Joe's self-introduction as a model in constructing her own. In fact, as
this sequence of self-introductions proceeds, the structure of
participants' introductions becomes stabilized, and all participants use
the same slots as those that Joe had used.

While the structure of Joe's self-introduction seems to be mediating
Katherine's own introduction, she uses that structure flexibly to situate
herself explicitly with regard to the MQP, which Joe had not done.
Katherine uses the "graduation date" slot explicitly to motivate her
participation. In saying that she is "supposed to be" graduating in the
summer, Katherine expresses some doubt about this outcome. The
doubt is due largely to the fact that the MQP is a necessary hurdle to
get over in order to graduate; as Katherine says, "so doing the MQP will
be great." It is important to note that Katherine is here adopting a
positive orientation to the project; that is, she is identifying with the
MQP as an aspect of her own "identity-making life project" (Lave,
1996). However, perhaps realizing that in so doing she might potentially alienate herself from her partner, she goes on to say, "Get it over
as soon as possible," indexing the same kind of orientation to school
expressed in Joe's wish to "just quit school altogether." Thus, without
explicitly saying so, Katherine is indexing an identification with Joe and
his values.

However, while Katherine has adopted a positive orientation to the
project, at least in part, her identification with the project is in terms of
what it means within her identity as a *student*, rather than her identity
as an *engineer*. And so, immediately after Katherine's apparent comple-
tion of her turn, Jack attempts to elicit a different identity from Katherine, one situated within the official context in which she is a project
manager and design integrator of a team engineering project. In line
193, Jack says "Just back from co-op wi:th," starting a sentence that
Katherine is clearly supposed to complete. Jack has recruited Katherine

for this project because of her experience working with a variety of CAD (computer aided design) software programs, experience that Jack expects to be quite crucial in completing this project. Jack thus guides Katherine toward a statement of her identity that is more appropriate for what he treats here as the relevant context. In line 194, Katherine completes the sentence started by Jack, and goes on to report, somewhat modestly, her CAD experience. Jack then, in line 199, goes on to explicitly locate this expertise in the project, saying "She's our ProCAD (.) guru," with the use of "our" implying that Katherine's expertise in CAD is relevant for the entire project team. It is worth noting Katherine's slight laugh in response to this turn, perhaps in discomfort at being singled out by Jack as a "guru."

After the turns of four other students, two of whom are participating in a similar MQP, and two of whom are "experts," Bill Lewis, one of the "experts," takes his own turn:

	Bill:	Um I'm (.) Bill Lewis, I'm a manufacturing student, graduating
		this year, (.) u:h I worked on the MQP (team) last year, (.)
		I co-op'ed at Aerospace Inc., so if you need any turbine blades
		for your car,
		[I know how to make them.=
240		[((laughter))
	Bill:	=Um (.) I know a lot about off road type vehicles of (.) a lot of
		sorts so (.) I a- I'm familiar with this type of racing. And so um
		(.) I wou- I would be good resource (.) if you have any questions.
		(.) And um (.) I want- just wanna build another truck too mostly
		though.
245		((laughter))

Bill is faced in his self-introduction with the rather sensitive task of constructing an identity as "expert"—his official role in the project—and thus differentiating himself from Joe and Katherine, who as fellow Tech students, and even fellow seniors, are his peers. He is, after all, only slightly ahead of them in the curriculum, having completed his own MQP just three months earlier. I suggest that Bill uses his self-introduction to both construct and minimize this potential split in ways that index alignment with both his official role and the emerging norms of the Micro Truck team.

We can clearly see elements of others' self-introductions in Bill's own introduction. For example, he uses the opening three "slot" structure used by other participants by stating his name, major, and graduation date. In addition, like Katherine, he mentions his co-op experience, and jokingly relates that to his role in the project. In addition, Bill's fellow "expert," Rob, has just completed his turn by saying that "I've worked on the truck before and now I just want to build another one and keep playing because I got a lot of good ideas that we didn't get to do." Bill uses aspects of Rob's turn when he says, in line 244, that "I want- just wanna build another truck too mostly though." In these ways, Bill's identity on this occasion is clearly locally constructed, in that "who he is" depends in part on the local context, right down to his position at the table.

Bill uses this emerging framework in interesting ways to orient himself to the kinds of oppositions that Joe and Katherine were orienting themselves to. An important aspect of Bill's self-introduction is his construction of relationships to others, and specifically to Joe and Katherine. Bill sets up an explicit opposition between himself, on one hand, and Joe and Katherine, on the other. He accomplishes this largely through the use of an *I:you* pronominal opposition (Wortham, 1994; cf. O'Connor, 2001). The use of these pronouns indexes a division between two interactionally relevant groups. More-over, Bill "characterizes" (Wortham, 1994) the groups he has indexed in terms of expert and non-expert identities. For example, in lines 238-239, he says, "so if you need any turbine blades for your car, I know how to make them," where *I* is associated with knowledge, and *you* is associated with lack of knowledge. Later, in lines 241-243, he again indexes these knowledgeable and non-knowledgeable "epi-stemic stances" (Ochs, 1996), when he says, "I know a lot about off road type vehicles of (.) a lot of sorts so (.) I a- I'm familiar with this type of racing. And so um (.) I wou- I would be good resource (.) if you have any questions." Here, he refers to himself as "knowing a lot," while presupposing that Joe and Katherine might know less, and might therefore have questions that he can answer.

It is interesting that, in addition to his use of his self-introduction to differentiate himself from Joe and Katherine, he also uses it to construct himself as the same kind of person as Joe and Katherine, identifying himself in important ways with the values they have indexed in their own turns. First, in his first use of the pronominal opposition to position himself as knowledgeable and Joe and Katherine as lacking knowledge, in lines 237-239 he does so by jokingly referring to his knowledge of how to make turbine blades as a result of his co-op. This knowledge is irrelevant to this project, and so does little to differentiate Bill from the others in any way that is meaningful or threatening here. It is also noteworthy that the knowledge that Bill is referring to here is *practical* and not purely theoretical knowledge; that is, it is knowledge of how to *make* turbine blades. This aligns Bill with the practical identity adopted by Joe in his self-introduction.

Bill further mitigates his claims to expertise in the final line of his turn, saying that "I want- just wanna build another truck too mostly though." Here, as he had earlier in stating that he knows how to "make" turbine blades, Bill, like Joe, aligns himself with the practical side of the theory/practice opposition. Moreover, he does so in a way that distances himself from his official identity as an "expert." That is, his *primary* interest is to "build another truck," and not to serve as an expert consultant to Joe and Katherine. Just as they are using the MQP as a means to the end of practical goals—leaving behind the school-based world of theory for the work world—so Bill is using the knowledge he gained from his own MQP for his own practical goals—building another truck.

One further source of alignment between Bill and the MQP students is relevant for my purposes here. That is, when Bill says, in line 243, that "I would be good resource (.) if you have any questions," he is indicating that the separation between himself and Joe and Katherine is only temporary. He is willing to share his knowledge to help them complete their own MQP, and thereby attain the expert status that he has achieved. We will see in the next section that this orientation toward the difference between expert and novice is not shared by all.

This first analysis has been intended to show how, as an interaction proceeds, participants use language to construct identifications and alignments both with and against the official model of the project, and how this contributes to the making and remaking of the context of the interaction. From an official perspective, successful participation in self-introductions involves relating oneself to the official model of the project, and specifically, as suggested by Jack's efforts to guide students' identifications, to do so by making clear what expertise or "core competencies" each participant is bringing that will benefit the project as a whole. However, these official identities do not exhaust the possibilities for successful participation, as we saw through the emergence of other, unofficial, criteria for successful performance of a self-introduction. That is, participants also oriented to the project from other perspectives, most notably from the perspective of the kinds of persons who de-emphasize expertise and "professionalism," and who instead align themselves with working-class norms, values, and activities. These unofficial identities, rather than being rejected as inappropriate, were instead validated by Jack and by other participants. In fact, throughout the Micro Truck Project, Tech students continued to align themselves with the practical, "hands-on," aspects of the project, and continued playfully to resist more academic and school-affiliated kinds of identities. In this way, the Consortium, with its attempt to elevate the status of activities that are traditionally devalued in engineering, was offering a place for students with these kinds of working-class affiliations to form positively valued identities. However, these identities are not equally valued in all contexts, and in the next section I examine what happens when these locally constructed identities are made relevant in interaction with students from a higher status school, who adhere more closely to some of the more traditional values of engineering.

Contesting Identities of Expertise

In this section, I examine segments of a videoconference that took place about three weeks after the initial project meeting at Tech that was analyzed in the previous section, and about two months before the scheduled end of the project. The videoconference is between Joe and Katherine, the Tech project managers, and Alex, Tina, and Luis from the Institute. The Institute students were recruited for the project with the understanding that they would be in charge of the Consortium truck's control system. These students were interested in working with sophisticated, state-of-the-art microprocessors in designing the truck's control system, and they were offered substantial financial resources by the Consortium for this task. Tina, in an interview, made it clear that this offer was important in persuading the Institute students to participate.

My aim in this section is once again to show how unofficial identities are made relevant in the interaction, and how, over the course of the interaction, this results in participants identifying themselves and others with regard to some of the central goals of the consortium. This time, however, rather than resulting in alignments being constructed among participants, as in the Tech meeting, participants from the two schools differentiate themselves in ways that line up with traditional views of engineering expertise and traditional status differences between the two schools. This is an active process in which Tech students become identified as less "educated" persons than their counterparts at the Institute.

Before turning to the transcript, it is worth clarifying that the Micro Truck Project is scheduled to culminate on April twenty-seventh, with a race at Tech that is modeled after the annual National Micro Truck Competition. The Tech competition is scheduled to include the five-school Consortium truck, as well as vehicles entered by another Consortium team, by the experts at Tech, and by any Consortium sub-teams that choose to produce their own vehicle. At the start of the first segment to be examined here, Tina, from the Institute, asks a question that aims to clarify this point:

	Tina:	I have a question though. Um on April twenty seventh (.) who are we actually going to race (.) against? Um if all five of us (scho:ols)-
990	Joe:	Our experts are currently building their o:wn (.) super car, (..)

		u:m plus I believe some of the other schools'll be making their own to bring up and- to race against (.) the actual consortium car.
	Kath:	Right so if you wanna make a car, you're welcome to bring it and race against it.
995		(..)
	Tina:	So there's other schools that (.) are gonna like- (.) you're gonna invite or something?
		(.)
		To- to participate (.) in this particular race on April twenty seventh?
1000	Kath:	Right. We're gonna invite [all the consortium scho:ols,
	Tina:	[(like)
		(.)
	Kath:	um as well as our experts from last year, and anyone at Tech who wants to make a car. They're welcome to come down (.)
1005		and test it on our track.
		(.)
		Uh for the quadfest o:n the twenty seventh.
	Joe:	Yeah. These schools are makin- de- they're desi:gning their parts, but at the same time I think they're also building their own cars
1010		also to come up.
		(..)
	Alex:	And now now there's something that's- that's sort of bothering us right here. Uh (.) y- you call- the- the- the two- the two guys that were there that you called experts, (.) they <u>are</u> building their
1015		own vehicle. And we- (.) we're sort of uh (.) a bit uh touchy on sharing information, as far as u:h what- what sort of processor we're actually gonna use, and (.) its speed. Uh because I believe that they were actually gonna use a microprocessor themselves. (.) And uh (.) since we are- tha- that was my question that was
1020		geared towards uh (.) when I- when I asked you u:h (.) what do you want to actually acco- wuh- what do you want us to accomplish, as far as (.) uh is it gonna be a competitive vehicle, or is it just (.) to assemble something and (.) sort of (.) he:y compete. Because if it's- if it's- if it's actually gonna be a competitive vehicle, (.) u:h I feel that we shouldn't share anything
1025		with uh (.) the experts.

Tina's question at the start of this transcript in line 988 brings up a topic that the Institute students have been trying to introduce for several minutes—that is, the arrangements for the final competition. By asking, "Who are we actually going to race against?," Tina is trying to establish the identity of the five-school team's competitors. Joe and Katherine respond in lines 990 through 1010 by explaining who the other participants will be. What is important here is that several of the participants in the Consortium's five-school team, including the experts, are also expected to be building their own truck to compete with the Consortium truck. These participants, then, have multiple potentially relevant identities, which include not only their project identities, such as "expert consultant," but also "competitor" identities. It is important to note that, while these multiple identities might be viewed as reflecting a conflict of interest, Joe, Katherine, and Jack Sanders, the Tech faculty advisor, regarded this possibility as irrelevant to the official model of the project. They emphasized collaboration, not competition, among the various teams.

It is important to note that, in contrast to the Tech team's emphasis on collaboration, the Institute students have already shown signs that they are not particularly aligned with the collaborative goals of the project. In fact, at one point relatively early in the project, the Institute students suggested in an email message to another Consortium school—the only one approaching the Institute in prestige—that the five-school project be disbanded, and each school produce its own truck for the competition. This resulted in a firm rebuke by the faculty advisor at that school, and the Institute's students continued as members of the five-school team. However, they repeatedly resisted efforts by other sub-teams to include them in their design work. Even in a case in which there was a question about a serious potential conflict between the Institute's control system and another team's steering mechanism, the Institute students repeatedly failed to respond to the other team's emails attempting to work out the problem.

In light of this, it is significant that, beginning at line 1012, Alex uses the experts' multiple possible identities as a basis for challenging the official model of the project. He foregrounds a role for "the experts" that is not a part of their official identities; that is, the experts are not only "consultants," they are also "competitors." He uses this as a rationale for why he does not want to "share anything" with the experts. This is of interest here in that it challenges the direction of the flow of knowledge that was behind the use of "experts" in this project to begin with. Alex is effectively questioning just who is in a position to learn from whom. It is important to note that the students from the Institute have made very clear earlier in this meeting that they have access to their own "experts," that is, electrical engineering faculty members at the Institute. What seems to be going on here is that the Institute students are protecting their privileged access to the expertise of their own faculty. In their view, the expertise of Tech students is in no way the equal of the expertise of Institute faculty members, and, thus, the Tech "experts" are in a position to "learn from" the Institute students. This challenge to the expertise of "the experts" is quite overt when Alex refers, in lines 1013–1014, to "the two guys that were there that you called experts," suggesting that, although Katherine and Joe might take "the experts" to be experts, Alex is not so willing to accept their expertise. It is important to note that Alex is apparently holding Katherine and Joe accountable for the designation of "the experts."

In addition, Alex is adopting a different orientation to the nature of knowledge and expertise than is reflected in the official model of the project. That is, in assuming that the experts are not necessarily benign guides and that they might instead attempt to gain some personal advantage from their position, he is treating knowledge as a valuable commodity that is the source of power and is therefore to be protected from others rather than freely shared.

Finally, I briefly consider Katherine and Joe's response to Alex's challenge. After a short exchange in which Joe responds to Alex and Alex elaborates on his position, Katherine provides a rationale for the participation of the experts:

	Kath:	I think the experts are more there for you to ask questions? They're not gonna be- (.) (say) when you send (.) Jim and myself (.) things about your ca:r, we're not gonna share it with
1050		them. I me:an (.) if they ask we'll (.) give em general knowledge, but we're not gonna give em- these are the blueprints to what (.) the Institute's doing. We're just gonna- you know (.) it's more for y- it's a one wa:y- (.) more for you to ask them questions than for them to ask you questions.
1055	Tina:	Okay.
	Kath:	It's just their expertise cause they did it once. (.) They're not really-
	Tina:	Okay.
	Joe:	Right. (.) They've- they've been there, they've raced a car, they
1060		know what the atmosphere is, they know what some of the other cars are like, (.) you know you can plug em questions about that, (.) but other than that I mean (.)
	Kath:	Right.
	Joe:	It's f- basically between (.) us and you.

Here, Katherine responds to Alex's challenge by reasserting the official structure of the project. In line 1047, she echoes Jack's assertion that the experts are "people you can go to with questions" when she says, "I think the experts are more there for you to ask questions?" She goes on to establish a basis for the experts' designation as experts when she says, "It's just their expertise cause they did it once." Here, she establishes a very limited basis for the status of the experts. That is, their expertise is grounded in practical experience, in that "they did it," that is, raced in the competition, and in limited practical experience at that: "they did it *once*." Joe, in lines 1059–1062, provides a similar justification for the status of the experts when he talks about the experts' experience at the competition. Thus, both Katherine and Joe are grounding the experts' status not in their having demonstrated their competence as engineers—the rationale for Tech's MQP requirement—or even in knowing "a lot about off road type vehicles of a lot of sorts," but rather in the highly situated conditions of the Micro Truck Competition.

This is particularly interesting in light of the fact that the Institute students are not treating the Micro Truck Competition as any special basis for expertise. In fact, one of the Institute students, Tina, told me in an interview midway through the project that she and her Institute teammates were quite certain that the design they were interested in pursuing would not be possible within the time constraints. Rather than changing their intended design to meet the deadline, however, Tina claimed that her team planned to pursue this design for as long as it took, regardless of whether they had finished in time for the competition. It was clear that the intellectual aspects of the design experience, and not collaboration with other schools in the "project realization process," was what primarily motivated the Institute students. Thus the limited practical basis Katherine and Joe give for the experts' status as experts is largely meaningless to the Institute team.

CONCLUSION

In this chapter, I have attempted to illustrate one way in which some of the concepts and methods of linguistic anthropology can be used to inform analyses of learning contexts, and to contribute to our understanding of processes of the cultural production of educated persons. My specific aim has been to show how the construction and contestation of "identities of expertise" takes place through the interplay between presupposing and entailing indexicality in a learning context.

In the analysis of the Tech students' construction of identities during self-introductions, I showed how participants used language to construct identifications and alignments both with and against the official model of the project. Through their playful resistance to the efforts of their faculty advisor to guide their participation toward a statement of their identities in terms of the official model, students aligned themselves with practical, "hands-on" aspects of the project, and constructed working-class identities for themselves, against the norms of "professionalism" that would typically characterize this genre. These identities came to have entailments for the interaction, as they were received positively, both by other students and by the advisor. In this way, participants renegotiated the possibilities for successful self-introductions and positively valued identities in this context. I also showed, however, that these working-class identities, constructed against typical views in engineering of what it means to be an expert, were later devalued during a videoconference with students from the Institute, a higher-status school. This devaluation was itself an emergent feature of the interaction, as Institute students brought "into play" potential but backgrounded—and to the Tech students, irrelevant—identities of the "experts," and used these as the basis for rejecting claims to expertise grounded in practical experience. Thus, in these interactions, participants were "learning relations among the major social identities and divisions" (Lave, 1996, p. 151) in their chosen profession of engineering, and at the same time participating in reproducing some of those same social identities and divisions.

A central point here is that when we do not privilege official understandings of context, it becomes possible to examine how participants not only act into an official context, but also orient to it from the perspective of other, unofficial and sometimes competing contexts. These negotiations are a central part of processes of cultural production, and attention to them can help us to maintain a symmetrical stance on the analysis of activity, and thus to adopt "an inclusive focus on all participants equally, as each contributes to the making of differences of power, salience, influence, and value of themselves and other participants" (Lave, 1996, p. 162).

NOTES

Research presented in this chapter was supported by the National Science Foundation Cooperative Agreement DMI-9413089 under the interagency Technology Reinvestment Project. The views expressed here are solely those of the author. I would like to thank Annie Allen, Betsy Rymes, and Stanton Wortham for helpful comments on earlier versions of this chapter.

1. All unattributed quotes in this section are taken from the Production Consortium's grant proposal.

APPENDIX: TRANSCRIPTION CONVENTIONS

Symbol   **Significance**

.   Falling pitch

?   Rising pitch

,   Slight rise in pitch, indicating "more to come"

~   Falling-rising pitch

-     Truncation

(.)   Pauses of less than 0.5 second

(..)   Pauses of greater than 0.5 second (number of dots indicates relative length of pause

=   Latching of speakers' utterances

[Onset of segments of overlapping speech

::   Lengthened segments (e.g., I don't kno::w)

{(( ))}   Non-lexical phenomena that overlay the lexical stretch (e.g., {((laughter)) text}.

(( ))   Non-lexical phenomena, vocal and nonvocal, that interrupt the lexical stretch (e.g., text ((laughter)) text)

(inaud)   Unintelligible speech

di(d)   A good guess at an unclear segment

(did)   A good guess at an unclear word

REFERENCES

Bauman, R., & Briggs, C. L. (1990). Poetics and performance as critical perspectives on language and social life. *Annual Review of Anthropology, 19*, 59–88.

Brown, J.S., Collins, A., & Duguid, P. (1989). Situated cognition and the culture of learning. *Educational Researcher, 18* (1), 32–42.

Collins, A. (1992). Toward a design science of education. In E. Scanlon & T. O'Shea (Eds.), *New Directions in Educational Technology*. Berlin: Springer.

Collins, A., Brown, J.S., & Newman, S.E. (1989). Cognitive apprenticeship: Teaching the crafts of reading, writing, and mathematics. In L.B. Resnick (Ed.), *Knowing, Learning, and Instruction: Essays in Honor of Robert Glaser*. Hilldale, NJ: Erlbaum.

Duranti, A. (1997). *Linguistic Anthropology*. New York: Cambridge University Press.

Duranti, A., & Goodwin, C. (1992). *Rethinking Context: Language as an Interactive Phenomenon*. New York: Cambridge University Press.

Engeström, Y., & Cole, M. (1997). Situated cognition in search of an agenda. In D. Kirshner & J. A. Whitson (Eds.), *Situated Cognition: Social, Semiotic, and Psychological Perspectives*. Mahwah, NJ: Erlbaum.

Greeno, J. G., & the Middle School Mathematics Through Applications Project Group. (1997). Theories and practices of thinking and learning to think. *American Journal of Education, 106*, 85–126.

Gumperz, J. J. (1982). *Discourse Strategies*. New York: Cambridge University Press.

Hanks, W.F. (1996). *Language and Communicative Practices*. Boulder, CO: Westview.

Lave, J. (1990). The culture of acquisition and the practice of understanding. In Shweder, R., Stigler, J., & Herdt, G. (Eds.), *Cultural Psychology*. New York: Cambridge University Press.

Lave, J. (1993). The practice of learning. In S. Chaiklin & J. Lave (Eds.), *Understanding Practice: Perspectives on Activity and Context*. New York: Cambridge University Press.

Lave, J. (1996). Teaching, as learning, in practice. *Mind, Culture, and Activity, 3*, 149–164.

Lave, J., & Wenger, E. (1991). *Situated Learning: Legitimate Peripheral Participation.* New York: Cambridge University Press.

Levinson, B.A., & Holland, D. (1996). The cultural production of the educated person: An introduction. In B.A. Levinson, D.E. Foley, & D.C. Holland (Eds.), *The Cultural Production of the Educated Person: Critical Ethnographies of Schooling and Local Practice.* Albany: SUNY Press.

McDermott, R. (1993). The acquisition of a child by a learning disability. In S. Chaiklin & J. Lave (Eds.), *Understanding Practice: Perspectives on Activity and Context.* New York: Cambridge University Press.

Nespor, J. (1994). *Knowledge in Motion: Space, Time, and Motion in Undergraduate Physics and Management.* London: Routledge Falmer.

Ochs, E. (1996). Linguistic resources for socializing humanity. In J.J. Gumperz & S.C. Levinson (Eds.), *Rethinking Linguistic Relativity.* New York: Cambridge University Press.

O'Connor, K. (2001). Contextualization and the negotiation of social identities in a geographically distributed situated learning project. *Linguistics & Education, 12,* 285–308.

Packer, M.J., & Goicoechea, J. (2000). Sociocultural and constructivist theories of learning: Ontology, not just epistemology. *Educational Psychologist, 35,* 227–241.

Rymes, B. (2001). *Conversational Borderlands: Language and Identity in an Alternative High School.* New York: Teachers College Press.

Silverstein, M. (1992). The indeterminacy of contextualization: When is enough enough? In A. DiLuzio & P. Auer (Eds.), *The Contextualization of Language.* Amsterdam: John Benjamins.

Silverstein, M., & Urban, G. (1996). The natural history of discourse. In M. Silverstein & G. Urban (Eds.), *Natural Histories of Discourse.* Chicago: University of Chicago Press.

Varenne, H., & McDermott, R. (1998). *Successful Failure: The School America Builds.* Boulder, CO: Westview Press.

Wenger, E. (1998). *Communities of Practice: Learning, Meaning, and Identity.* New York: Cambridge University Press.

Wertsch, J.V. (1991). *Voices of the Mind: A Sociocultural Approach to Mediated Action.* Cambridge, MA: Harvard University Press.

Wertsch, J.V. (1998). *Mind as Action.* New York: Oxford University Press.

Wortham, S. (1994). *Acting Out Participant Examples in the Classroom.* Amsterdam: John Benjamins.

4

Linguistic Anthropology and Language Education

A Comparative Look at Language Socialization

Agnes Weiyun He

Although it is true that contemporary concepts such as indexicality and creativity from linguistic anthropology have not yet directly influenced mainstream educational research and practice, a branch of linguistic anthropology known as language socialization (LS), which rests on a theory of indexicality, has already made an important impact on language education in particular. My overall goal in this chapter is twofold: one is to review critically and comparatively the notions of indexicality and creativity as expounded in LS, drawing impetus from conversation analysis (hereafter, CA). The other is to use language education as both a site and a set of practices in education to demonstrate what an enriched LS perspective can contribute. I suggest that LS's notions of indexicality and creativity can be enriched by adding CA notions of intersubjectivity and emergence. I discuss further how both theoretical issues and everyday practices in language education can be reconceptualized with an intersubjective, emergent account of LS.

WHAT IS LANGUAGE SOCIALIZATION?

Grounded in ethnography, LS, as a branch of linguistic anthropology, focuses on the process of becoming a culturally competent member through language use in social activities. As formulated by Ochs and Schieffelin (Ochs, 1990, 1996; Ochs & Schieffelin, 1984; Schieffelin & Ochs, 1986a, 1986b, 1996), LS is concerned with (1) how novices (e.g., children, second language learners) are socialized to be competent members in the target culture through language use, and (2) how novices are socialized to use language. This approach focuses on the language used by and to novices (e.g., children, second language learners) and the relations between this language use and the larger cultural contexts of communication—local theories and epistemologies concerning social order, local ideologies and practices concerning socializing the novices (e.g., rearing children, teaching students), relationships between the novice and the expert, the specific activities and tasks at hand, and so forth. Most work in LS has focused on analyzing the organization of communicative practices through which novices (especially children) acquire sociocultural knowledge. Methodologically, it examines audio-/video-recorded, carefully transcribed, recurrent socialization activities and relates the grammatical, discursive, and non-verbal details of interaction to the construction of social and cultural ideologies that define a community.

By its very conceptualization, LS is centrally concerned with human development and growth in areas where language and culture intersect. In other words, it views education not just as a physical site (e.g., formal schooling), but more important as a set of practices—how learning takes place in and through language, regardless of the setting. Although earlier work in LS has focused on non-school settings such as traditional cultures, non-American cultures, everyday encounters such as play time or dinner time (e.g., Goodwin, 1990; Heath, 1983; Ochs, 1988; Ochs & Taylor 1992; Schieffelin, 1990; Schieffelin & Ochs, 1996), more recent research guided by LS has also studied formal educational settings such as physics laboratories (Ochs et al., 1994) and to second /foreign/heritage language teaching and learning in the classroom (Duff, 2000; He, 2000, 2001, in press; Kanagy, 1999; Ohta, 1999; Poole 1992).

The theory of LS rests on a theory of indexicality. Indexicality, as a number of linguistic anthropologists such as Ochs (1990), Duranti and Goodwin (1992), and Wortham (this volume) argue, is central to the linguistic and cultural organization of social life, something that constitutes language as a context-bound, interactively accomplished phenomenon. From sociolinguistics, among other fields, we have learned that a single linguistic form may index some contextual dimension (e.g., honorific forms can index social and affective relationships between the speaker and the addressee or between the speaker and the referent). Or, a set of linguistic forms may index some contextual dimension. As isolated linguistic features often have a wide range of indexical possibilities (e.g., mispronunciation can index speech by a child, an elderly person, a foreign language speaker, or simply a slip of tongue), it is often the case that a combination of several indexes narrows the indexical scope in terms of identities of and relations between the language users, and/or dispositions of the language users, and/or the activities at hand (e.g., [s] deletion along with high pitch might index a child English speaker, etc.).

In contrast to the view that language forms *directly* index some sociocultural contexts, within the framework of LS, indexicality is conceived of as a property of speech through which sociocultural contexts (e.g., identities, activities) are constituted by particular stances and acts, which in turn are indexed through linguistic forms (Ochs, 1990, 1992, 1993). That is to say, from an LS perspective, the indexical relationship between linguistic forms and sociocultural contexts is often achieved indirectly, instead of directly (i.e., one or more linguistic forms indexing some contextual dimension). According to LS, "A [a] feature of the communicative event is evoked indirectly through the indexing of some *other* feature of the communicative event. . . . [T]he feature of the communicative event directly indexed is conventionally linked to and helps to constitute some second feature of the communicative event, such that the indexing of one evokes or indexes the other" (Ochs, 1990, p. 295). Further, it is not random that some features of the communicative event bear a direct or indirect relationship to linguistic forms. Major sociocultural dimensions include social identities of the participants, relationships among participants, affective dispositions of participants (feelings, moods, and attitudes of participants toward some proposition), epistemological dispositions of participants (beliefs or knowledge vis-à-vis some proposition, e.g., the source of their knowledge or the degree of certainty of their knowledge), social/speech acts and activities, and genre. Ochs (1990) argues that among these dimensions *affective* and *epistemological dispositions* are the two contextual dimensions used recurrently to constitute other contextual dimensions. Hence this two-step indexical relationship can be illustrated in Figure 4.1.

The advantages of this model can be seen in the analysis of the Chinese heritage language classrooms that I have been studying for the

Linguistic forms→affect/stance→contextual features (identity, activity)

Figure 4-1.   Indexical relationship between language and sociocultural context.

past few years. In terms of linguistic forms, teachers in these classrooms consistently embed their commands for the students to act according to the teacher's wishes within three-phased moralized directives (He, 2000), as seen in example (1). Setting and background information can be found in the section titled "The Case of Chinese Heritage Language Learning." Data transcriptions can be found in Appendix A. Grammatical gloss can be found in Appendix B.

(1) [TWATL:931] directive: respect for parents' efforts
((In the middle of a class, several students, especially B2 and B5, appear tired or bored. They are sitting sideways, kicking their legs, and not paying attention to Tw, the teacher.))

```
1     Tw:->    A: baba mama hua le hen DA de liqi
                PRT father mother spend PERT very big POS effort
                Ah, your parents spent lots of efforts
2                cong HEN YUAN de difang ba nimen song lai >shi bu shi<?
                from very far POS place PTP you send COMP right NEG right
                sending you here from distant places, right?
3                (.5)
4     Tw:       Hai zai waitou deng zhe nimen,
                even at outside wait DUR you
                They are even waiting for you outside
5     ->        ruguo nimen meiyou haohao xuexi meiyou dedao eh:::
                if you NEG well study NEG gain
                If you do not study hard, and learn something, eh:::
6                meiyou dedao dongxi de hua, (.2) a,
                NEG gain thing PRT case PRT
                if you don't get anything
7                na jiu bu heSUAN le
                then CONJ NEG worthwhile PRT
                then it is not worthwhile
8                (.4)
9     Tw:->     A, suoyi (.2) women YIDING yao zuo hao::.
                PRT therefore we surely should sit well
                Ah, so, we must sit well.
10               ((B2 and B5 stop kicking, sit straight, facing Tw))
```

Noticing that some students are not sitting well and not paying attention, Tw first points out the efforts the parents made sending the children to weekend Chinese language schools (lines 1-4). The import of the statements is not transparent until the next utterances in which she projects the negative consequences of the students' behavior (lines 5-7). Only finally does she issue a directive (line 9). Note that the problem itself (that some students are not sitting well and not paying attention) is never formulated overtly; rather, it is embedded in negative conditional clauses (if-not clauses in lines 5 and 6). This way Teacher Wang uses the opportunity of asking her students to sit well to inculcate the idea that children should be filial, grateful to their parents by meeting their expectations. In other words, her directive is grounded in a moral appeal: if you don't study hard, your parents' efforts will be wasted; and if that happens, you are not a good child.

So here we see a three-phased directive pattern, namely, Orientation→Evaluation→Directive. Specifically, the teacher first orients the students to some state of affairs, which in turn renders the students' behavior problematic, then she formulates negative consequences that may result from the students' problematic behavior, and only then does she issue a directive to correct the behavior. Thus, rather than simply issuing directives, the teacher weaves cultural values and ideology in the prefaces so as to warrant the directives for desirable behavior.

Moralized directives like (1) index both an affective disposition and social identity. They directly index affective dispositions of being moral and authoritative and indirectly index the social identity of the speaker—that of a parent or a teacher, as in the Chinese culture parent/teacher roles, which are largely defined in terms of or constituted by moral and authoritative dispositions. Confucian teachings, which have provided dominant educational and social ethos for the major part of Chinese history, are primarily concerned with moral conduct as the basis of social harmony. It is thus the teachers' and the parents' prerogative as well as responsibility to socialize the students/children into the various virtues (known as *li*) that regulate all human conduct.

Although "teacher" is a universal social role, the communicative practices of teachers vary considerably across cultures and societies (see He, in press). In other words, there is not a one-to-one mapping relationship between three-phased moralized directives (language forms) and the social identity of the teacher (cultural context). Instead, the relation of moralized directives to the identity of the Chinese teacher is constituted and mediated by the relation of language forms to stances (e.g., moral and authoritative), activities, and other social constructs. As such, students in these classes come to understand teacher-related meanings in part through coming to understand certain recurrently displayed stances (e.g., upholding moral values such as filial piety).

The LS approach to indexicality provides a systematic account of how language relates to cultural context. In the diaspora situation of teaching/learning a heritage language in the adopted culture, it is possible that the teachers may fail to achieve the identity of "teacher" through failure to act and feel in some way expected, desired, or preferred by the students or through the failure of the students to ratify the teachers' displayed acts and stances. With LS, we can examine how different displays of and reactions to certain acts and stances (e.g., moralizing) construct different identities and relationships. It also allows us to examine the construction of multiple yet compatible/congruent identities, blended and blurred identities in multilingual, multicultural, immigrant contexts.

TOWARD AN INTERACTIONALLY ENRICHED LANGUAGE SOCIALIZATION PERSPECTIVE: INSIGHTS FROM CONVERSATION ANALYSIS

One might argue, however, that, although it is feasible to directly link some linguistic features with some affective or epistemological dispositions (the first step in the indexical relationship in the LS model), it appears more challenging to grasp the constitutive relationship between affective or epistemological stances and other contextual features such as social identities and interpersonal relationships (the second step in the LS theory of indexicality). In data segment (1), for example, one could suggest that the moral and authoritative stance can in fact index a number of different social identities other than the Chinese teacher—parents in Chinese, Jewish, and other cultures; old-fashioned school teachers; priests; and so forth. Thus the analytical challenge becomes this: How can we ascertain that it is one specific cultural and situational context and not any other that is invoked by certain affective and epistemological dispositions?

The LS answer to the question is that one needs to consider the preexisting local context. For example, Ochs (1992) argues that the relation of language to the participant's gender identity is constituted and mediated by the relation of language to stances, social acts, and other social constructs. As such, novices come to understand gender meanings through coming to understand certain pragmatic functions of language and coming to understand local expectations vis-à-vis the distribution of these functions and their variable expression across social identities. For example, the sentence-final particle "wa" in Japanese indexes an affect of gentle intensity, which in turn is in Japanese society associated with the female voice and thus indexes the female gender identity. Along this line of argument, we might say that it is the Chinese heritage language classroom context that warrants the connection between the moral and authoritative stance with the role of the teacher. But the logic here runs the risk of being circular—the local context determines to which contextual features the affective and epistemological stances are linked, and yet these very stances constitute those contextual features.

To address this question and to avoid the circularity in LS, I suggest that we consider two additional concepts from CA: intersubjectivity and emergent context, both of which are constructed through moment-by-moment interaction among the participants. These two concepts may enable us to ground cultural context in the interactional production of acts and stances.

Intersubjectivity

Ochs (1990, pp. 302-303) presents an integrated socialization model for the theory of LS. On the one hand, this model recognizes the social and psychological dominance of the expert vis-à-vis the novice and the impact of this fact on the novice's understanding of the world. On the other hand, this model allows for the expert to be influenced by the novice through the medium of joint social activity; as the expert inducts the novice, the expert's knowledge may also be transformed by the responses of the novice. Schematically, this model looks like that shown in Figure 4-2.

While the account of socialization as co-constructed and interactively accomplished is integral and essential to LS theory, it is not yet sufficiently presupposed in empirical LS studies. As I discuss elsewhere (He, in press), research drawing upon LS tends to emphasize the efforts made by the experts (e.g., mothers, other caregivers, teachers) to socialize the novices (e.g., children, students). Little visible, however, are the reactions and responses of the novices. Consequently, the process of socialization in empirical LS studies is often characterized as smooth and seamless; novices are often presumed to be passive, ready, and uniform recipients of socialization; and cultural and situational con-

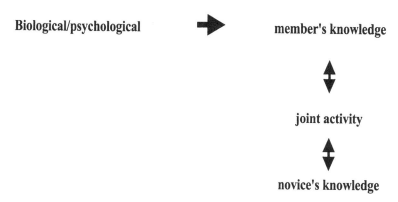

Figure 4-2. Integrated socialization model (Ochs, 1990, p. 303).

texts are often taken as an *a priori* given, which can be overlaid on the analysis of data.

Yet we know that in any kind of social action and interaction, including language socialization, there exist clashes of ideas, goals, dispositions, expectations, and norms of interaction between the experts and the novices (Chaiklin & Lave, 1993; Erickson & Shultz, 1982; He & Keating, 1991; Jacoby & Gonzales, 1991; Latour, 1987). For socialization to take place, the expert and novice need to negotiate their differences through interaction. Even in idealized cases where the expert and novice share the same goals, expectations, and norms of behavior, socialization cannot be accomplished without the co-construction by the novice, as any constitution of action, activity, identity, emotion, ideology, or other culturally meaningful reality is inherently a joint achievement by all the participants (He, 1995; Jacoby & Ochs, 1995).

Here I would like to highlight and reinforce the dialogical, interactional perspective within LS theory and complement it with analytical tools from parallel perspectives such as CA (Atkinson & Heritage, 1984; Drew & Heritage, 1992; Sacks, 1992; Sacks, Schegloff, & Jefferson, 1974), ethnomethodology (Garfinkel, 1967), practice theory (Bourdieu, 1977), and sociohistorical psychology (Vygotsky, 1986). From these perspectives, the encounter between any expert and novice is first and foremost an activity in which the participants try to make sense of what each other is saying. In other words, the participants take it to be a constant objective in their encounter to achieve a shared understanding of what each other means. Language learning problems and solutions, for example, become problems and solutions when students and teachers together identify and articulate them as such. Interpersonal and cultural knowledge is revealed and reconstructed as interaction between the participants unfolds. The participants' understanding of what each other means is dialogically based, in the sense that meaning is jointly constructed through discourse by both parties. Such joint construction of meaning is neither objective nor subjective, but rather intersubjective. It transcends the polarity between an objectivism, which prescribes that there exists some permanent, ahistorical, independent meaning, and an anything-goes relativism. The goal of the participants in any socialization setting is not to work toward an absolute objectivity, but toward an intersubjectivity, which is achieved through and mediated by language use.

If we assume that meaning is intersubjectively constructed and that the interpretation of meaning is sensitive to language use in interaction, we must then appreciate and analyze the consequences of interactive language use. As is true of any other setting, intersubjectivity between the participants in the contexts of language socialization is not achieved automatically. It takes interaction to arrive at intersubjectivity. By interaction, I mean not only what the participants say to each other in terms of their words (lexicon) and sentence patterns (grammar), or lexicogrammar, but also the speech exchange system that regulates who speaks when for how long and related matters. At the same time as it is a meaning-making activity, a language socialization activity is an instance of interaction, in which two parties (e.g., caregiver and child or teacher and students), through talking to each other, influence each other and react to each other, affectively and cognitively. As interaction, these socialization encounters take on an emergent quality as the novice and the expert jointly build their discourse moment-by-moment.

What this means for LS empirical research is that, in actual analyses of joint activities between the expert and the novice, we need to make salient the reactions and responses of the novice to various socialization efforts and to examine how an intersubjective orientation to cultural/situational contexts and other realities is established, maintained, or altered moment by moment.

Emergence

To understand the construction of emergent contexts, we can turn to CA for guidance. CA has been developed as an approach to "the analysis of the practices of reasoning and inference that inform the production and recognition of intelligible courses of action" (Goodwin & Heritage, 1990, p. 287). CA concentrates on drawing principles, or systematics, of spoken discourse by examining the ongoing social and conversational activities displayed in language use. Rather than speculating about the idealized characteristics of social action, CA empirically investigates actual, naturally occurring social actions and their sequential organization. Rules used to account for the orderly and collaborative nature of interaction are seen as those that the participants themselves use to make sense of their moment-by-moment interaction. It is a generic approach to the analysis of social interaction that was first developed in the study of ordinary conversation but that has been applied to a wide spectrum of other forms of talk in social institutions.

From CA, we learn that conversation, or talk-in-interaction, is systematic and dynamic. It is systematic because there is describable order in the seemingly random and chaotic ways in which speaking turns are distributed and sequenced. It is dynamic because each new turn or turn-constructional-unit creates a demand and an opportunity for the participants to re-assess and re-structure their mutual understanding. Interaction is therefore a vehicle through which intersubjectivity is constantly built and rebuilt, with the potential of shifting from moment to moment. Reciprocally, intersubjectivity provides the basis for interaction; each speaking turn or turn-constructional-unit is oriented to the intersubjectivity established thus far.

CA and LS converge in their mutual concern with context. A CA take on context is to focus on how the participants themselves orient to, manage, and sustain context in actual, real-time interaction. The specification of context must be derived from orientations exhibited by the participants themselves. Hence, for example, to claim that some interaction has a socialization character, the relevance of socialization must be shown to inhabit the details of the participants' conduct. To say that the teacher in data segment (1) is engaged in values education by organizing her directives in specific ways, we need to verify that statement by examining textual evidence indicating that the students are in fact taking the teacher's utterances to be both directives and moral inductions. Accordingly, words, phrases, utterances, turns, and sequences are not treated as isolated, self-contained artifacts. Instead, they are forms of action situated in specific sequential contexts, they are oriented to these specific contexts, and they have the potential to either maintain or alter these contexts.

Although LS recognizes that context is in part created and sustained through concrete human actions and interactions and is subject to change as language use unfolds, emergent context is not the exclusive concern for LS. LS also considers other types of contexts that may not be immediately observable, recoverable, or reconstructable in the moment of interaction. The norms, dispositions, preferences, cultural models, or folk theories of the observed group may be among these not-immediately-available contexts. As a result, LS studies have tended to resort to the researcher's knowledge of these not-immediately-available contexts as primary and often sole resources in analyzing socialization data. What is often missing from empirical LS studies is the participants' orientation to and co-construction of emergent contexts. From a CA standpoint, however, context is exclusively seen as an intersubjective, interactively constructed, local, situated phenomenon. As such, it defies generic descriptions as something that contains variables X, Y, and Z. CA's adherence to emergent contexts, I suggest, can be more substantively and systematically incorporated in LS studies, for it can help us understand how sociocultural knowledge is re-enacted and reproduced through interaction and ground claims about the relevance of the sociocultural context in the participants' (not merely the researcher's) orientation to such context.

Having highlighted the interactional, dialogical perspective in LS theory and complemented it with analytical tools from CA, I will next consider how an interactionally enriched LS perspective may illuminate broad, fundamental issues in language education and discuss how it may help us analyze classroom data.

WHAT CAN LS OFFER TO LANGUAGE EDUCATION IN GENERAL?

By language education, I refer to the learning and teaching of a foreign, second, or heritage language. For a long time, language learning and teaching has been predominantly guided by research from language acquisition, a field that has focused largely on the language learner—what and when the learner can listen/speak/read/write. Based on research results concerning the stages and sequences of the language learning process, language textbooks are written, language testing instruments are designed, and language teachers are trained. In other words, language learning has for a long time been seen as a purely cognitive process that occurs within the individual learner. Acquisition implies a unidirectional path in which the learner is constantly attempting to approximate the native speaker of the target language.

LS, on the contrary, considers language learning and teaching as a social, cultural, and interactional process that inherently involves both the learner/novice and the teacher/expert. Within this theoretical perspective, the very process of language learning and teaching has the potential to transform not only the language learner but also the language teacher (either within or outside the classroom). LS has appealed to the community of language education for several reasons. First, it interfaces with some of the primary concerns of language acquisition research, such as the impact of the acculturation of the learner on his/her second language acquisition (Schumann, 1978). Second, its ethnographic orientation and the importance it attaches to context show strong affinity with various sociolinguistic approaches to language learning (e.g., Bayley & Preston, 1996; Rampton, 1997, 1999, 2000). Third, its focus on communicative practices resonates with the more interactionally and ethnomethodologically oriented approaches to second/foreign language acquisition (Hatch, 1978; Markee, 2000; Pica, 1994; Pica, Doughty, & Young, 1986; Pica, Young, & Doughty, 1987). Fourth, its emphasis on developmental cultural competence and its theory of indexicality contribute directly to the understanding of the learner's language use throughout the developmental stages (Kasper, 2000).

Not only has LS been appealing, but it has also been challenging to the field of language education. While the central concern of (second) language acquisition research has been with when, how, and why language learners understand and use linguistic forms in the target language, LS research has largely focused on culturally and/or developmentally relevant communicative practices and activities, which both contribute to language learning and are shaped by language use

(Ochs & Schieffelin 1995). Consequently LS research also contrasts with language acquisition research. LS reconceptualizes language education in a number of ways. It redefines what it means to know a language, advances an indexical (rather than correlational) view concerning language and culture, enables us to see the acquisition of language forms in a culturally accountable way, and takes ordinary interaction to be the primary sites for socialization.

What It Means to Know a Language

It is true that more recent language acquisition research has also focused on the comprehension of linguistic forms in terms of both language universals and pragmatic functions of language. The emphasis, however, has remained on acquiring a self-contained, fixed set of morpho-syntactic or phonetic forms. On the other hand, LS considers language practice as a set of indexicals participating in a network of semiotic systems and treats language acquisition and socialization as an integrated process. Linguistic meanings and meaning makings are therefore necessarily embedded in cultural systems of understanding. An account of linguistic behavior (speaking and listening) must then draw on accounts of culture. Accordingly, the knowledge of a language includes a set of norms, preferences, and expectations relating linguistic structures to context, which language users draw on in producing and interpreting language (Ochs, 1988).

For example, the acquisition of modal elements in language is a particularly interesting area developmentally. Epistemic modality (e.g., *must* in "Everything that goes up must come down" or *can* in "Too much of a good thing can be bad") provides children with a resource for developing the capacity to infer, predict, generalize, and hypothesize; and deontic modality (e.g., *should* in "When playing with your friends, you should always take turns" or *can* in "Yes you can call me Sandy") provides a resource for children's exploration and understanding of social obligations, responsibilities, constraints, and cultural and moral values. While most acquisition studies on children's use of modal language have largely focused on the timing and frequency of isolated instances of production (Dittmar & Reich, 1993), an LS approach would argue that (1) it is not context-free frequency but rather the understanding of the degree of situational relevance and cultural meaningfulness that indexes the learner's competence, and (2) children's acquisition and use of modal language are an integral part of a more general socialization process.

He (2001) documents, for instance, that teachers in Chinese heritage language schools frequently mark and mask an imperative with modals of low obligation, as in (2):

(2) [TSCDL:951] "may = must"

((All seven students are practicing writing characters on the blackboard. Each student has a limited space to use.))

1	Ts:->	Hao, xie wan le keyi ca diao.
		Good write COMP PRT may erase COMP
		good, when you are finished writing, you may erase it.
2		(.4) ((Ss write and erase))
3	Ts:	Zai xie zhangda de zhang(3).
		Next write "zhangda" POS "zhang"
		Next, write "zhang" as in "zhangda" (third tone).
4		(.2)
5	Ts:	Zhangda de zhang.
		"zhang" as in "zhangda".
6		((Ss write))
7	Ts:	Ok hao, zhangda de zhang xie wan mei?
		Good "zhangda" POS "zhang" write finish NEG?
		Ok, good, have you finished "zhang" as in "zhangda"?
8		((Ts waits for Ss to finish writing and then erasing "zhang"))
9	Ts:->	Hao xiaopengyou keyi xie zhang(1).
		Good little friends may write "zhang"
		Good, my little friends may now write "zhang" (first tone).

Two instances of *keyi* (may) statements are found in (2). In line 1, Ts states that the students may erase what they have written before writing the next word on the blackboard. In fact, since all seven students are sharing the blackboard, each of them has enough space to write only one word/phrase. That is to say, they *must* erase one before they write another; if they don't, there will hardly be enough space for everyone. Ts, however, presents her directive to erase the current word as optional rather than obligatory. Similarly, in line 9, Ts states that the students *may* now write the next word while in fact there is no room for negotiation as to what the students should write next.

Clearly, in cases like (2), language forms that indicate preferences or permissions also indicate directives. In other words, the preference/permission function and the directive function coalesce. The logical steps that the teacher takes to issue directives are thus the following:

- presenting a preference/permission
- eliminating all other options
- asking the students to implement the preference/permission as a directive

To be able to construct an interpretative frame for the semantic meaning of *keyi* (may or can) to license the pragmatic inference "One must do X," the students need to understand not merely the dictionary meaning of these modals but also to draw on an understanding of the classroom and cultural context. They must understand the ongoing teaching/learning activity and the local ideology and practice that allows (or even prefers) those in the power position (including teachers) to remain ambiguous in their stances and that requires those not in the power position to make speculations and draw inferences regarding their interlocutors' references, intentions, dispositions, and goals (He, 2001).

How Culture/Context Relates to Language

Acquisition research has typically adopted a correlational approach to the relationship between the learning or use of certain language forms and certain aspects of cultural contexts. It has treated culture/context as *a priori* variables to be correlated with language forms or to be invoked to account for variations in language use (Young, 1999). This can be seen in the work of second language acquisition (SLA) variationists who have used quantitative, correlational analyses to express the relationship between variable linguistic forms in the learner's developmental language (i.e., interlanguage) and co-occurring elements of social and linguistic context. For instance, Bayley (1996), in a study of final [t/d] deletion in the speech of Chinese-English bilinguals, found that speakers whose social network consisted predominantly of other Chinese delete final [t/d] more often than speakers who reported a mixed Chinese and American network. But acquisition studies like this do not tell us how a *particular* pragmalinguistic feature is related to the *particular* grammatical knowledge implicated in its use. It is precisely this question that Bardovi-Harlig (2000) recommends to SLA researchers' attention. Similarly, SLA pragmatics studies have typically matched learners' performance of a *particular* pragmatic feature, mostly a speech act, with the performance of that speech act by native speakers, on the one hand, and a *general* measure of L2 proficiency, on the other—a standardized proficiency test like the TOEFL, grade level, or even measures that are related to proficiency by inference only, such as length of residence or study. Such studies have found repeatedly that high general proficiency is not matched by native-like performance in the examined pragmatic feature (Kasper, 2000).

What is missing is a theory of indexicality (as discussed in the first section above). From an LS perspective, a language learner's acquisition of linguistic forms requires a developmental process of delineating and organizing contextual dimensions in culturally sensible ways. Indexical knowledge, as Ochs (1996) argues, is at the core of linguistic and cultural competence and is the locus where language acquisition and socialization interface. A language socialization model decries reductionistic visions that view the sociocultural context as "input" to be quantified and correlated with learner's grammatical patterns. Instead, it accounts for learner's grammatical development in terms of the indexical meanings of grammatical forms. The underlying assumption is that "in every community, grammatical forms are inextricably tied to, and hence index, culturally organized situations of use and that the indexical meanings of grammatical forms influence children's [and learners' in general] production and understanding of these forms" (Ochs & Schieffelin, 1995, p. 74). In this model, learners are viewed as tuned into certain indexical meanings of grammatical forms that link those forms to, for example, the social identities of interlocutors and the types of social events. This model relates learners' use and understanding of grammatical forms to complex yet orderly and recurrent dispositions, preferences, beliefs, and bodies of knowledge that organize how information is linguistically packaged and how speech acts are performed within and across socially recognized situations (Ochs & Schieffelin, 1995, p. 74).

Let's now return to data segment (1) and take a look at the identity of the teacher. LS research asks, "what kind of social identity is Tw attempting to construct in performing this type of moralized directive and in expressing the stance of upholding moral values?" In the sociolinguistic variationist approach to language acquisition, the question becomes "how does Tw being a teacher speak?" While social identities have a sociohistorical reality independent of language behavior, an intersubjective, emergent account of LS maintains that in any given situation, at any given moment in interaction, the participants are not passively enacting some prescribed social identities, but are actively (re)constructing their identities (Ochs, 1993). Even in highly institutionalized and/or ritualized settings, the participants are agents in the re-production of their own and their interlocutors' social identities (He, 1995, 1997).

What Constitutes Evidence of Learning

While acquisition research has focused on frequency in output as evidence of learning (Kasper, 2000; Young, 1999), socialization research has looked for culturally meaningful practices across settings and situations (Ochs & Schieffelin, 1995). Within a sociocultural perspective, LS views language acquisition "as increasing competence in both the formal and functional potential of language. By functional, I mean the multiplicity of relations between language and context, including that in which language creates context" (Ochs, 1988, p. 13). Over developmental time, language learners acquire repertoires of language forms associated with contextual dimensions (e.g., role relationships, acts, events).

Consider data segment (2) again. As directives masked with modals of low obligation are used by persons of power and authority (e.g., teachers, parents, or any elderly person), a student who has acquired the meaning of the modal verb *keyi* (can/may) may in fact not be using the form in his/her speech to the teacher in the same manner the teacher does to the students, because it would be pragmatically and culturally inappropriate. Hence frequency in output alone will lead to a misguided interpretation of the student's acquisition of modals. From an LS perspective, we need to ask the following questions: (1) In what contexts is the modal form *keyi* used by children? (2) What is the impact, if any, of the sequential organization of interaction on the children's (non-)use of *keyi*? (3) What is the impact, if any, of the local activity on the children's (non-)use of *keyi*? (4) Do the children and their teachers differ in their use of *keyi* in terms of 1-3? (5) What stances are exhibited by the (non-)use of *keyi*? and (6) How are these stances associated with social roles, identities, responsibilities, and obligations in the local Chinese community?

The Function of Interaction

In cases where interaction is at all considered within acquisition research, it is largely seen as a means to acquire morpho-syntactic forms (Day, 1986; Hatch, 1978; Krashen, 1980; Long, 1981; Pica et al., 1986, 1987; Varonis & Gass, 1985). LS, on the other hand, views interaction as language practices that serve as resources for socializing social and cultural competence (Goodwin, 1990; Heath, 1983; Ochs, 1988; Schieffelin, 1990). In this view, interactional competence itself (He & Young, 1998; Kramsch, 1986; Markee, 2000; Young, 2000) embodies both cultural competence and linguistic competence.

As discussed previously, when the interactional, dialogical perspective in LS theory is complemented by analytical tools from CA, it is in a position to account for the (re-)creation of moment-by-moment, emergent contexts. In the context of language education, an interactionally enriched LS perspective may illuminate the process of language learning and teaching in two important ways: (1) by recognizing the important role of the language learner/novice—their reactions and responses to socialization efforts/attempts—in language socialization processes, and (2) by recognizing the important role of the teacher/expert in the construction of language proficiency in the learner. In the remainder of the chapter, I turn to an empirical case from language education to illustrate how an interactionally enriched LS perspective can elucidate some issues in the construction of teacher-learner (expert-novice) relations and the construction of the learner's language proficiency.

THE CASE OF CHINESE HERITAGE LANGUAGE LEARNING

Research Context

For the past few years, I have been studying discourse in Chinese heritage language schools from an LS perspective. Data presented in this chapter were collected in two Chinese heritage language schools in two different cities in the United States, where evening or weekend Chinese language classes are offered for children whose parents come from China or Taiwan and are pursuing professional careers in the United States. These children were either born in the United States or came to the United States with their parents at a very young age. Most of them go to mainstream English-speaking schools on weekdays. While many of them are bilingual in Chinese and English in the oral form, some are already English-dominant, and few have opportunities to learn how to read and write in Chinese. Their parents send them to these Chinese language schools for the children to acquire literacy in the heritage language. Combining elements from family, community, and school, heritage language schools like these function as an important vehicle for ethnic minority children to acquire heritage language skills and cultural values (Bradunas & Topping, 1988; Cummins, 1992; Fishman, 1966; Wang, 1996). The corpus includes (1) thirty hours of audio- and video-recorded class meetings involving four teachers in four different classes and a total of thirty-five children (aged 4.5 to 9), (2) classroom observations, and (3) interviews with parents, teachers, and school administrators.

My overall research questions are these: Are Chinese-American children currently being socialized into traditional Chinese values, particularly with respect to interpersonal role relations and ways of speaking in the classroom? If so, what are the specific ways in which this socialization takes place? What are the children's responses to this socialization? These questions presuppose a pre-existing knowledge of what constitute "traditional Chinese values" in the classroom context, which entail teacher-student relationships, ways of assessing learner competence, and classroom discourse patterns, among other aspects. It is thus very convenient and tempting to impose this pre-existing knowledge in the analysis of actual data. However, I will show that, with intersubjectivity and emergent contexts in mind, these questions in language socialization can be explored in an interactionally as well as a culturally accountable way.

Students' Co-Construction of the Teacher's Expert Role

Originating in the teachings of Confucius and Mencius two thousand years ago and sustained throughout Chinese history is the notion of *shi tao zun yan*—the supremacy of the Way of the teacher. The teacher in a traditional Chinese classroom is someone who is the indisputable, unchallenged center and authority of knowledge. The student accordingly is someone who is expected to listen, observe, and follow the teacher's instructions. In data segment (3), I aim to show that the expert-novice relation between the teacher and the students in the Chinese heritage language classes is not a clear-cut case of whether or not it represents an instance of "traditional" classroom practice; instead, it may in fact take on a highly emergent quality as the participants ratify, reverse, reject, or make irrelevant their prescribed role identities moment-by-moment.

The scenario in (3) concerns the choice of script between *jiantizi*, the simplified script, which is the official script used in mainland China, and *fantizi*, the traditional (un-simplified) script, which is typically used in Taiwan and elsewhere. While the heritage language schools I observed adopted textbooks published in mainland China (in *jiantizi*), they also provided their students with supplementary reading materials published elsewhere, such as Taiwan and Hong Kong. As a principle, the schools I observed accept any choice made by the instructor or by the students who may have a preference due to family influence. In the case of (3), the teacher, who received her education in mainland China before moving to Taiwan (and then the United States), chooses to use *jiantizi*. Student G5 comes from Taiwan and prefers *fantizi*.

(3) [TCCDL:953] choice of script
((Tc is walking around to check each individual student's writing.))

1	Tc:	zhe ge zi uh dui ma?
		This MSR character PRT correct Q
		Is this character uh correct?
2		((pointing to G5's writing))
3	G5:	umm::
4	Tc:	zhao shushang de xie
		follow book PRT write
		Write the character exactly as it appears in the book.
5		((G5 opens the textbook and looks for the character and then opens another book, a storybook; Tc moves on to other students. In a few minutes, Tc returns to G5.))
6	G5:	Laoshi, zhe ben shu shuo wo dui le
		teacher this MSR book say I correct PRT
		Teacher, this books says I'm right.

```
7              ((G5 points at the storybook; Tc looks.))
8      Tc:     zhe shi zhe shi sheme shu- nali de?
                This COP this COP what book where PRT
                What is this is this book- where does it come from?
9      G5:     cong tushuguan jie de
                from library borrow PRT
                [It is] borrowed from the library. ((The reading room in this
                Chinese language school.))
10     Tc:     zhe bu shi jiantizi >>women xue de shi jiantizi<<
                this NEG COP we learn PRT COP
                This is not jiantizi, what we're learning is jiantizi.
11     G5:     chen laoshi shuo fantizi jiantizi dou ok
                teacher say all ok
                Teacher Chen said that fantizi and jiantizi are both fine.
12              ((Teacher Chen is the school principal.))
13     Tc:     na hao.
                Then good.
                Okay then.
14              (.2)
15     Tc:     Rang wo kan ni xie dui ma.
                Let I see you write correct Q
                Let me see whether you write it correctly.
16              ((G5 hands in the storybook to Tc; Tc checks G5's writing
                against the storybook.))
17     Tc:     hao.
                Good.
```

This segment of interaction can be fruitfully analyzed in its four phases.

- Phase I, lines 1-5: Here Tc is being a teacher/expert by casting questions (line 1) and providing instructions (line 4), and G5 ratifies Tc's expert status by considering her question (line 3) and following her instruction (line 5).
- Phase II, lines 6-9: The expert-novice relation is neutralized if not reversed in this phase, as G5 introduces another expert-source, the storybook (line 6), and legitimizes it (the book is from the school reading room, line 9); Tc, on the other hand, is the less knowledgeable in terms of the background of the book (line 8).
- Phase III, lines 10-13: here upon hearing Tc's negative assessment of the script used by the storybook (and also by G5 who followed the book, line 10), G5 clearly challenges and rejects Tc's expert view by invoking Teacher Chen, the School Principal, who sometimes also substitute-teaches this class (line 11). Tc accepts the challenge and relinquishes her expert status (line 13).
- Phase IV, lines 15 to 17: Tc resumes her expert role by verifying G5's writing against the storybook (lines 15-16) and provides assess-

ment of G5's work (line 17). G5 corroborates Tc's resumed expert status by complying with her acts (line 16).

In terms of sequential organization, lines 1-6 constitute the first question-answer sequence, with a delay by the student (line 3) and an insertion by the teacher (line 4). Tc's question in line 1 was not responded to by G5 until line 6, when she gathered support for her writing. Lines 7-9 is the second question-answer sequence; this time there is no delay in G5's answer to Tc's information-orientated question. Lines 10-13 is an expanded assessment sequence, in which Tc presents the first assessment, G5 provides the second assessment (which does not align itself with the first assessment), and Tc follows up by aligning with G5. Lines 15-17 is a directive sequence, in which Tc issues a directive, G5 complies, and Tc follows up with an assessment.

By attending to interactional details moment by moment, we are able to see that, first, the teacher's expertness and authority is not presupposed to the same degree at all times and is not readily accepted by the student at all times. In other words, the teacher's expert and authority status is emergent as interaction unfolds. Interaction may maintain or alter the teacher's status. Second, a classroom discourse pattern that allows delayed responses and second assessments by the novice (the student) may change the expert's (teacher's) behaviors, perhaps more effectively than a discourse pattern that relies on the teacher's modeling and the students' imitation (cf. He, 1997). Finally, I suspect moments like (3) are not unique to the Chinese heritage language classes I observed; they permeate classroom interactions (whether or not language is the subject matter) everywhere. With a view that identity (expert, novice, teacher, student) is not a static entity, but something that takes the participants' efforts to accomplish jointly, we are then able to have a firm grasp of the creative and transformable nature of language use.

Teacher's Co-Construction of Learner's Language Proficiency

Intersubjectivity and emergence account for more than social identities and interpersonal relationships between the teacher and students in the classroom. These notions also shed new light on the construction of the learner's language competence. Predominantly, the community of language education has viewed second/foreign language competence as individual traits (Canale, 1983; Canale & Swain, 1980) that can be measured independently (Bachman, 1990; Bachman & Palmer, 1996; see He & Young 1998 for a critique). With an LS framework (although LS has not yet directly addressed issues having to do with language assessment) and an enhanced sensitivity toward the co-constructed nature of emergent communicative context, we may argue that language competence resides in the intersubjectivity co-constructed with target language users (Jacoby & McNamara, 1999; Lazaraton, 1994; He & Young, 1998). A brief example below shows how the teacher's language use at a given moment helps to shape the student's ability in reading *pinyin* (phonetic representation of Mandarin Chinese).

(4) [TWATL:934] san-pin-liang-du

1	Tw:	Yixiu ni lai duyidu.
		You come read
		Yixiu, you try.
2		((pointing to *pinyin* "bian" on the blackboard))
3	G4:	b-ian bian
4	Tw:	san-pin-liang-du a jizhu san pin
		PRT remember three sound-unit
		San-pin-liang-du ah, remember it's three phonemes.
5		((san-pin-liang-du is a pedagogical jargon indicating three
		consecutive phonemes strung together.))
6	G4:	b- b-
7		((G4 looks at Tw and then down))
8	Tw:	shi b-an ban haishi b-I-an bian na?
		COP or Q
		Is it b-an ban or b-I-an bian?
9	G4:	b-I-an bian.
10	Tw:	hen hao.
		Very good.
		Very good.

In (4), when called upon to read *bian*, G4 first gave a two-phoneme "b" and "ian" reading (line 3). At this point, Tw reminded G4 of a *pinyin* principle called *san-pin-liang-du* (the reading of three consecutive phonemes, which are rare in Mandarin compared to the common two-phoneme constructions), which, instead of helping G4, inhibited her from making another attempt to read the vowel components (line 6). Subsequently, Tw provided G4 with an either/or choice (line 8) and G4 was able to successfully choose and read aloud the correct form (lines 9-10). Hence G4's lack of ability (line 6) and reduced ability (line 6 as compared to line 3) to read *bian* was in part due to Tw's introduction of an abstract rule (line 4). Similarly, G4's success in finally being able to pronounce all the phonemes in *bian* (line 9) was interactively made possible by Tw's inclusion of the correct form in her previous speaking turn (line 8). To pass any judgment on G5's performance without considering the sequential contexts of her interaction with the teacher will be misleading.

Clearly, language assessment does not take place solely in the class-room. Analyses such as the preceding one can be extended to account for the perception of language proficiency of children, second/foreign language learners by members of the target culture in any socialization contexts and in any stage of language development (cf. He, 1998; Lazaraton, 1996).

In this section, I have considered how an enriched interactional, dialogical perspective on LS may provide new explanations of some classroom data, whether in the context of language teaching or language testing. On the one hand, insights from traditions such as CA that are parallel to LS have made it possible and compelling for us to have a more empirically sensitive and nuanced view on the interactional construction of emergent context. On the other hand, empirical concerns in language education provide us with a strong motivation to seriously and systematically take into account the impact of moment-to-moment interaction in language socialization activities.

CONCLUDING REMARKS

The discussion in this chapter has been driven by two main motivations. One is to focus on one linguistic anthropological model—LS—to examine its theory of indexicality, and to enrich it with an emphasis on the role of interactive language use in constructing emergent contexts. I have argued that when put in the actual context of data analysis, the LS theory of indexicality runs the risk of being circular. Further, while LS in theory promotes a dialectical, dialogical perspective on socialization, actual empirical LS studies have not yet systematically and methodically documented the co-constructed, interactive nature of socialization activities. To overcome the potential circularity in the LS model of indexicality and to operationalize the bi-directional, interactional perspective inherent in LS theory, I have suggested that the notions of intersubjectivity and emergence from parallel analytical traditions be incorporated in LS theory and practice.

The other motivation for this chapter is to make relevant to the field of language education the benefits of an interactionally enriched LS perspective. I have discussed how LS may illuminate some central concerns in language education such as the entailment of knowing a language, the relation between language learning and cultural development, and the evidence of language acquisition. I have also used Chinese heritage language classrooms as an example to show how ordinary day-to-day practices in language teaching and learning may reveal important information about the jointly constructed nature of expert-novice role relations and language proficiency assessments when examined from an interactionally enriched LS perspective. Although I have limited my discussion to the area of language education, LS is centrally concerned with education in its broadest sense: all forms and sites of human growth and development accomplished and mediated by language use. In this sense, LS epitomizes linguistic anthropology of education.

NOTE

Research reported in this chapter was made possible by a research grant from the Spencer Foundation ("Language socialization of Chinese American children," Principal Investigator Agnes Weiyun He) and by a National Academy of Education/Spencer Postdoctoral Fellowship, to both of which I am extremely grateful. The views expressed are exclusively my own. I am also thankful to the editors of this volume for their very helpful comments.

APPENDIX A: TRANSCRIPTION SYMBOLS

CAPS   emphasis, signaled by pitch or volume
.   falling intonation
,   falling-rising intonation
°   quiet speech
[ ]   overlapped talk
-         cut-off
=   latched talk
:   prolonged sound or syllable
(0.0)   silences roughly in seconds and tenths of seconds (measured more according to the relative speech rate of the interaction than to the actual clock time)
(.)   short, untimed pauses of one tenth of a second or less
( )   undecipherable or doubtful hearing
(( ))   additional observation
T: at the beginning of a stretch of talk, identifies the speaker; T is for teacher, G for girl, B for boy, Ss for whole class.
< >   slow speech
> <   fast speech

APPENDIX B: GRAMMATICAL GLOSS

COMP directional or resultative complement of verb

CONJ   conjunction

COP   copula

DUR   durative aspect marker

EMP   emphatic marker

LOC   locative marker

MSR   measure

NEG   negative marker

PERT   perfective aspect marker

POS   possesive

PRT   sentence, vocative or nominal subordinative particle

PTP   pre-transitive preposition

Q   question marker

REFERENCES

Atkinson, J. M., and Heritage, J. (Eds.). (1984). *Structures of Social Action: Studies in Conversation Analysis*. Cambridge: Cambridge University Press.
Bachman, L. F. (1990). *Fundamental Considerations in Language Testing*. Oxford: Oxford University Press.
Bachman, L. F., & Palmer, A. S. (1996). *Language Testing in Practice: Designing and Developing Useful Language Tests*. Oxford: Oxford University Press.
Bardovi-Harlig, K. (2000). *Tense and Aspect in Second Language Acquisition: Form, Meaning and Us*. Malden, MA: Blackwell.
Bayley, R. (1996). Competing constraints on variation in the speech of adult Chinese learners of English. In R. Bayley & D. R. Preston (Eds.), *Second Language Acquisition and Linguistic Variation* (pp. 97–120). Philadelphia: Benjamins.
Bayley, R., & Preston, D. R. (Eds). (1996). *Second Language Acquisition and Linguistic Variation*. Philadelphia: Benjamins.
Bourdieu, P. (1977). *Outline of a Theory of Practice*. R. Nice (Trans.). Cambridge: Cambridge University Press.
Bradunas, E., & Topping, B. (Eds.). (1988). *Ethnic Heritage and Language Schools in America*. Washington: Library of Congress.
Canale, M., & Swain, M. (1980). Theoretical basis of communicative approaches to second language teaching and testing. *Applied Linguistics, 1*, 1–47.
Chaiklin, S., & Lave, J. (Eds.). (1993). *Understanding Practice*. Cambridge: Cambridge University Press.
Cummins, J. (1992). Heritage language teaching in Canadian schools. *Journal of Curriculum Studies, 24*, 281–286.
Day, R. R. (Ed.). (1986). *Talking to Learn: Conversation in Second Language Acquisition*. Rowley, MA: Newbury House.
Dittmar, N., & Reich, A. (Eds.). (1993). *Modality in Language Acquisition*. Berlin: de Gruyter.
Drew, P., & Heritage, J. (Eds.). (1992). *Talk at Work*. New York: Cambridge University Press.

Duff, P. (2000, October). Language socialization in high school social studies: The construction of knowledge in multicultural discourse communities. Paper presented at the Annual Meeting of the National Academy of Education, New York City.

Duranti, A., & Goodwin, C. (1992). *Rethinking Context.* Cambridge: Cambridge University Press.

Erickson, F., & Shultz, J. (1982). *The Counselor as Gatekeeper: Social Interaction in Interviews.* New York: Academic Press.

Fishman, J. A. (1966). *Language Loyalty in the United States: The Maintenance and Perpetuation of Non-English Mother Tongues by American Ethnic and Religious Groups.* The Hague: Mouton.

Garfinkel, H. (1967). *Studies in Ethnomethodology.* Englewood Cliffs, NJ: Prentice-Hall.

Goodwin, C., & Heritage, J. (1990). Conversation analysis. *Annual Review of Anthropology, 19,* 283–307.

Goodwin, M. H. (1990). *He-Said-She-Said.* Bloomington: Indiana University Press.

Hatch, E. (1978). Discourse analysis and second language acquisition. In E. Hatch (Ed.), *Second Language Acquisition: A Book of Readings* (pp. 402–435). Rowley, MA: Newbury House.

He, A. W. (1995). Co-constructing institutional identities: The case of student counselees. *Research on Language and Social Interaction, 28*(3), 213–231.

He, A. W. (1997). Learning and being: Identity construction in the classroom. *Pragmatics and Language Learning, 8,* 201–222.

He, A. W. (1998). Answering questions in LPIs: A case study. In R. Young & A.W. He (Eds.), *Talking and Testing: Discourse Approaches to the Assessment of Oral Proficiency* (pp. 101–116). Philadelphia: Benjamins

He, A. W. (2000). Sequential and grammatical organization of teacher's directives. *Linguistics and Education, 11*(2), 119–140.

He, A. W. (2001). The language of ambiguity: practices in Chinese heritage language classes. *Discourse Studies, 3*(1), 75–96.

He, A. W. (in press). Novices and their voices in Chinese heritage language classes. In R. Bayley & S. Schecter (Eds.), *Language Socialization and Bilingualism.* Clevedon, U.K.: Multilingual Matters.

He, A. W., & Keating, E. (1991). Counselor and student at talk: A case study. *Issues in Applied Linguistics, 2*(2), 183–210.

He, A. W., & Young, R. (1998). Language proficiency interviews: a discourse approach. In R. Young & A. W. He (Eds.), *Talking and Testing: Discourse Approaches to the Assessment of Oral Proficiency* (pp. 1–24). Philadelphia: Benjamins.

Heath, S. B. (1983). *Ways with Words.* New York: Cambridge University Press.

Jacoby, S., & Gonzales, P. (1991). The constitution of expert-novice in scientific discourse. *Issues in Applied Linguistics, 2*(2), 149–182.

Jacoby, S., & McNamara, T. (1999). Locating competence. *English for Specific Purposes, 18,* 213–241.

Jacoby, S., & Ochs, E. (1995). Co-construction: An introduction. *Research on Language and Social Interaction, 28,* 171–183.

Kanagy, R. (1999). Interactional routines as a mechanism for L2 acquisition and socialization in an immersion context. *Journal of Pragmatics, 31,* 1467–1492.

Kasper, G. (2000). Four perspectives on L2 pragmatic development. Plenary address presented at AAAL, March, Vancouver, Canada.

Kramsch, C. (1986). From language proficiency to interactional competence. *Modern Language Journal, 70,* 366–372.

Krashen, S. D. (1980). The input hypothesis. In J. E. Alatis (Ed.), *Current Issues in Bilingual Education* (pp. 168–80). Washington: Georgetown University Press.

Latour, B. (1987). *Science in Action*. Cambridge, MA: Harvard University Press.

Lazaraton, A. (1994, March). Question turn modification in language proficiency interviews. Paper presented at AAAL, Baltimore.

Lazaraton, A. (1996). Interlocutor support in oral proficiency interviews: The case of CASE. *Language Testing, 13*, 151–172.

Long, M. (1981). Input, interaction and second language acquisition. In H. Winitz (Ed.), Native language and foreign language acquisition: *Annals of the New York Academy of Sciences, 379*, 259–278.

Markee, N. (2000). *Conversation Analysis*. Mahwah, NJ: LEA.

Ochs, E. (1988). *Culture and Language Development*. Cambridge: Cambridge University Press.

Ochs, E. (1990). Indexicality and socialization. In J. W. Stigler, R. Shweder, & G. Herdt (Eds.), *Cultural Psychology: Essays on Comparative Human Development* (pp. 287–308). Cambridge: Cambridge University Press.

Ochs, E. (1992). Indexing gender. In A. Duranti & C. Goodwin (Eds.), *Rethinking Context* (pp. 335–358). New York: Cambridge University Press.

Ochs, E. (1993). Constructing social identity. *Research on Language and Social Interaction, 26*, 287–306.

Ochs, E. (1996). Linguistic resources for socializing humanity. In J. J. Gumperz, & S.L. Levinson (Eds.), *Rethinking Linguistic Relativity* (pp. 407–437). Cambridge: Cambridge University Press.

Ochs, E., Jacoby, S., & Gonzalez, P. (1996). "When I come down I'm in the domain state": Grammar and graphic representation in the interpretive activity of physicists. In E. Ochs, E. A. Schegloff, & S. Thompson (Eds.), *Grammar and Interaction*. Cambridge: Cambridge University Press.

Ochs, E., & Schieffelin, B. B. (1984). Language acquisition and socialization: Three developmental stories. In R. Schweder & R. LeVine (Eds.), *Culture Theory: Essays on Mind, Self and Emotion* (pp. 276–320). Cambridge: Cambridge University Press.

Ochs, E., & Schieffelin, B. (1995). The impact of language socialization on grammatical development. In P. Fletcher & B. MacWhinney (Eds.), *The Handbook of Child Language* (pp. 73–94). Cambridge, MA: Blackwell.

Ochs, E., & Taylor, C. (1992). Science at dinner. In C. Kramsch & S. McConnell-Ginet (Eds.), *Text and Context: Cross-disciplinary Perspectives on Language Study* (pp. 29–45). Lexington, MA: D.C. Heath.

Ohta, A. S. (1999). Interactional routines and the socialization of interactional style in adult learners of Japanese. *Journal of Pragmatics, 31*, 1493–1512.

Pica, T. (1994). Research on negotiation: What does it reveal about second-language learning conditions, processes, and outcomes? *Language Learning, 44*, 493–527.

Pica, T., Doughty, C., & Young, R. (1986). Making input comprehensible: Do interactional modifications help? *International Review of Applied Linguistics, 72*, 1–25.

Pica, T., Young, R., & Doughty, C. (1987). The impact of interaction on comprehension. *TESOL Quarterly, 21*, 737–758.

Poole, D. (1992). Language socialization in the second language classroom. *Language Learning, 42*, 593–616.

Rampton, B. (1997). A sociolinguistic perspective on L2 communicative strategies. In G. Kasper & E. Kellerman (Eds.), *Communication Strategies: Psycholinguistic and Sociolinguistic Perspectives* (pp. 279–303). London: Longman.

Rampton, B. (1999). Dichotomies, differences and ritual in second language learning and teaching. *Applied Linguistics, 20*(3), 316–340.

Rampton, B. (2000). Instructed foreign language rituals in and out of class. Plenary address presented at AAAL, Vancouver, Canada.

Sacks, H. (1992). *Lectures on Conversation*. (Vols. 1 and 2). Cambridge: MA: Blackwell.

Sacks, H., Schegloff, E. A., & Jefferson, G. (1974). A simplest systematics for the organization of turn-taking for conversation. *Language, 50*, 696–735.

Schieffelin, B. (1990). *The Give and Take of Everyday Life*. New York: Cambridge University Press.

Schieffelin, B., & Ochs, E. (Eds.). (1986a). *Language Socialization Across Cultures*. New York: Cambridge University Press.

Schieffelin, B., & Ochs, E. (1986b). Language socialization. *Annual Review of Anthropology, 15*, 163–191.

Schieffelin, B., & Ochs, E. (1996). The microgenesis of competence. In D. Slobin, J. Gerhardt, A. Kyratzis, & J. Guo (Eds.), *Social Interaction, Social Context, and Language* (pp. 251–264). Mahwah, NJ: Lawrence Erlbaum.

Schumann, J. H. (1978). The acculturation model for second language acquisition. In R. Gingras (Ed.), *Second Language Acquisition and Foreign Language Teaching*. Arlington, VA: Center for Applied Linguistics.

Varonis, E. M., & Gass, S. M. (1985). Non-native/non-native conversation: A model for negotiation of meaning. *Applied Linguistics, 6*, 71–90.

Vygotsky, L. (1986). *Thought and Language*. Cambridge, MA: MIT Press.

Wang, X. (Ed.). (1996). *A View from Within: A Case Study of Chinese Heritage Community Language Schools in the U.S.* Washington: National Foreign Language Center.

Young, R. (1999). Sociolinguistic approaches to SLA. *Annual Review of Applied Linguistics 19*, 105–132.

Young, R. (2000). Interactional competence: Challenges for validity. Paper presented at a joint symposium on "interdisciplinary interfaces with language testing," AAAL and LTRC, March 2000, Vancouver, Canada.

5

Relating Word to World

Indexicality During Literacy Events

Betsy Rymes

> Can learning take place if in fact it silences the voices of the people it is supposed to teach? . . . The answer is: Yes. People learn that they don't count.
>
> Henry Giroux, 1992, p. 15

As methodological pendulums swing wildly and politicized education reform climates grow hot then cold, as teachers change their books and their seating arrangements, as laptops are issued, as blackboards change to whiteboards, and even as the complexion and language backgrounds of students change dramatically, a certain feature of classrooms may change very little. It is likely that certain students, those who have always struggled through school, will continue to do so. From one perspective, this persistent inequity in the classroom is rarely affected by policy changes because inequity is handed down from societal injustice at large. While certain critical theoretical perspectives on education (e.g., Freire, 1970; Giroux, 1992; Hooks, 1994) investigate, theorize, and practice education by first analyzing injustices outside the classroom, a linguistic anthropological perspective combines this awareness of larger societal patterns with a close look at how the particularities of interactions shape who gets to learn inside a class-room. Linguistic anthropology provides analytic tools to investigate and critique interactions inside, around, and relevant to these class-rooms. The promise linguistic anthropology holds for education, then, is in the analytical insights it provides into the relationship between larger sociocultural patterns and the (re)production of inequity, on the level of person-to-person interaction, inside the classroom (Philips, 1993).

This link between macro-level power inequities and micro-level interactional positioning is not new (cf., Duranti & Ochs, 1988; Foster, 1995; Heath, 1983; Philips, 1993), and lately it has taken the form of work on the social construction of identity through classroom dis-course and narrative (Gee, 2001; Rymes & Pash, 2001; Wortham, 2001). Despite this growing body of work, however, there is some resistance to micro-level analysis of discourse. One reason for this may be that taking the words of one teacher and a few students and putting them under the analytical microscope could be construed as "epistemic violence" (Bransen & Miller, 2000; Spivak, 1993) or ethically dubious (DeStigter, 2001). Close analysis of a transcript can be viewed as reading *into* what people are saying, appropriating their words for our own agendas. We don't want to ascribe a certain identity to a person, or suppose they have certain goals or intentions based only on their words. But this is what people (including teachers and students) do every day in interaction. Every day, in school, teachers and students interpret each other's words, read into them, and act according to their own presuppositions and expectations. The every-dayness of this activity is why it is so powerful, and why close micro-analysis is so important—not to reproduce the assumptions and the "reading into" that goes on everyday, but to uncover this process and explore how this "reading into" reproduces unequal power relations that exist in society more generally.

This chapter focuses on this process. Unlike earlier work on commu-nicative competence and its relevance to classroom discourse, this chapter does not describe an ethnography of "ways of speaking" (Hymes, 1972) that could be generalized to all the children in this reading group, or to a certain socioeconomic, linguistic, or ethnic de-mographic. It describes the particularities of a few interactions, and the implications of those processes for learning. For example, choosing between the words "happy" and "gay," or deciding to use the word "dude" in a certain way, might make or break someone's apparent competence during a classroom interaction. And, by incorporating students' use of those words into a reading lesson, a teacher constructs a particular stance toward learning and social issues. These are inciden-tal, interactionally contingent micro cues. But one reason we—and in this *we* I include myself as a researcher as well as the teacher and students participating in the interaction—care about and attend to these cues is that they are linked to educational outcomes and, in turn, to power relations in society at large.

More specifically, by examining literacy events in two very different classroom settings, I argue that certain micro interactional phenomena construct a limiting portrait of what literacy can or should be. In one of these literacy contexts, the teacher follows a carefully scripted phonics program, and in the other the teacher freely selects children's literature trade books as well as themes and activities to accompany these books. Both of these teachers were seeking the best practices to help struggling readers—those who were already falling far behind their peers. Of course, neither of these teachers intended to reproduce the failure of linguistic and ethnic minorities, and they drew on varied methodologies to avoid doing so. However, students' experience of the reading process is not necessarily related to the methodology teachers intend to follow. Nor are children's experiences with reading success or failure necessarily related to teachers' overarching goal to provide equal educational access to language minority students. Instead, it may be that children's success as readers is crucially affected by the stance these teachers take in interactions as students use words of a text (like "gay" or "dude") to index worlds outside that text. The analyses that follow show this process in action, describing how micro-level linguistic practice structures these students' experiences of reading. As the chapter shows, linguistic anthropology can provide the first step to reforming the kinds of interactions that go on in classrooms and the way literacy is constructed through those interactions.

BACKGROUND: SETTING AND PARTICIPANTS

I examine these issues through classroom interactions that involve Rene (all names here are pseudonyms), a second language learner and native of Costa Rica, and his changing classroom peers. For two years, I made weekly trips to Rene's elementary school in Northeast Georgia to observe, tutor, videotape, and, in the process, try to understand Rene's struggle through classroom practices designed to facilitate his progress as a reader.

When the study began, in 1998, Rene was repeating second grade because of reading difficulties. During this year his teacher, on her own initiative, decided to try a literature-based reading approach with Rene and several other struggling readers in the classroom. (All of the other struggling readers were native English speakers.) During these reading sessions, Rene's teacher read books aloud to children and encouraged them to enter into the story by describing pictures, talking about their own experiences, and drawing and writing stories related to the topics in that week's book. During the second year of the study (1999-2000), Rene, despite limited progress in his reading, was promoted to third grade, and the school created an English for Speakers of Other Languages (ESOL) pullout program for the increasing numbers of second language learners. During the second year, in the ESOL pullout group, reading lessons consisted primarily of phonics instruction. This was accomplished by playing a carefully sequenced series of card games.

On the surface, there appears to have been a drastic change in curriculum between the first and second year of my study. The school developed an ESOL program (as mandated by the state and federal government); reading instruction switched from literature-based whole-language activities to phonics card games and rule recitation. Rene's reading group transformed from a single-grade group of native English speakers to a multi-grade group of second language learning peers. However, despite the contrast in methodological approaches practiced by these reading teachers, my research suggests that there were some profound similarities in how reading interactions were accomplished during these two years. These similarities become clear on a closer look at how the world outside the text and the practice of reading itself are indexed in these reading groups.

The analysis that follows analyzes the similarities between the two classrooms and the discursive mechanisms that facilitate these similiarities. First, I outline the linguistic anthropological concept of indexicality and its relationship to literacy events.

THEORETICAL BACKGROUND: INDEXICALITY AND LITERACY

What is the role of indexicality in literacy? I argue that literacy events are constructed, in part, through patterns of indexical practice. Cues within interaction suggest both how a text is to be understood and how, in general, the practice of reading is legitimately accomplished. To build this argument I briefly outline the role of indexicality in literacy.

Indexicality

Generally speaking, to say that utterances are indexical is to say that their meaning, rather than being arbitrary or purely symbolic, is tied to context. In some cases, the context-bound nature of reference is obvious. For example, certain words (like the pronouns *you* and *me*, or the demonstratives *this* and *that*) are obviously indexical because the referential meaning of *you* and *me*, or *this* and *that* depends primarily on the situation in which I use such words. While pronouns like *you* and demonstratives like *that* are most clearly indexical as individual words, all language is indexical to a degree. Linguistic forms do carry some decontextualizable symbolic content, but there is also an element of word-meaning that is construed through context. Gee (1999) gives the example of *coffee*. At first glance, this word seems very different from a word like *you* or *this*. Its meaning doesn't seem to depend on the context of utterance—that is, its meaning appears to be more symbolic. But Gee uses the two utterances, "The coffee spilled, get a broom" and "the coffee spilled, get a mop," to illustrate how the meaning of the word *coffee* changes according to the words that surround it. This is because the words around the word *coffee* (like *broom* or *mop*) act as indexical cues that tell us what aspects of context are relevant to our understanding of that word—the words *broom* and *mop* presuppose different kinds of coffee spills.

Indexical cues can also create new contexts. For example, imagine that someone sees the coffee spill and, instead of demanding a mop or a broom, says, in a joking voice, "The coffee spilled, *Mrs. Olson!*" For those familiar with old Folger's coffee commercials, *Mrs. Olson* cues a new context for coffee—the homey kitchen in which she serves up a rich, mountain-grown brew. In this utterance, *Mrs. Olson* functions as an entailing (or "creative") indexical (Silverstein, 1976), creating a new relevant context for interpreting the word coffee. In addition, the use of Mrs. Olson as a term of address entails or creates a new addressee identity. Suddenly, the person who spilled the coffee is constructed as a matronly Swedish homemaker. The use of *Mrs. Olson* might also simultaneously create an identity for the speaker as someone old enough to have been around for those Mrs. Olson commercials, someone who watched enough TV to have some lasting familiarity with her, and someone who bothers remembering such characters. The use of *Mrs. Olson* and its co-occurrence with a light-hearted tone of voice might also transform the speech situation from one that foregrounds the annoyance of spilled coffee to one that foregrounds a casual joking relationship. All these possibilities arise from the potentialities of creative indexing.

Of course, how the people in the interaction understand this utterance will also depend on a common (presupposed) social history that includes an awareness of Mrs. Olson, what sort of coffee she drinks, what kind of kitchen she runs, and whether she seems funny. So, which particular meaning an utterance like "The coffee spilled, Mrs. Olson!" entails and what identities it constructs for the participants will also be partially determined through the talk that follows that utterance and how meanings are taken up in interaction. In this way, indexical meaning, in addition to having presupposing and entailing elements, is also emergent in interaction. That is, how indexes function, in particular events, is determined over the course of an interaction.

Indexes not only provide cues to referential meaning and participant identities in the speech situation (as discussed previously), but they also provide cues about how language should be attended to in any given interaction. The surrounding context of the utterance "the coffee spilled" helps people in conversation to understand more precisely what the word *coffee* refers to, but also, more fundamentally, whether the word coffee is treated as meaningful at all. If, in response to "The coffee spilled . . ." I said, "Shh!," I would be constructing the utterance not as meaningful commentary, but as an intrusion. The meaning of the word *coffee* in this last imaginary interaction, then, is constructed as unimportant. It doesn't matter if the person is referring to coffee beans or a double-tall latte. Their utterance is simply something outside the realm of current concern. In this case, "Shhh" is a (not so subtle) indexical cue to participants that the referent of *coffee* is irrelevant.

To say that language is indexical, then, is to say that what a word means is context-dependent, how words are used can create new relevant contexts, and whether any of this meaning-making potential is realized at all, is dependent on the kinds of interactions people have around those words. Furthermore, as He (this volume) has argued, indexical meaning accrues through multiple interactions (Ochs & Schieffelin, 1984). The way meanings are indexed over the course of a single interaction and in repeated, patterned interactions influences how people understand (and create new understandings for) both words and events.

Indexicality and Literacy

The practice of indexical meaning making in interaction is critical for understanding literacy events. An analysis of indexicality illuminates the processes that construct reading *not* as a neutral practice, but as a practice that builds on the (presupposed) background assumptions and practices—both oral and written—that surround it. This understanding of literacy has been explored in the theoretical deconstruction of the orality/literacy dichotomy, as well as in empirical investigations of multiple literacies.

In 1973, Hymes made the important claim that literacy, like speaking, is not a skill that can be isolated from the speech community within which it occurs, or from the kinds of interactions that surround it. This theoretical claim called for empirical work, not only ethnographies of diverse ways of speaking, but also ethnographies of diverse ways of writing and reading and the speech communities within which these activities take place. In this way, Hymes encouraged researchers to begin to explore the accumulated habits and assumptions surrounding reading and writing.

Hymes' recognition of literacy as a cultural practice, linked to oral activity, also opened up a discussion and investigation of multiple literacies. Nearly twenty years ago, Heath's *Ways with Words* firmly established that "mainstream ways" of both reading and talking about print, while often privileged in classrooms, are just one of many sorts of literacy event. Since then, there has been a growing theoretical understanding of culturally variable forms of literacy (e.g., Delpit, 1995; Ochs, 1988; Pérez & McCarty, 1998; Street, 1993). Studies of cross-cultural literacies have illustrated clearly that "pedagogised literacy" (Street, 1993) is just one form of literacy, one that builds on a certain set of assumptions about what sorts of meanings are to be taken from texts, as well as how texts are to be talked about.

However, and this is one way in which the linguistic anthropology of education can contribute to the study of literacies, literacy events not only build on sets of assumptions and previous practices, but they also have the possibility of making new, "creative" meanings. While a classroom literacy event may indexically presuppose certain mainstream habits, indexicality can also be entailing. What a literacy event comes to be will develop in unique and situationally contingent ways through classroom interaction. There may be some regularities to what classroom literacy events look like, and these regularities make it possible to characterize something like "pedagogized" or "mainstream" literacy events. Likewise there may be some regularities in "home"-based literacy events, including those that diverge from typical school events. But there is also contingency and particularity in each school literacy event, and certainly in the kinds of literacy events that children engage in outside of school (Dyson, 1997; Hicks, 2001; Hull & Schultz, 2002; Street, 1995).

How literacy events come to be organized can be traced, in the emergent particular, by analyzing how meaning is construed indexically. So, just as Hymes' original concept of a community-specific, normative "communicative competence" (Hymes, 1972) benefits these days from a more situationally contingent understanding (Wortham, this volume), our understanding of "pedagogized" or "mainstream" literacy events also benefits from an understanding of the situational contingency of these events. Pedagogized literacy events may vary each time they occur, and understanding the particularity of each such occasion might lead to an understanding of how interaction during literacy events shapes children's futures as readers.

In this chapter, to understand how participants in classroom reading events construct literacy to be a certain kind of activity, I examine how the meaning of reading texts is indexically cued in interaction. I look at two different sorts of classroom contexts to see how indexical meanings and understandings about what is appropriate for a literacy event emerge. Although each context yields literacy events that are constructed through different indexical patterns, both communicate a similar message about reading and what it is for: it is unrelated to students' experiences outside of the literacy event.

RELATING A TEXT TO A WORLD DURING THE PHONICS LESSON

Ironically, the clearest case of the context-dependent nature of word meaning can be found in the phonics lessons that Rene, during the second year of the study, attended daily. I say "ironically" because the teacher's intention during the phonics lessons was expressly to limit the context that students would draw on, teaching students to focus exclusively on the phonological context and the rules of word "decoding." These phonics lessons were the meat of the ESOL pullout program Rene went to for about fifty minutes each day. The purpose of these sessions was to provide special reading instruction suited to Rene's language learning needs and those of the several other second language learners at the school. The teacher approached this goal by using a phonics card game. To play the game, each student would take a turn picking a card from a deck in the center of the table. Each card had a word printed on it, and each deck of cards was carefully organized to contain only words that exemplified the phonological rules under study, in addition to those already mastered.

The sterile classroom environment (a small, unadorned meeting room within the school library) also pushed the students to use only phonological context to understand the meaning of these words. Each word was read off the card. There were no pictures on the cards or around the room that might provide extra-textual clues. The students didn't read the words in sentences, but saw them in isolation. Students were to read the words in the absence of cues to non-phonological contexts for understanding them. However, as might be expected, this didn't prevent the students from drawing on contexts even more distant from the literacy event. New contexts for words like *dude* and *witch* were brought into the classroom as students incorporated the phonics words into their interactions. Though the teacher attempted to limit available context, students themselves provided indexical cues that potentially created new contexts for understanding the limited text available around the phonics game-playing table. When this happened, the literacy event changed drastically.

For example, in the following interaction, during the first weeks of phonics game play, Oswaldo picks a card with the word "Dude" written on it. For the teacher's purposes, this word is relevant only as an instantiation of the "magic e" rule being studied. According to this rule, "magic e" changes vowel sounds from short to long, so students were instructed to first cover the "e" and pronounce the short voweled word, (*dud* in this case) and then reveal the e and pronounce the long-voweled word (*dude*):

Dude

Teacher: Did you sound it out? Are you stu:ck?
            [Okay.
Rene: [Where? Hh.
Teacher: ((*covering up the –e- spelling the word first*)) -d- -u- -d-. [du:h -
            u:hd
Oswaldo: [du:hd
Teacher: Yes, du:hd. ((*uncovering the –e-*)) If you add the -e-, the- the -
            u- is gonna go oo:. Du:h oo:d.
Oswaldo: dude.
Teacher: dude.

Here the teacher has supplied the rule and Oswaldo successfully utters the letters *d* , *u*, and *d,* as they are affected by the context of magic *e*: "*Dude.*" Despite the efforts of the teacher to keep the children focused exclusively on phonological context, however, students bring their own associations to bear on the texts (the word cards) in the phonics lesson. As students draw cards from the stack, as they pronounce them carefully, and as they articulate the phonological rules guiding their pronunciation, they also find ways to link those words to contexts broader than the phonological. For example, just after successfully pronouncing "dude" in the interaction, Rene chimes in with his own, more broadly contextualized version of the word:

Dude (continued)

Oswaldo: dude.
Teacher: dude.
Rene: ((laughs)) Hey du:de! ((laughs))
Teacher: ((laughs))

By adding just *hey* to the word *dude* and lengthening the long *u* even more, Rene supplies indexical cues that presuppose a particular understanding of the word *dude*. As in Gee's (1999) imaginary case of *coffee*, which takes on different meanings when followed by *broom* or *mop*, the word *dude* takes on new meaning when it is preceded by the word *hey*. The word *hey* acts as a cue to which kind of context is relevant to understanding *dude*. By using the word *dude* to call out to a hip and funny guy, the imaginary recipient of the greeting, "Hey du:de!," Rene also creates a new sort of addressee, just as *Mrs. Olson* entailed a funny kind of addressee in the coffee example. In this particular classroom interaction, even though Rene has strayed from the exclusively phonological context the teacher would like students to be using, she picks up on the humor in Rene's use of *dude* and she laughs along.

A month later, this word came up on a card again, and another student supplied "hey" and "How you doin'" as indexical cues for the possible meanings for dude. This time, however, the teacher didn't laugh:

Dude 2
Oswaldo: ((picks a card and reads it)) Dude.
Teacher: Ye:s.
Jose: Hey du:de. (.) How you doin'?
Teacher: Remembe:r (.) don't talk at the same time.

This second interaction surrounding the word *dude* as it came up during the phonics game is more representative of the teacher's response to these playful student attempts to provide context outside the phonological rules. Indeed, in every other recorded example of student-generated external meaning, the teacher responded either by silencing them directly or by ignoring their comments.

In the example below, the word *chancy* came up from the stack, to illustrate both the *–c- -h-* cluster and a short single vowel sound followed by consonants. Rene, once again, cues another context:

Chancy
Teacher: -c- -h[- says. (.) (Shh) ((teacher is hushing other students))
Student: [(ca:n)
Rene: a:n (.) (cha:n)
Teacher: Cha:n (.) –c- -y-.
          (2.0)
Rene: Chances.
Teacher: Cha:n::c:y.
Rene: Chancy.
Rene: Ohp! ((looking at David and smiling)) [Pokémon.
David: [It's a Pokémon.

As this interaction illustrates, Chancy is a troublesome word when phonological cues alone supply the context for its reading. Rene bumbles his first attempt ("chances"), before the teacher supplies the correct articulation. But as in the *dude* example, once the word *Chancy* is fully articulated, it prompts Rene to add to it, and to provide indexical cues that entail another relevant context. *Chancy* sounds like the name of a Pokémon character that the other students recognize. David chimes in, verbalizing his recognition of the Pokémon character. (Ironically, Chancy the Pokémon is actually spelled *Chansey*, which contradicts the phonics rules under consideration.) Rene's reference to Chansey the Pokémon has entailed another context—the context of kids' interest in Japanese animation. Just as *Mrs. Olson* entails a realm of hominess, "the richest kind" of coffee, and addressees who recognize this allusion, *Chansey* potentially entails a *children's* realm of fanciful pocket monsters, each with distinct personality traits, powers, and needs (Figure 5-1).

Figure 5-1. "Chansey! It's a Pokémon!"

But, as the interaction continues, it becomes clear that this is a context that the teacher would prefer not to discuss explicitly. Instead, she proceeds with elicitation of the phonological rules guiding the word's pronunciation.

Chancy (continued)

Rene:	Chancy.
Rene:	Ohp! ((looking at David and smiling)) [Pokemon.
David:	[It's a Pokemon.
Teacher:	And you have to tell me [why the -a- is sho:rt.
David:	[Chancy. (.) I got it.
Teacher:	You need to li:sten. ((looking at David))
Rene:	Cause the -c:- (1.0) The -y-.

As Rene and David both recognize the word and its meaning through reference to the world of Pokémon, the teacher insists that they make meaning of this word through phonological context alone, and the interaction transforms into a duel over which forms of context should be used to decipher meaning. This exchange illustrates the multiplicity of oralities and literacies that are potential in any reading event. It also shows the distinction between mainstream and non-mainstream, schooled and non-schooled, forms of literacy events breaking down. A *Pokémon* is a quintessentially mainstream figure. It even seems to be the sort of icon that Heath uses in her landmark article to characterize the mainstream literate environment, filled with "animals that represent characters found in books. Even when these characters have their origin in television programs, adults also provide books that either repeat or extend the characters' activities on television" (Heath, 1982, p. 49). In the interaction described previously, however, the potential for *Chansey* to become integrated into a literacy event is cut short. The context of diverse and beloved pocket monsters and the literacies that surround them is not relevant to this literacy event. Instead, this context comes to be treated (by students and teacher alike) as a disruption in the lesson.

In another duel over relevant context, the students use the word *witch* to index the even more mainstream and traditional world of children's fairy tales. Again, the teacher insists that the word *witch* be deciphered by reference to phonological context alone, while students insist on realizing its broader indexical potential:

Witch

Teacher:	((taking her turn and reading the card)) (.) **wuh-itch. Wi:tch.**
Jose:	You're a **witch**. ((in a high squeaky witch-like voice))
Rene:	You're the **whi:ch (which?)**?
Jose:	Hee-hee-hee-hee-hee
Teacher:	((moving to next word)) Qua-[it (.) Quit.

Although the teacher performs a reading of this word that draws on phonological decoding alone ("wuh-itch. Wi:tch"), Jose immediately contextualizes the word in a sentence, and with his high-pitched imaginary witch voice ("You're a witch"). By bringing the index *you* into the conversation and directing his utterance to the teacher, Jose indexically creates an addressee for his comment and turns his addressee into a witch! But, by pitching his voice high, he gives implicit directions for how to take his comment: it is a funny joke, not a cruel or disrespectful insult. This light-hearted context is further solidified as Rene picks up on the non-serious tone and indexes yet another meaning of this word, creating a "who's on first" type of punning confusion by calling out, ambiguously, "you're the *which*? (witch?)" The teacher, however, as in the previous two examples, ignores the joke, and any indexed meanings that could move reading outside of the merely phonological context. Coincidentally, the next word card she picks and sounds out, *quit*, might also be read as a directive to the joking students, but only if its creative indexicality and the addressees that it potentially entails were considered relevant to this interaction.

As illustrated in the preceding examples, these second language learners have a control of the English language (as well as appropriate use in varied social contexts) far beyond the words on these phonics cards. Furthermore, in these last two examples, the students are (whether intentionally or not) playing with the homonymic character of these words: *Chansey/chancy, witch/which*. But homonyms are words that phonics rules alone cannot accommodate. Further context must be invoked to understand which word is appropriate. Students' references to the multiplicity of meanings and their recognition of sound similarities across different homonyms are evidence of their own facility with the affordances of words (Gibson, 1979). Despite the evidence of their clear desire to link written words to worlds outside the text, however, these students' indexical cues are always relegated to the margins of the game.

This pattern could be represented generally as follows:

1) Teacher and/or student sound out a word (e.g., "Dude")→
2) Student supplies indexical cues to point to extra-textual context (e.g., "hey du:de!")→
3) Teacher treats these cues as irrelevant by ignoring them or explicitly silencing them (e.g., "don't talk at the same time")

This pattern of indexical cueing occurred roughly once or twice during each lesson I recorded. More significantly, with only one exception, it occurred *every* time a student cued extratextual context. In other words, with the exception of the first excerpt in this chapter, the teacher *never* treated extratextual indexing initiated by the students as relevant to the literacy event underway.

This pattern indicates not only how student contributions are systematically silenced, but also how *reading* is constructed in this group. By repeatedly silencing students' links to broader context, this teacher constitutes the reading process itself as unrelated to externally indexed meaning. Just as the meaning of "the coffee spilled" becomes a moot point if I simply say "SHHH!," the students' contextualizations of words in the phonics game are rendered meaningless through repeated interactions in which the teacher silences or ignores these additions. While one of the teacher's goals is to teach children to read by teaching them the phonological rules used to decode words, she simultaneously banishes any other forms of meaning-making from the reading process. Furthermore, by silencing these alternative indexical processes, she constructs these interactions as disruptions to the legitimate reading lesson. In this literacy event, *dude* or *witch* or *chancy* are decodable fragments. Their status as indexes to the students' worlds of experience is not relevant in this context. Thus, reading itself is constructed as unrelated to the socially meaningful worlds and experiences of these learners.

RELATING A TEXT TO THE WORLD DURING LITERATURE READING

It may seem obvious that the interaction surrounding text in a phonics lesson would discourage making associations with meaning outside the text. What may be surprising, however, is that similar indexical patterns occurred in the literature-based reading group and led to the same indexical constitution of the reading process as irrelevant to students' own experiences of the text and the world.

During the first year of this study, 1998-99, Rene's school did not have special services for their ESOL students. Nevertheless, his teacher wanted to do something different for Rene, who, repeating second grade, still was not reading in English (or Spanish) at a first-grade level. Therefore, she took a courageous step. She jettisoned the school-sanctioned phonics program and, based on her own knowledge of children's literature and reading pedagogy, created a special group for him and the other struggling readers in her class. She intended to use children's trade books (rather than the regimented basal readers and phonics exercises prescribed by the school) to instill in Rene and his peers a love of reading and an appreciation for children's literature. One of her key strategies for drawing the children into these books was to elicit their own experiences related to themes brought up in the books. She usually would scaffold this process by modeling how she relates the books under consideration to her own life.

As I watched her reading sessions unfold throughout the year, however, I found that, even as students were coaxed to share their own experiences, students' experiences were co-constructed as irrelevant. I say "co-constructed" because, as will become clear in the examples, both teacher and students played a role in achieving this outcome. The co-constructed irrelevance of the particulars of student experience occurred in two general interaction types, described in detail in the next two sections. In both of these types of interaction, students' description of their own experiences is effaced *despite* the teachers' intentions, which she described to me during many of our weekly conversations, to incorporate students' experiences into reading lessons whenever possible.

Teacher Relates the Text to Her World

In one type of interaction during the literature-based reading lessons, despite the teacher's intent to draw on students' experiences related to the text, the teacher's *own* experiences are the only ones legitimized. On such occasions, this legitimizing of the teacher's experiences was a joint accomplishment of the students and teacher in interaction. As the teacher struggled to draw on students' experiences related to a particular theme, students would resist, supplying one-word answers at best, prompting the teacher to provide her own examples. So, as this teacher modeled her own entry into the textual world, the students, instead of following this as a model to use to draw on their experiences, would often fall back on teacher-elaborated meanings and use them as their own. This process resulted in the implicit message that there were particular sorts of experiences students *should* be bringing to reading—those of the teacher. The following examples discussed illustrate this process. (For a fuller and more ethnographic account, see Rymes & Pash, 2001.)

In all the literature-reading lessons, the teacher asks children, in one way or another, to relate the text to their own experiences outside the text. Students did this eagerly during the phonics lesson, although, as illustrated in the preceding examples, in that context such linkages are rarely legitimized as relevant to reading. In the literature-based lessons, pulling this extra-textual context into the discussion is an explicit goal of the teacher. However, as illustrated next, at times she has difficulty getting the students to do so. As she reads from the book *My Little Island* (Lessac, 1985), in which a boy from a Caribbean island takes a friend to his birthplace and shows him the indigenous pleasures of his life there, she explicitly directs students to make the sorts of connections the phonics teacher was banishing. In the section of the story under discussion here, the theme of festive foods comes up, as the characters consume a large island-style lunch, including "goat-water stew." The teacher tries to illustrate that, although this dish sounds funny to the children in the reading group, it is quite a familiar treat for the children in the story. She encourages this reading by eliciting their own experiences of special meals, asking them what they like to eat on big celebration days.

In the following interaction, as Damon still puzzles over the odd sound of goat-water stew, the teacher questions another, particularly quiet student, Jamarcus, about the kinds of foods that he likes to fix for special days.

You Like Steak?

Teacher:	Let's see, what do you fix Jamarcus?
Damon:	((to nobody in particular)) <u>Goat</u> <u>water</u> <u>stew</u>
Teacher:	((Still addressing Jamarcus)) What do you eat on special occasions.
Jamarcus:	((Shakes his head))
Sally:	Uhm.
Teacher:	What's your favorite dish.
Jamarcus:	((Shrugs his shoulders and looks away))
Stephanie:	I like-
Teacher:	Uh-a ste:ak?
Jamarcus:	((Nods yes))
Stephanie:	I like [(hot wings)
Teacher:	[Steak. (.) Okay.

Here, as is common during these read-aloud sessions, the teacher tries to use the text as a springboard to student-generated meanings. And she brings Jamarcus into the interaction by addressing him directly, "What do *you* fix, Jamarcus?" By doing so, she may, potentially, not only demystify the experiences on the Caribbean island, but also communicate to students that their own lives are legitimate background to understanding a story and relating to characters. But the message that emerges in this interaction is quite the contrary.

As Jamarcus resists the teacher's questions, remaining silent, she gradually scaffolds an appropriate answer for him, rephrasing her question slightly each time. After she receives no response to her first question, she tries again with, "What do you eat on special occasions?" and then "What's your favorite dish?" This relatively open-ended question still elicits only minimal response from Jamarcus, so, finally, the teacher narrows her inquiry into a yes/no question about whether his favorite dish is steak. When the teacher supplies this answer, Jamarcus nods obligingly. Despite the more spontaneous answer volunteered by another student, Stephanie, the teacher focuses on the answer she has elicited from Jamarcus and then moves on. That the teacher ignored Stephanie's blithely volunteered "hot wings" suggests her concern was focused on drawing out Jamarcus, who was always the more reticent student. These were good intentions, but the result was an interaction the teacher did not intend. A presumably open query for student experience led to a narrowed question, and, then, to the teacher's offer of her own experience for students to use as if it were theirs. Finally, the student's one-word (or, in this case, one head-nod) response is treated as sufficient engagement.

This pattern occurs not only during actual reading, but also during post-reading writing activities related to the books. After reading the book, *Cinnamon, Mint, and Mothballs* (Tiller & Aki, 1993), which describes a boy's sensory delight during a visit to his grandmother's house, the teacher urges the students to write generally about their own grandmothers. Again, she wants the book to be a springboard into the lives of the students. As suggested by the minimal student discussion that follows her reading, however, the students have difficulty using it as such. To urge Rene to begin writing, the teacher has questioned him about his own grandmother and he has been reticent. The excerpt below begins with the teacher asking Rene if he shows off to his Spanish-speaking grandmother by speaking English. After receiving minimal response from Rene, she then goes on to detail what her *own* son, Sam, does, when his grandfather visits:

Write Down That
Teacher: Did you:: show off?
Rene: I speak to her and (she'll go) wha::t?
Teacher: That's what=
Damon: Ms. Miller
Teacher: =Sam does when his grandfather comes or grandmother comes. He will (0.4) he says grandaddy listen to me play the piano. Or grandaddy watch me do karate. Or grandaddy- he sho:ws off. All the things he's very proud of. Do you do you do that?
           (3.0)
Rene: ((pauses, makes facial expression, and nods))
Teacher: Yeah? Okay. Well write down that.

The teacher's directive to "write down *that*" efficiently closes down her session with Rene. While there is evidence that Rene started to make links to his own experience ("I speak to her and (she'll go) wha::t?"), when the teacher says "write down that," most of what the demonstrative *that* indexes is her own previous talk. She is simply linking her own experiences, not Rene's, to the text.

In this case, as in the previous example, there are also interactional contingencies that push the teacher to accept such a minimal response from Rene. In the "steak" example, the teacher's one-on-one line of questioning with Jamarcus, and her concern to involve him, took her attention from another student's answer to her original more open-ended question. In this example, as Damon's interruptive "Ms. Miller" indicates, there is also some pressure for this teacher to take note of other students, and here this pressure shapes the sort of interaction she has with Rene. She doesn't have the time to draw out Rene's experiences of his own grandmother more carefully. So the way this reading activity is structured also contributes to the interactional necessity to let the teacher's rendition of experience suffice.

However, and again against the teacher's genuinely good intentions, the interaction itself also indexes that the teacher's experiences and what her own son's granddaddy does are the kinds of experience that *should* be drawn on to make meaning out of the text under consideration. A multiplicity of interactional necessities lead to this prototypical pattern during these literature reading and writing activities, but the end result implicitly communicates that texts index only *certain kinds* of contexts. This is not a lesson the teacher intends the students to learn, but one implicated in interaction.

In the preceding excerpts, the teacher's own indexical cues to worlds outside the textual word are taken as the one set of legitimate external references. We see no student cueing of outside experience—nothing like the spontaneous indexing of Pokémon, witches, or dudes that came up (but was swiftly stifled) in the phonics lessons. This occurred despite the teacher's repeatedly stated desire (stated to me and, at times, to the children) to draw students out, to have them relate literature to their own lives, and through the process to bring literature alive to them. While in both settings the students' experiences are constructed as outside the process of reading, in the phonics class this is primarily accomplished through the way the teacher treats student-volunteered contributions. In these literature lessons, this devaluing of student experience is a more clearly collaborative achievement.

Paradoxically, students' reticence in these exchanges seems to arise out of the very intention of the teacher to penetrate their reticence. As mentioned, this teacher is taking a risk by treating reading as something other than basal readers and decoding exercises. The risk is not simply institutional. In fact, institutional risk was mitigated since the teacher had obtained permission from the administration to modify her curriculum. The primary risk, as illustrated in these exchanges, is interactional. She is working within a school culture in which literacy is typically administered in a series of tightly controlled basal readers and associated phonics exercises. More generally, she is working within a culture that treats schooling as a set of displays of learning, and talk of genuine experience as a disruption to that display (Rymes & Pash, 2001). This context brings with it a certain set of expectations from these students. The teacher in this case continually frustrates these expectations by asking questions that are not meant to lead to displays of "right answers," but to a portrayal of the particulars of the students' lives. The students' frustrated expectations are made evident in their reticence about responding to the teacher's often open-ended prompts (often they seem to be waiting for the teacher to provide the "right" answer). This reticence, in addition to the teacher's responsibility to attend to the needs of all the students, led the teacher to further scaffold student contributions.

The result is the following prototypical pattern:

1) Teacher prompts for experience➔
2) Students are reticent➔
3) Teacher provides example of her own relevant experience➔
4) Students use teacher example as their own experience.

As in the phonics lessons, this pattern indicates how the experience of reading is being constructed in this group. The difference here, however, is that student voices are not silenced after they say something. In these examples, *student voices are silent from the start*, in part, it seems, through the institutional expectations to which they have been inculcated *before* this teacher began her curricular innovation. But, instead of drawing them out, through her scaffolding of these difficult interactions, the teacher substitutes her own voice for theirs. Although this pattern, and certainly the content of these interactions, differs from patterns established during the phonics events, the way reading is constructed interactionally is similar: Reading need not be related to students' own lives. The teacher's life will suffice.

Students Really Do Relate the Text to Their World and Interests

There were rare moments, however, when students in the literature group were not "silent from the start." On these occasions, students initiated question sequences, using contexts outside the book and their own experiences, unprompted, to flesh out words they were reading inside the book. In this type of interaction, however, while students did volunteer their own additional readings of text under consideration, the interaction that followed didn't build on possible entailed meanings, but instead closed off entailments to focus students' attention back on the text.

For example, in the excerpt below, one student notices that in the story *My Little Island* whites are the minority (Figure 5-2):

Race of characters

Sally: They're whi:te and everybody else [is bla:ck.
Teacher: [Shh::.° ((*aside to other students*))
Teacher: Oh, so her friend is whi:te and everybody else is bla:ck in the picture.
Damon: ((*to Sally*))Hey don't be talking about that.
Teacher: ((*Suddenly serious in tone*))What is <u>wrong</u> with that?
Damon: Nu'n ((*Damon shakes his head*))
Sally: Nothin'
Teacher: Is there anything <u>wrong</u> with that?
Students: No. ((*Sally shakes her head*))
Teacher: No, I didn't think so either, but that was really=
Sally: (   )
Teacher: =neat that you. But look at there ((*pointing to the illustration in the book*)). It was neat that you pointed that ou:t.

Figure 5-2. "They're white and everybody else is black."

Here, Sally's remark ("They're whi:te and everybody else is bla:ck."), and Damon's response to it ("Hey don't be talking about that.") raise numerous tangled issues, and the issues rest on the ambiguity of *that*'s referent. Does it refer to Sally's bringing up the issue? The fact of whites being in the minority on this island? Race relations in society at large? Race relations in this reading group? There are multiple possibilities, but the interactional context points to some as more likely relevant. While nothing in Sally's utterance explicitly directs our attention outside the text and visual image, certain features of Damon's utterance and its contextualization provide cues for construing his *that* as presupposing a set of social issues beyond the pages of the literature book. If he were referring to the picture in the book exclusively, his swift directive *not* to talk about something would be nonsensical in this context, since talking about pictures is what this reading group does frequently. Furthermore, his dialect, African-American Vernacular English, indexes his own membership in the "black" category and, as such, it presupposes that the literacy event itself is taking place among a mixed-race reading group. So the reading group itself is implicated as a relevant context for discussion of issues of "black" and "white." (Indeed, one might ask, why is this group of "struggling readers" majority "black" when the school is majority "white"?)

The teacher's response to their exchange also provides evidence that *that* refers to a set of cultural norms that she does not want to address explicitly in this reading group. Her sudden response to Damon's command, accompanied by a distinct change in tone from vivacious storytelling to no-nonsense rhetorical questioning, also constructs his utterance as one that indexes issues that are not to be discussed in this setting.

Thus, despite the teacher's intention to use literature to include students' experiences in the reading process, her responses in this excerpt work to ensure that Sally's remark be treated as one about the picture alone. Immediately following Sally's remark, the teacher strategically adds the more specific "her friend" and "in the picture" to index that the source of understanding for this statement is the concrete picture in the book. Damon's nearly simultaneous statement, "Don't be talking about that," builds on Sally's observation to construct a moment in which race relations among the teacher and the diverse students are relevant to the characters and the text in a book they are reading. However, the teacher transforms the student-generated opportunity for links between text and their own lives into a rhetorical question with only one answer: "What is wrong with that?" To which Damon and Sally both respond, "nothing." As if to emphasize that there is only one answer, she repeats the question again, in yes/no format: "Is there anything wrong with that?" coaxing "no" out of the remaining students and an additional head-shake "no" from Sally. Whatever the referent for *that* here, the force of her rhetorical question ensures that whatever *that* is, it will not be discussed further. And her closing statement, during which she physically points to the picture in the book, solidifies the picture in the book as the appropriate context for construing the meaning of *that*. She praises Sally for "pointing *that* out" but ignores the possible entailments of *that* implicated through Damon's command (and her swift contradiction of it).

In contrast to her unsuccessful teacher-initiated attempts to draw students' lives into the story illustrated in the previous examples, in this excerpt the teacher is presented with an ideal opportunity, initiated by the students, to call on their own lives to understand the text under consideration. However, in this instance she seems reluctant to be drawn into students' perceptions of issues outside the text. Through this interaction, the teacher communicates that there certainly is nothing wrong with talking about the pictures in the book. But she seems hesitant to discuss race relations in the students' own lives or the reasons *why* there are often uneven distributions of black and white people, or, for that matter, why there are proportionately more black people on a Caribbean island. Ironically, Damon made these issues surface by commanding *not* to talk about them. And the teacher, despite her claim that there is nothing wrong with *that*, doesn't let them talk about it. Like the phonics teacher, but with regard to more touchy subject matter, she seems threatened by students' capacity to index certain kinds of context outside the text. And her responses, like those of the phonics teacher, rein in the context-creating entailments of *that*.

This complex intersection of student curiosity, socially complex topics, and the reading of children's literature could potentially be a site for transformative literacy events. It is during these moments—when the possibility of socially complex topics arises—that students can read text as contextualized within their own experiences in the world, and possibly as a source of knowledge about that world. However, in the preceding example, the specter of race prevented the teacher from capitalizing on the connections the students were (potentially) making.

In the next example, at a similar intersection of a socially complex topic and book reading, the word *gay* sparked a possible discussion on sexuality. Here, the teacher and students had been reading a book, *Crow Boy* (Yashima, 1976), about a shy and creative boy, who is ostracized by his peers in school.

The Word *Gay*
Teacher: Okay, together. ((*students read along in unison*)) "He showed
            how crows call when they are happy and gay"
Damon: What does *that* me:an?

Teacher:	Ha:ppy. Just really [happy.
Sally:	[But why do-
TC?:	Happy and ga:y.
Teacher:	I know, Well it's just another way of (.) saying that. Just like you would make [a:
Rene:	[A gay bird is like (.)
	[( )
Teacher:	[No this would be:. This is what they said when uhm excited and happy and elated.[All the words
Rene:	[When somebody says like "you're ga:y."
Teacher:	That's [not i:t.

Here, as with the words "black" and "white" in the previous example, the word "gay" entails new contexts, outside the immediate context of the text they are reading together. In the previous example, Damon's "Don't talk about *that*" presupposed the previous mention of "black and white," but it also had multiple potential entailments. Here, his "what does *that* mean" presupposes the previous reading of the word "gay," but also entails other possible meanings. What ensues is a familiar battle of competing contexts for interpretation. The teacher insists that the only appropriate context for the interpretation of this word is the sentence they just read together. In this context, gay means "happy, just really happy." But Rene articulates another possible context for this word by giving voice to someone who might taunt you on the playground ("When somebody says like, 'you're gay.'"). Being taunted on the playground, in fact, is a common experience of Chibbi, the main character in *Crow Boy*, the book they are reading. And a fuller discussion of this sort of ostracism would certainly be relevant to the text here. Damon's calling attention to one particular word children in *his* school use to taunt each other, and Rene's articulation of how this word is used, could have led to a felicitous link between the text and everyday experiences of the children reading it. However, immediately after Rene's enactment of the word *gay*, the teacher, with determined closure, excises this context from relevant consideration, by saying "That's not it." Again, despite her goal to elicit experiences from students to contextualize reading, she vetoes this experience as relevant context for construing the word "gay."

However, unlike the previous interaction, in which discussion of race issues outside the text is "successfully" silenced, in this interaction discussion of the word "gay" is more drawn out. The students are more insistent, and they won't let the teacher interactionally silence them. Even after the teacher's brusque "that's not it," Sally goes on to insist on an alternative meaning:

The Word *Gay* (continued)

Teacher:	That's [not i:t.
Sally:	[I thought it (me:ant).
Damon:	Ye:ah, I'm happy.
Teacher:	Ri:ght.
Sally:	So, I thought that it meant that a girl likes another girl. ((*laughter*))
Teacher:	We::l[l.
Rene:	[I'm happy.
Sally:	That's why it [(.) it was a long time ago.
Teacher:	[But we've heard it la:tely.
Sally:	That's what it was a long time ago.
Teacher:	We've read two book lately though and it's had the word in there hasn't it?
TC:	Ye:s.
Vanessa:	[Ye:s.
Teacher:	[Do you think some words, their meanings may change? (1.0)
Teacher:	That looks like o:ne, doesn't it? Or they may have mo:re than one meaning.
Sally:	When are we gonna do the scissors?
Teacher:	We (.) We're gonna do that in just a little bit. Okay. Next o:ne.

Sally, here, has followed Damon and Rene's lead, pursuing the alternative understanding of the word *gay*, and the battle over relevant context for its interpretation continues. The teacher enforces her meaning by validating Damon's utterance "I'm happy" with "that's right." Sally counters with the taboo definition of "gay," claiming that "happy" is an old definition for "gay." The teacher latches onto this rationale—yes, word meanings change—then shifts to a more accurate explanation, that some words "have more than one meaning." This is not only a more accurate explanation, but it is probably also more situationally appropriate and comfortable for the teacher. This is the kind of talk about language that is sanctioned in the context of school-based literacy. However, this explanation also serves to end any previous discussion. Sally, no longer hot on the trail of a definition of *gay* or how it applies to playground taunts or the story of *Crow Boy*, now asks when they can use scissors.

The result is that students leave the interaction with the understanding that the meanings they bring to a text will be treated as unrelated to the reading process. The result is *not* a discussion of how this book illustrates an issue endemic in schools—social cruelty and intolerance of difference. Although the discussion of the word *gay* might seem like a tangential reference when students first raise it, understanding the word *gay*—the students' own definition of it, and Rene's own contextualization of how this word might be used by peers—brings into the conversation a situation that mirrors the predicament of the book's protagonist. Indeed, as the teacher collects the reading books from her students, she summarizes the story's theme, saying it shows "how we should accept people's differences and that all of us are unique and have different talents don't we." Although this might have been a theme perfectly applicable during the discussion of the word *gay*, this particular sort of "difference" isn't admitted into the conversation as an *appropriate* contextualization for the text.

Instead, in these situations, in which students use indexical cues to suggest taboo meanings for text or pictures in a book, the teacher dismisses the cueing of contexts external to the text and eliminates the possibility of their relevance for understanding the text. In contrast to the previous examples from this literature-based reading group, in which the students were reticent to provide answers, these examples illustrate students actively contributing to the discussion, then being rebuffed.

But there are points of similarity between these two sets of examples. Both reveal the extent of the institutional and *interactional* risk this teacher has taken by choosing to infuse the curriculum with literature that might prove relevant to students' lives. While she had the courage to read this literature, she doesn't have the interactional experience to handle students' responses that arise from the content these books cover. Since this teacher is working within a school culture in which literacy content is controlled by the phonological features under study, the community provides no experience (for the teacher or the students) with discussions in which more complicated issues are raised through literacy events. In the first set of examples from these literature reading sessions, the teacher frustrated the students' expectations by asking them open-ended questions. In these examples, the students frustrate the teacher's expectations by providing overly open-ended comments about touchy issues like race and sexuality. In the first set of examples, students' frustrated expectations are made evident in their reticence about responding to the teacher's often open-ended prompts, when they seem to be waiting for the teacher to provide the "right" answer. In these "touchy issue" excerpts, the teacher seems to be the reticent one, closing down student inquiry in an attempt to return to the "right" kind of classroom interaction.

The recurrent pattern here could be represented as follows:

1) Teacher and/or students read text (e.g., "Gay")→
2) Student supplies open-ended indexical cues to point to extra-textual context (e.g., "When somebody says like "you're ga:y.")→

3) Teacher implicitly dismisses (or greatly minimizes) the cueing of contexts external to the text. ("That's not it.")

In contrast to the previous examples from the literature-based group, in which the teacher needs to pull information from students and ultimately provides her own, in these situations the students provide potential connections of their own that start the interaction, but the teacher closes down the indexical links being made by the students. Just as we saw in the phonics lesson, the participants in this example and the previous one seem to be battling over relevant contexts for interpreting what words or pictures mean. Here, the teacher insists that *gay* be understood only in the context of the happy crow, rather than in the broader context of playground taunts—or for that matter, the thematic context of the book. And during the discussion of *My Little Island*, even as the student utterances implicated larger contexts, the teacher insisted that the picture be the exclusive source of relevant context. The result in all these sorts of interactions, then, is that students and teacher participate in repeated interactions that imply reading is not related to their own experience in contexts outside the text.

In most of the literature-based lessons, the students resist by being silent from the start. Despite the teacher's attempts to elicit their experiences in the context of reading, they usually keep to themselves, or depend on teacher coaxing to mention outside experiences they relate to the texts they read. Even in the previous two examples, in which students are providing links to text that come out of their own experiences, they are nevertheless, if not completely silent, at least avoiding the lesson from the start. They are, after all, drawing attention to words and images that may be interesting to them only because they are known to presuppose topics that teachers don't like to discuss. In this way, by offering of troubling topics for discussion, these sessions accomplish much of the same implicit lesson as the phonics lessons. "Topics that teachers don't like to discuss" in the context of the phonics lessons is a far broader set. Those students need not reach far to index context that will be stifled by the teacher. They can achieve a playful camaraderie, through avoidance of the teacher's lesson, by a simple mention of a "dude" or a "witch." In both the phonics group and the literature-based reading group, however, teacher reactions to student-initiated extra-textual indexing communicate similar messages. Despite differences in content, teachers and students co-construct literacy events as events through which teachers, not the students, control what is relevantly cued context, and what is not. As a result, the topics (Pokémon), issues (race representation, sexuality), and even ways of speaking (Hey Dude!) of intrinsic interest to students, emerge as irrelevant to literacy development.

IMPLICATIONS: RELATIONSHIP OF *THIS TEXT* TO LARGER CONTEXT

If linguistic anthropology is to provide any meaningful insight to education, the relevance of micro-analysis, as in the examples given here, needs to be related to a broader social context. As Heath writes, "literacy events must also be interpreted in relation to the *larger socio-cultural patterns* that they may exemplify or reflect" (1982, emphasis hers). A superficial and sympathetic look might suggest that both reading groups examined here were working against the damaging and unjust sociocultural patterns of society at large. These teachers were intending to undo the damage caused by a system that too often fails students like Rene and his peers. And, indeed, the system was also helping these students by providing the resources to have small group instruction and, in the case of the second year, an ESOL "specialist" in the employment of the school. These teachers and the school personnel were also working to ensure that these children were not falling through the cracks.

But on closer inspection, despite the genuinely good intentions of teachers and administrators to ensure that these students would not fall through the cracks, in both cases students' contributions *were* falling through the cracks. The benefits of small group interaction and the camaraderie of fellow ESOL students in one case, and the focus on literature and students' experiences in another, were minimized, as literacy events in both reading situations were constructed as events in which the teacher's cues to indexical meanings were privileged. So, despite the possibility of equal opportunity provided through school administrative structures and innovative curricula, the interactions within these groups seemed to reproduce those larger sociocultural patterns that would have excluded these students in a less subtle way had no intervention been organized either by the teacher (in the case of the first year) or the school administration and federal law (in the case of the second year).

Nearly thirty years ago, Hymes called for "a great deal of ethnography" (1973, p. 71) with the goal of providing a catalogue of equally valid literacy and other cultural practices. However, a current linguistic anthropology of education recognizes that, in the rapidly changing field of cultural production within which children and teachers operate today, the exploration of multiple, pre-existing forms of communicative competence is not enough to unearth persistent inequities. As interaction in these reading events has illustrated, successful communication is shaped also by momentary contingencies. Educational researchers interested in all student voices still need to be able to account for exactly how student contributions enter and are taken up in interaction, and how contexts for learning are created and recreated everyday. Or, as Hicks has put it, how we are to put students' "social practices and identities in dialogue with new ones" (Hicks, 2001, p. 221). Clearly, the students discussed in this chapter are not using the same discourse patterns as their teachers. They do not chime in when these teachers want them to, and they do not always supply the relevant information and external experiences that these teachers will ratify. They do begin to make contributions that could be drawn on. However, drawing on students' own contributions is a complex process that is more fine-grained and situationally specific than simply recognizing and ratifying home-based "ways of speaking." It is also a process that can be examined, through interaction, during literacy events.

Just as the concept of "communicative competence" can benefit from analysis of its situational contingencies, so can the concept of "multiple literacies." The distinction between, for example, home-literacy knowledge or pedagogized literacy is an important starting point for understanding literacy events, but these days children do not come to school with one monolithic "home literacy." There are many potential contexts in any reading event, and these contexts are often created of the moment through the indexically entailing properties of language. Students may be very fluent in certain aspects of mainstream literacy, perhaps even more so than their teachers. *Pokémon* characters, for example, are quintessentially mainstream figures and, as we saw, the ESOL students indexed this mainstream world through their references to Chansey during the phonics lessons. But Chansey's presence, and its potential as a foundation for literacy, was swiftly covered over by the teacher's agenda and the students' familiarity with classroom order.

Despite higher-level social policy that mandates certain forms or methods of instruction and despite research that investigates and validates multiple literacies and ways of speaking, interactions that take place in "reformed" classrooms, if left unanalyzed, might persistently reproduce status quo approaches to literacy and, in turn, larger social inequities. Despite surface innovations, interactional patterns in both of these reading groups continued to construct literacy in limiting ways, as these groups practiced reading as if it were unrelated to the interests and experiences of the children learning to read, or, for that matter, to any aspect of a world outside the text and the teacher. The research here also suggests that, *if analyzed*, interactional contingencies can override larger social forces that structure reading in school as one limited kind of activity. Literacy practices can be expanded to incorporate student commentary when it occurs, often by some happy and unpredictable contingency. A discussion of the word *gay* and an elaboration on the spelling and meaning of *chancy* (and *Chansey*) might be far more memorable reading events than the regimented recitation of a literature story or a recall of that story through the teacher's life experiences or a series of cards in a phonics game. Regardless of policy or methodological mandates, if I want my students' voices to be valued, I can work with them to change how interactions work in my classroom.

It is my hope that the tools of linguistic anthropology of education can illuminate this process of change by closely investigating interactions between people, texts, and levels of social reality in schools. The promise of a linguistic anthropology of education is its capacity to relate the classroom word to a changing world.

REFERENCES

Bransen, J., & Miller, D. (2000). Maintaining, developing and sharing the knowledge and potential embedded in all our languages and cultures: On linguists as agents of epistemic violence. In R. Phillipson (Ed.), *Rights to Language: Equity, Power, and Education* (pp. 28–32). Mahwah, NJ: Lawrence Erlbaum.

Delpit, L. D. (1995). *Other People's Children: Cultural Conflict in the Classroom.* New York: New Press.

DeStigter, T. (2001). *Reflections of a Citizen Teacher: Literacy, Democracy, and the Forgotten Students of Addison High.* Urbana, IL: National Council of Teachers of English.

Duranti, A., & Ochs, E. (1988). Literacy instruction in a Samoan village. In E. Ochs, *Culture and Language Development* (pp. 189–209). Cambridge: Cambridge University Press.

Dyson, A. H. (1997). *Writing Superheroes: Contemporary Childhood, Popular Culture, and Classroom Literacy.* New York: Teachers College Press.

Foster, M. (1995). Talkin' that talk: The language of control, curriculum, and critique. *Linguistics and Education, 7,* 120–150.

Freire, P. (1970). *Pedagogy of the Oppressed.* New York: Herder and Herder.

Gee, J. P. (1999). *An Introduction to Discourse Analysis: Theory and Method.* London, New York: Routledge.

Gee, J. P. (2001). Identity as an analytic lens for research in education. *Review of Research in Education, 25.* Washington: American Education Research Association.

Gibson, J. J. (1979). *The Ecological Approach to Visual Perception.* Boston: Houghton Mifflin Company.

Giroux, H. A. (1992). *Border Crossings: Cultural Workers and the Politics of Education.* New York, London: Routledge.

Heath, S. B. (1982). What no bedtime story means. *Language in Society, 11*(1), 49–76.

Heath, S. B. (1983). *Ways with Words: Language, Life, and Work in Communities and Classrooms.* New York: Cambridge University Press.

Hicks, D. (2001). Literacies and masculinities in the life of a young working-class boy. *Language Arts, 78*(3), 217–226.

Hooks, B. (1994). *Teaching to Transgress: Education as the Practice of Freedom.* New York: Routledge.

Hull, G., & Schultz, K. (2002). *School's Out! Bridging Out of School Literacies with Classroom Practice.* New York: Teachers College Press.

Hymes, D. (1972). On communicative competence. In J. B. Pride & J. Holmes (Eds.), *Sociolinguistics* (pp. 269–93). Harmondsworth, U.K.: Penguin.

Hymes, D. (1973). Speech and language: On the origins and foundations of inequality among speakers. *Daedalus, 102*(3), 59–85.

Lessac, F. (1985). *My Little Island*. New York: Harper Collins.

Ochs, E. (1988). *Culture and Language Development: Language Acquisition and Language Socialization in a Samoan Village*. New York: Cambridge University Press.

Ochs, E., & Schieffelin, B. (1984). Language acquisition and socialization: Three developmental stories. In R. A. Shweder & R. A. LeVine (Eds.), *Culture Theory: Essays on Minds, Self, and Emotion* (pp. 276–320). Cambridge: Cambridge University Press.

Pérez, B., & McCarty, T. (1998). *Sociocultural Contexts of Language and Literacy*. Mahwah, NJ: Erlbaum.

Philips, S. U. (1993). *The Invisible Culture: Communication in Classroom and Community on the Warm Springs Indian Reservation*. Prospect Heights, IL: Waveland Press.

Rymes, B., & Pash, D. (2001). Questioning identity: The case of one second language learner. *Anthropology and Education Quarterly 32*(3), 276–300.

Silverstein, M. (1976). Shifters, linguistic categories, and cultural description. In K. Basso & H. A. Shelby (Eds.), *Meaning in Anthropology* (pp. 11–55). Albuquerque: University of New Mexico Press.

Spivak, G. C. (1993). *Outside the Teaching Machine*. London: Routledge.

Street, B. V. (1993). *Cross-Cultural Approaches to Literacy*. New York: Cambridge University Press.

Street, B. V. (1995). *Social Literacies: Critical Approaches to Literacy in Development, Ethnography, and Education*. London, New York: Longman.

Tiller, R., & Aki, S. (Illustrator) (1993). *Cinnamon, Mint, and Mothballs: A Visit to Grandmother's House*. San Diego: Browndeer Press.

Wortham, S. (2001). *Narratives in Action: A Strategy for Research and Analysis*. New York: Teachers College Press.

Yashima, T. (1976). *Crow Boy*. New York: Viking.

6

"Imagined Competence"

Classroom Evaluation, Collective Identity, and Linguistic Authenticity in a Corsican Bilingual Classroom

Alexandra Jaffe

When Petru Paulu entered the village school at age three, he spoke only one of the two languages of the classroom: Corsican. But now, in 2000, as a six-year-old first grader, he speaks French just as well as his classmates who learned it as a first language. The older children remember when he spoke no French, and they tell me about it. Over the last two years, two more children—a brother and sister—have come to the school with Corsican as their first language. Just like Petru-Paulu, Cesaru (5) and Stella-Maria (3) have learned French fast. On occasion, however, the fourth and fifth graders address these smaller children in Corsican: comforting the littlest ones when they cry, giving them directions or advice when the entire school is out together on a field trip. These brief exchanges between children are the only spontaneous, extrascholastic uses of Corsican between children that I observe all year. The children play in French. And it is the language of play that my (anglophone) daughter (aged 6) tells me that she wants to know better. She asks me, after three months in the bilingual school, why one of the teachers keeps speaking to her in Corsican "when I'm here to learn French."

Petru Paulu's older sister, Vanina (10), also learned Corsican before French. The two sibling pairs in the school come from families with deep political and cultural commitments to promoting Corsican language and identity. Their decision to speak only Corsican to their children in the early years sets them apart from most other Corsican parents. For Cesaru and Stella Maria's parents, it was a choice that involved a good deal of personal effort and discipline, since neither of them had been raised exclusively in that language. Out of the twenty-seven children in the school, these four children, along with the two children of one of the teachers, are the only students who hear and use Corsican systematically in the home.

Near the end of the 1999-2000 school year, I ask the children to identify the language competencies and preferences of all the people in the school, showing them photographs of themselves, the teachers, myself, and a few parents and asking them to tell me what language(s) each person understands, speaks, speaks best, and prefers. Almost all of them say that Petru Paulu, Vanina, Stella Maria, and Cesaru speak Corsican better than French, and that they prefer Corsican to French. This is despite the fact that almost all of the French-dominant children's (successful) communication and interaction with these children is in French, a language in which none of the children with Corsican as a mother tongue exhibits the slightest weakness. In fact, Vanina is one of the most accomplished speakers and writers of French in her class. The children are also sure that their teachers prefer Corsican to French and—despite the teachers' demonstrated command of French and the authoritative role they play in the teaching of French—attribute higher levels of Corsican versus French competence to them.

In this chapter, I look closely at Corsican-language literacy work in one of the classes in this bilingual school. Following a well-established theme in the linguistic anthropology of education, I explore the interplay between the macro-level of language ideologies and politics and the micro-level of classroom interaction. Specifically, I focus on minority language linguistic competence—both "real" and "imagined"—and how it is related to issues of individual and collective cultural identity and authenticity. I approach these issues through close analysis of a familiar participation structure, IRE, as it is used by one of the teachers in this school. I go on to relate evaluative practice surrounding Corsican at the micro-interactional level to the overall patterning of literacy practices in the classroom in both Corsican and French. Schools like this one face a key challenge: teaching a language that many of the schoolchildren do not know while at the same time authenticating their legitimate cultural claims to "own" that language (Henze & Davis, 1999). In the data analyzed next, we see one teacher responding to this challenge in the everyday discursive management of competence—and problems of competence—in the classroom. In the following section, I sketch the macro-level practical and ideological contexts that influence bilingual curricula and pedagogical practice in Corsican schools.

THE ETHNOGRAPHIC CONTEXT: LANGUAGE PRACTICE AND IDEOLOGY

Practice

As the account of Petru Paulu and the other corsophone children in the school illustrates, bilingual education on Corsica is not about teaching Corsican to children who already know the language. The percentage of children with Corsican as a mother tongue in this particular school (6 of 27, or about 22%) is actually higher than the average, which I would estimate at less than 10% for the general population. These small numbers of Corsican-speaking children result from *language shift*, from Corsican to French, that began at the turn of the twentieth century and accelerated after World War II. The French school as an institution played a significant role in this shift, whose roots are both economic and ideological. From an economic perspective, access to French language education enabled many Corsicans in an agro-pastoral economy to gain access to white-collar jobs and to raise their standard of living. Often, these new job opportunities took them away from the island. Several generations of Corsicans have raised children (and chosen spouses) in French-speaking milieux on the French mainland and in the French colonies. These life trajectories have contributed to language shift toward French.

Corsican language education is part of an effort to reverse language shift, to teach children a language of cultural heritage that is no longer the language of their daily interactions. This does not mean that Corsican is absent from Corsican social life. Many of the children in the village school I describe hear Corsican quite frequently. More than 50% of their parents and a higher percentage of their grandparents speak Corsican, although some of them do not use it often, and many of them use it to speak to people other than their children. While there is no doubt that today's generation of children, overall, is exposed to less Corsican than in the past, the home language patterns described previously are not new. In fact, both of the teachers in this village school (aged 39 and 42) also grew up in households where Corsican was spoken frequently by parents, but not to them. Like the parents of Stella

Maria and Cesaru, both teachers made a concerted effort (seeking out informal opportunities to speak and taking Corsican language classes) in their late teens and early twenties to turn the passive knowledge of Corsican they acquired in childhood into active speaking competence.

The teaching of Corsican in the public schools dates back to 1975, when Corsican was included in the French Deixonne law, which permitted up to three hours a week of instruction in "regional languages of France." This option allowed motivated teachers in some schools to teach some Corsican, but did not translate into anything like a systematic Corsican education program across the school system. New national educational directives issued in 1995, however, paved the way for the systematic implementation of Corsican-language teaching in all schools. This has included efforts to recruit and place Corsican-speaking teachers at all grade levels with the goal of assuring that children in all classrooms receive three hours a week of instruction in Corsican. It also made possible the opening of bilingual village schools like the one I studied and the establishment of bilingual tracks in larger schools in the towns and cities. In 2000, there were seventeen bilingual sites (whole schools or tracks). During the next few years, Corsican educational authorities plan to increase the number of these sites to twenty-nine, which would create one complete bilingual school or track (preschool through fifth grade) feeding each of the island's twenty-nine middle schools. The official guidelines for the curriculum in these schools is that up to 50% of classroom instruction (13 hours per week) can be conducted in Corsican, and that Corsican can be used to teach any subject area except French. In practice, teachers have a great deal of leeway in the amount of Corsican they use in class, because the Corsican language inspectors of the Academy have an advisory rather than a coercive role. In the school I studied, the teachers used Corsican at least 50% of the time. Through the first grade, it was used in all subject areas, including some French literacy work. In the second through fifth grades, it was used in all subject areas in equal proportions to French, with the exception of French grammar and spelling.

Ideology

Contemporary work on language ideologies in linguistic anthropology addresses collectively held ideas about what language is and how linguistic forms are connected to social and cultural identities and hierarchies.[1] Ethnographic research in this area has described in detail how dominant language ideologies at the societal level are manifested, reproduced, and sometimes challenged in everyday discursive practices. Let me take up, in turn, the ideological underpinnings of (a) the relationship between language and identity and (b) the relationship between language and power.

Language and Identity

In the Corsican case, the very existence of bilingual classrooms is based on an unquestioned assumption that language and identity are indexically linked. Such an ideology not only takes for granted that Corsican stands for corsicanness but also assumes that both language and identity are fixed and unproblematic categories. These assumptions can be traced to histories of language practice on Corsica and the ways in which they have been shaped by dominant (French) language ideologies. Here, schools played a significant role within a larger and powerful French discourse in which the use of French (and more important the use of "good French") is linked with identity (being French) and moral value (being a good French citizen). French schools both articulated this ideology in explicit terms and engaged Corsican schoolchildren in practices that implicitly ratified it. It is important to note that the "essential" connection between language and identity was both asserted in public discourses and created and reproduced by the State's ideological regimentation of linguistic practice through key institutions like the schools. Over time, this combination of power and practice *made* language competence and cultural membership congruent. That is, in their successful pursuit of white-collar jobs and social advancement, Corsicans experienced their integration in the French cultural and economic system through the French language.

But Frenchness was not simply built on the positive association with French. It was also constructed in opposition to non-French languages and cultures. Because of this oppositional logic, the very same processes that linked French to the acquisition of French identity reinforced the connection between Corsican and Corsicanness. In this respect, the Corsican language revitalization effort—which ultimately led to the opening of bilingual schools—appropriated the basic structure of a dominant discourse about language and identity, insisting on the primordial link between Corsican and Corsicanness in order to resist the domination of French, to make claims for minority language rights, and to mobilize Corsicans to reverse minority language shift (Jaffe, 1999).

The link of language and identity is also connected experientially and ideologically to practice—specifically, to the issue of linguistic competence. We see this link operating implicitly in the schoolchildren's linguistic evaluations of their corsophone peers described above: they equated mother tongue with both language dominance (competence) and language preference. That is, they understood people to have one and only one primary linguistic identity, which is predicated on a certain level of competence. There is also an implicit competence threshold for identity in the Corsican bilingual schooling agenda, which, although it does not specify how much Corsican competence is "enough," assumes that some level of societal practice of Corsican is crucial for the maintenance of collective Corsican cultural identity.

As several recent studies of multilingual and multicultural schooling contexts show (Heller, 1999; Rampton, 1995), however, these dominant ideologies of linguistic identity are not reproduced without modification or challenge in pedagogical and communicative practice. In the Corsican case, bilingual schooling in and of itself highlights tensions associated with embracing essentialist ideologies of language identity in conditions of minority language shift. That is, while the "essential" language–identity relationship is a key motivation for teaching Corsican in schools, minority language shift creates a social context in which language competence and cultural membership are *not* congruent. As we have seen, Corsican bilingual schools are an effort to correct this "problem" of incongruence between practice and cultural identity by teaching Corsican to Corsican children who are largely French-dominant. The existence of these schools thus foregrounds minority language loss as a problem for individual and collective cultural identity. This is reflected indirectly in public debates about Corsican over the last twelve years. In these debates, there has consistently been a segment of the population that has opposed the systematic, obligatory teaching of Corsican because it rejects the very notion that there is incongruence between practice and collective identity. People who take this position refute the proposition that the language shift is significant and/or that language shift cannot be reversed through informal practices in social and familial contexts outside the school (Jaffe, 2001).

Language and Power: Parity and Differentiation

The disparity between Corsican language use and competence and the symbolic value of Corsican as a heritage language influences Corsican literacy practices in the bilingual classroom in a number of ways. On the part of the teachers it creates a heightened awareness of the socially and politically contingent relationship between linguistic signs and social identities. This awareness is manifested in two, sometimes competing curricular/pedagogical strategies that respond to the dual objectives of Corsican bilingual education: (1) the political goal of creating institutional and symbolic parity between the dominant and the minority language and (2) the cultural goal of giving the minority language a privileged, differential value as a language of cultural identity.

Creating parity. The first category of pedagogical strategies in the bilingual curriculum is aimed explicitly at challenging the unquestioned status of French as a dominant language and the relegation of Corsican to a subordinate position in the classroom. The teachers in this school made a conscious effort to legitimate Corsican by creating parity in the pedagogical functions of Corsican and French in the curriculum, striving for equality in both the number of hours and the subject areas taught in each language. In fact, if anything, the teacher of the younger children used more Corsican than French to try to compensate for the dominance of French outside the classroom. The drive for parity also motivated the teacher of the older children's extensive efforts to create Corsican language materials in the high-status subject areas of science and math; in fact, she was the co-author of a Corsican-language primary-school text on Corsican fauna.

As far as subject areas are concerned, literacy is a crucial symbolic arena for the display of linguistic legitimacy, since texts in the minority language serve to demonstrate the existence of norms and standards in Corsican and the equal authority of Corsican and French as written codes. Next, we will see a number of evaluative practices surrounding the reading and writing of texts in Corsican that send an implicit message to the children that they are equally constrained by authoritative rules in Corsican as by those in French.

Creating difference. While Corsican experiences of French language domination have led them to try to establish and police authoritative language standards for Corsican—to make it like French—those same experiences have also given Corsican value *in opposition to* the dominant code. This means that the authoritative presentation of linguistic standards for spoken and written Corsican in the classroom sometimes conflicts with the bilingual schools' goal of "giving back" ownership of a code whose value has been experienced, historically, as not-French— as a code of intimacy and inclusion that is spoken voluntarily and not subject to formal, academic criteria of judgment. Corsican experiences of French language and literacy have also created sensitivity to a theme in a large body of educational research: the ways in which dominant literacies can alienate non-mainstream speakers. That is, official or schooled literacies are always linked to social and linguistic hierarchies; in schools, dominant ways of speaking and writing are privileged, and the linguistic skills that non-mainstream children bring to the classroom are either sanctioned or go unrecognized (Cazden, 1988; Collins, 1991; Gee, 1991; Heath, 1983; Michaels, 1991; and Street, 1995; among many others). Students who do not come to school with mainstream linguistic capital often do not acquire it through schooling, since successful participation in school literacy practices is based on middle-class cultural capital. That cultural capital includes patterns of inquiry, norms of interaction, and modes of learning that much schooling takes for granted as universal, rather than culturally specific ways of being and criteria of value. The result is that non-mainstream learners often never achieve legitimacy (in Lave & Wenger's 1991 sense) as participants in dominant discourses and literacy practices. Their failure is thus bemoaned but taken for granted in schools, which are fundamentally conservative social institutions that reproduce social inequality.

In contrast, teaching a minority language in a context of language shift and revitalization both foregrounds the political dimension of literacy instruction and specifically rejects its potential for alienation and linguistic disenfranchisement. With regard to the Corsican language, the bilingual school is *not* a gatekeeping institution, as the teaching of Corsican is defined explicitly as being about strengthening and forging collective cultural ownership of oral and literate practices in the language. In this respect, the classroom is engaged in reinforcing the oppositional value of Corsican as "not-French." In pedagogical terms, this oppositional value involves creating new models of *learning as apprenticeship* that acknowledge the social and cultural basis of standards of linguistic competence (Lave & Wenger, 1991).

This desire for differentiation is expressed in contrasting emphases in the evaluative frameworks and criteria used to define Corsican versus French competence in the classroom. I claim that the teacher structures and evaluates oral work during Corsican literacy activities to confer competence and cultural ownership of Corsican on a group of children with very uneven levels of linguistic skills in that language. That is, Corsican competence is defined and evaluated less as an individual relationship with a fixed, authoritative, and abstract code and more as a collaborative product created through socially situated practices.

In the following analysis, I look at how this minority language identity work is accomplished through the management of sameness to and difference from French in participation structures and evaluative practices surrounding work on a Corsican text.

CORSICAN LITERACY WORK

Background

In the spring of 2000, Pierrette, the teacher of the older group (ages 7 through 11) of children in the village school, selected a story about two cats that she had found in two French-language collections of Corsican traditional tales. She synthesized the plot elements and, working loosely from both texts, translated the story into Corsican.

This translation/adaptation was one of a large portfolio of Corsican teaching materials she and the other teacher in the school had created in over six years of extensive teaching in Corsican (which began even before the school was officially declared a bilingual site). Sometimes, these translations were used in parallel with the French versions of a text. That is, the children worked on the same subject or theme in both languages. This time, however, Pierrette presented only the Corsican version to the children, which she introduced by reading it to them out loud in class.

By the time work on the story of *Pedilestu è Mustaccina* (the two cats' names) began, I had spent three months of daily, full-time observation in the school, in one or the other of its two classrooms. I had been videotaping for about a month. I videotaped all kinds of lessons, in Corsican and in French, and at all different moments of the day and in all different kinds of lessons—from math to language to physical education.

I began taping work on *Pedilestu è Mustaccina* the day after the teacher read the children the story; the data analyzed below comes from the transcript of the first twenty-five minutes of approximately forty minutes of discussion on that day. The following is an extract (followed by a translation) from the full story, which represents the portion of the text discussed in this lesson:

PEDILESTU E MUSTACCINA
I dui ghjatti

Un ghjattu Pedilestu è una ghjatta Mustaccina campavanu cù u so vechju patrone in un casale cù un tettu à teghje. Pudianu andà in tutte e pezze di a casa, fora di u granaghju. U patrone li dava à manghjà bè è eranu felice.

Cum'è à tutti i ghjatti, li piacia à caccighjà i topi. L'accadia à spessu chì i topi eranu numarosi à entre in casa.

D'inguernu Pedilestu è Mustaccina ùn surtianu micca. Un facianu chè à ghjuca cù un ghjumellu di canapu o à fallà e scale dopu à una castagna. Durmianu ind'è u scornu di a sala, vicinu à u fucone.

A u principiu di u veranu, i dui ghjatti ricumminciavanu à dorme tesi à u sole è à appichjassi à l'alburi di l'ortu. Un ghjornu, mentre ch'elli eranu incalpacati nantu à a un ghjambone, Pedilestu vede chì a scala chì permettia di ghjungje à a finestra di u granaghju era firmata appughjata contra u muru di a casa.

—Veni cù mè, dice u ghjattu, ci avemu da campà.

—A sai puru ch'ella hè difesa! risponde Mustaccina.

—Veni subbitu chì u patrone ùn c'hè.

Collenu a scala è ghjunghenu in granaghju. Quantu robba da manghja! Castagne, spighe di granone, noce è amandule.

Pedilestu, videndu a so amica avvicinassi da l'amandule li dice:

—O Mustaccì, ùn ti scurda di scurticà le nanzu di manghjà le.

—Perchè?

—Perchè chì a chjoppula hè dura è risicheghja di strangulà ti!

—Feraghju cum'è tù dici.

Di scurticà l'amandule impedisce à Mustaccina di manghjane quant'ella vole. Tandu si scorda di u cunsigliu di Pedilestu.

Pedilestu and Mustaccina
The Two Cats

Pedilestu the cat and the (female) cat Mustaccina lived with their old master in a big house with a slate roof. They were allowed to go in all of the rooms of the house except the loft. Their master fed them generously and they were happy. Like all cats, they liked to hunt mice. They got to do this often because many mice came into the house.

In the winter, Pedilestu and Mustaccina didn't go out. They spent the day playing with a ball of wool or dashing down the stairs chasing after a chestnut. They slept in the corner of the big room, near the fireplace.

When spring came, the two cats began to sun themselves outside and to climb the trees of the garden. One day, while they were perched on a branch, Pedilestu saw that the ladder that went up to the window of the loft had been left leaning up against the wall of the house.

"Come with me," said the cat, "what a treat we'll have."

"But you know that it is forbidden!" responded Mustaccina.

"Come quickly, while the master is not there."

They climbed up the ladder and entered the loft. What bounty they saw! Chestnuts, ears of corn, walnuts and almonds.

Pedilestu, seeing his friend going towards the almonds, said,

"O Musty, don't forget to shell the almonds before eating them."

"Why?"

"Because the shell is hard and it might strangle you!"

"I'll do what you say."

Shelling the almonds, however, prevented Mustaccina from eating as many as she liked. By and by, she forgot Pedilestu's advice.

In the lesson described here, the teacher passed out a paper to all of the children on which she had written a series of questions that addressed, in chronological order, the principal facts recounted in the story. These are her questions:

QUESTIONS

*Cumu si chjamanu i dui ghjatti?	**What are the two cats called?**
* Induve campavanu?	**Where did they live?**
* Induve pudianu andà?	**Where were they allowed to go?**
* Chì caccighjavanu?	**What did they hunt?**
* Chì facianu d'inguernu?	**What did they do in winter?**

* Induve durmianu?	**Where did they sleep?**
* Chì si passa un ghjornu?	**What happened one day?**
* Chì c'era in u granaghju?	**What was in the loft?**
* Chì dà cum'è cunsigliu u ghjattu à Mustaccina?	**What advice did the cat give to Mustaccina?**
* Ella, piglia in contu stu cunsigliu?	**Did she heed his advice?**

Framing of the Event

Next, Excerpts I through III from the transcript show how the teacher discursively framed the upcoming pedagogical activity and its ground rules. In Excerpt I, she makes reference to the fact that they are engaging in a typical mode of functioning in the class: they will be answering the list of questions orally in preparation for writing a summary of the story.

Excerpt I[2]

Maria:	*C'est tout ce qu'on a fait hier!*
	It's everything we did yesterday!
Tea:	Ghjustu à puntu, ghjustu ghjustu cusì. Avà di modu avera da pruvà à risponde di modu precisu à ogni...ogni dumande, micca inseme..innò unu, ci vulerà à pisà u ditu, perchè sè vo parlate tutti inseme, allora cusì, quand'emu fattu, emu trovu tutte e risposte à e dumande o Pasquà, tandu seremu capace di fà ciò chè tu ai dettu nanzu.
	Exactly, exactly. Now, in a, now we need to try to respond in a precise manner to each, each question. Not all together. No, one person, you need to raise your finger because if you all speak at once, well that way... when we are finished, finding all the answers to the questions oh Pierre, then we'll be able to do what you said before.
Pierre:	Di fà
	To do...
Teacher:	Chì femu di modu generale per prisentà u racontu.
	What we normally do in order to present the story
Martin:	*un compte-rendu*
	A summary,
Child:	*un résumé*
	a resume.
Teacher:	*un*...ai dettuu...riassuntu.
	A...you said it, a summary.

In the comment made by the teacher in Excerpt II, below, she emphasizes what is also common procedure in her classroom: that the children are to refrain from writing anything down until all the answers have been formulated (and perfected) orally:

Excerpt II
(Stopping a child from writing):
Teacher: QuìAghju dettu sta prima parte si face à bocca, scrivimu
              micca e risposte per avà hein.
              Here...I said that this first part will be done orally, we won't
              write the answers right now, eh.

On other occasions, the teacher had explained that the reason she did
not want children to write was that it prevented them from paying full
attention to what was being said. Excerpts I and II, therefore, reinforce
for the children their responsibilities both as active speakers and as
active listeners in work that is oriented towards producing a collective
text.

   In the classroom sequence in the following excerpt (III), one of the
children (Andrea) has been called on to read the very first question
on the xeroxed list. The teacher then calls on another child, Pierre,
to answer the question. The teacher's comments in this sequence
frame the exercise as being just as much about *how* the children
express themselves as it is about providing accurate answers about
story content.

Excerpt III

1	Andrea:	Cumu si chjamanu i dui ghjatti?
2		**What are the two cats called?** (softly)
3	Teacher:	Tuttu u mondu a capitu? Cumu si chjamanu i dui ghjatti?
4		Allora per risponde, pruvete da fà, da fà una risposta sana.
5		Sana, sana. Iè.
6		**Everyone has understood? What are the two cats called?**
7		**Now, to respond, try and make your answer complete.**
8		**Complete, complete. Yes.**
9	Pierre:	Dui ghjatti si chjamanu.
10		**Two cats are called.**
11	Teacher:	Un aghju micca intesu.
12		**I didn't hear.**
13	Pierre:	I dui ghjatti si chjamanu Pedilestu è Mustaccina.
14		**The two cats are called Pedilestu and Mustaccina.**
15	Teacher:	Bravu. Qualè chì ripeta sta risposta? Jeanne, cumu ellu ci
16		vole.
17		**Good. Who will repeat the answer? Jeanne, take care to do**
18		**it right.**
19	Jeanne:	I dui ghjatti si chjamanu Pedilestu è Mustaccina.
20		**The two cats are called Pedilestu and Mustaccina.**
21	Teacher:	Pedilestu hein! è Mustaccina. Brava. Voli pruvà tù? Allez.
22		**Pedilestu, eh and Mustaccina. Good. Do you want to try?**
23		**Go ahead.**
24	Sandrine:	I dui ghjatti.si chjamenu [dyamenu]....

25		The two cats....are called...
26	Teacher:	Si chjamanu.[dyamanu]
27		Are called (correction of pronunciation)
28	Sandrine:	Si chjamanu [dyamanu] Pedilestu è Mustaccina.
29		Are called Pedilestu and Mustaccina.

We see the focus on form and delivery in several places. First of all, on line 6 (in the translation), the teacher asks, "Everyone has understood?" This question, I would argue, is more or less a rhetorical one, since she leaves no room for a negative answer and follows the question immediately with instructions to "make a complete response." Pierre shows that he has understood this as a request for a complete sentence, because when the teacher tells him "she didn't hear" his response (line 12) he repeats it, adding in the article ("**The** two cats....") he left out the first time. Second, she has two children repeat the correct answer. Taken together, the teacher's directions take the children's comprehension for granted and frame the event as being to a great extent about using complete sentences and pronouncing accurately.[3] This framing implies the parity of Corsican and French in the classroom, both as known languages and as languages with clear standards of practice. This message is reinforced by the teacher's evaluative moves, below.

Evaluation

The excerpts below highlight the teacher's evaluative moves throughout the twenty-five-minute stretch of questions and responses that follows the format established previously (children responding to the written questions read out loud by their classmates). These evaluations concern four main linguistic categories: pronunciation, delivery, grammar, and usage, as well as criteria of attention and involvement that are not strictly linguistic. These evaluations both reveal the teacher's criteria of competence in Corsican and implicitly attribute certain kinds of competence to the children. Let me first take up the issue of pronunciation.

Pronunciation

For the most part, pronunciation is corrected as it is at the end of Excerpt III, by the teacher repeating, correctly, the word that has been mispronounced by the child, often with added emphasis on the syllable with the offending sound. In Excerpt IV, however, the teacher makes explicit the rule behind her correction of the pronunciation of *granaghju* [loft/granary]:

Excerpt IV:

1	Martin:	Chì c'era in u granaghju [in u granaju]?
2		**What was there in the loft?**
3	Teacher:	Ùn hè micca u granaghju [u granaju], hein! O dici chì c'era
4		in granaghju [in granaju] o in u granaghju [u ranaju].
5		**It isn't in the loft [u granaju]}, hein! Either you say it was**
6		**'in loft' [in granaju] or 'in the loft' [in u ranaju].**
7	Martin:	In u granaghju [in u ranaju].
8		**In the loft [in u ranaju].**
9	Teacher:	Eccu, hein! Torna sta lettera, una bella cambiarina.
10		**There you are! That letter again, a nice 'cambiarina'.**

In explaining why Martin's pronunciation of "granaghju" as [granaju] is incorrect, the teachers uses the term *cambiarine* [changers] that is given by Corsican linguists to the graphemes whose pronunciation changes depending on their context.[4] One phonological rule governing the pronunciation of the *cambiarine* is that in post-vocalic contexts, unvoiced consonants are voiced, and voiced consonants become semi-vowels or, as in the case of the /g/ in "granaghju," disappear.

The teacher's evocation of the *cambiarine* is significant as a reference to explicit literacy instruction. It is a contextualization cue—an indexical language form that presupposes socially relevant knowledge, identities, or interactional frames. This contextualization cue does at least two things. First, it brings Corsican into the interaction as a formal and authoritative code. Against the backdrop of the students' and teacher's shared classroom practice, which includes a great deal of explicit instruction on French grammar and orthography, this is an index of Corsican's symbolic parity with French. The reference to the *cambiarine* thus makes relevant formal, structured properties of Corsican. It also takes for granted, and thus makes relevant, students' participation in this kind of literacy instruction in Corsican. That is, the utterance "una bella cambiarina" [a nice changer] presupposes the student's knowledge of this phonological and orthographic feature. While the most common correction strategies of pronunciation errors that we see at the end of Excerpt III and in lines 5 and 6 (of the translation) in Excerpt IV simply tell the children they are wrong, the evocation of the *cambiarine* recontextualizes the student's oral error as a temporary lapse by a person who knows the rule. In effect, then, it valorizes knowing the rule as a form of linguistic competence. Participation in schooled discourses about the minority language—literacy talk—thus mitigates deficits in the children's ability to participate in extra-academic, informal discourse in Corsican. In this minority language revitalization context, metalinguistic discourse is thus not a school-based language practice that alienates children by disregarding their existing linguistic knowledge. Rather, it is a language practice around Corsican that allows children to share in a collective discourse involving the minority language.

This form of linguistic competence is not, however, the kind of competence enjoyed by native speakers of Corsican. As the author of a Corsican language learning method comments in his recorded preface to the cassette tapes included with the manual, while native speakers cannot name the *cambiarine* or articulate the rule for their use, they never make a mistake in their pronunciation. These extra-scholastic definitions of authentic pronunciation ("native speaker" identity) also affect pedagogical practices and student performances inside the class. First of all, the *cambiarine* are one of the features of spoken Corsican that distinguishes it from standard Italian. In terms of the relation between spelling and pronunciation, the *cambiarine* also distinguish Corsican from French, in which few consonants have variant pronunciations.

The *cambiarine* are also highly charged markers of linguistic identity and competence. Pronunciation "mistakes" in public discourse (like the media) are often brandished in popular discourse as incontrovertible proof of a speaker's (or of a category of speakers') lack of legitimate claims to know Corsican. The teacher was also aware that most adult Corsican speakers will make no allowance for "spelling pronunciations" in the language since they have, for the most part, little or no experience with Corsican in its written form. Thus her vigilance over pronunciation of the *cambiarine* was also related to the critical importance of pronunciation in the social evaluation of Corsican competence. As a consequence, she never gave the children written texts in Corsican "cold," that is, before they had heard and/or spoken the words. In this way, she tried to compensate for the children's French dominance by building an oral baseline around every text presented and paying close attention to pronunciation when those texts were read out loud.

Children's overgeneralizations show that they too understood the *cambiarine* as key indices of "speaking Corsican." For example, Jeanne was corrected once in this lesson on her pronunciation of "si passa": she said [si pasa], failing to voice the /p/ as [b] in the intervocalic context (as [si basa]). She also, of course, heard Martin's pronunciation of "granaghju" corrected in Excerpt IV. The next day in class, she pronounced "in granaghju" incorrectly as [in ranaju]. This error is not a spelling pronunciation (which, in the case of the *cambiarine*, causes children to put in sounds that should not be heard) but an omission of a sound based on overgeneralization of a phonological rule.

In summary, "micro-level" evaluative practice surrounding pronunciation both responds to and provides alternatives to "macro-level" criteria of competence and language identity that exist outside the classroom. The extra-scholastic criteria are related to ideological models of linguistic authority and authenticity developed in response to dominant political ideologies of language. The teacher responds to these models by striving for competencies that will be recognized as authentic by native speakers, as well as by validating school-based learning of Corsican as a formal code.

Delivery

This lesson also illustrates another general feature of this teacher's classroom, which has to do with performance esthetics. In both Corsican and French, she places a great deal of emphasis on the children's delivery when they read out loud, recite poems, or say lines in a play. We see this emphasis in Excerpt V, where the teacher draws Jeanne's attention to question intonation (line 6):

	Excerpt V	
1	Teacher:	Qualè chì leghje a seconda dumanda? Jeanne.
2		**Who wants to read the second question? Jeanne**.
3	**Jeanne:**	Induve campanu.
4		**Where do they live**.
5	Teacher:	Induve campanu? Ghjè una dumanda. Induve campanu?
6		Maria.
7		**Where do they live? It's a question. Where do they live?**
8		**Maria.**

We see the same thing in the following excerpt, in the teacher's comment to Martin (line 10) that he has not read the text correctly as a question.

	Excerpt VI	
1	Teacher:	Martinucciu voli pruvà?
2		**Martin[5], do you want to try?**
3	Martin:	Chì si passà...un ghjornu. (pianu)
4		**What happened...one day. (softly)**
5	Teacher:	Ripete.
6		**Repeat.**
7	Martin:	Chì si passà un ghjornu.
8		**What happened one day.**
9	Teacher:	Ùn hè micca una dumanda què!
10		**That isn't a question!**
11	Martin:	Ah! *ouè*! chì si passà un ghjornu?
12		**Oh! *Yeah*! What happened one day?**

In Excerpt VII, the teacher evokes a more general issue of "smoothness" of delivery, asking Sandrine to "try to say it in one breath" (line 7) and modeling the way it should be said at the end of line 8.

Excerpt VII:

1	Sandrine:	Chì facianu ... d'inguernu?
2		**What did they do....in winter?**
3	Teacher:	Senza fighjà, senza fighjà u [unintelligible], chì facianu
4		d'inguernu? Prova tù d'un soffiu. Chì facianu
5		d'inguernu? stà à sente: "chì facianu d'inguernu?"
6		**Without looking, without looking [...] what did they do in**
7		**winter? Try to say it in one breath. What did they do in**
8		**winter. Listen: "What did they do in winter?"**
9	Sandrine:	Chì facenu [faenu] d'inguernu?
10		**What do they do in winter?** [wrong tense, mispronunciation
11		of a *cambiarina*]
12	Teacher:	Chì facianu [fajianu] d'inguernu?
13		**What did they do in winter?**
14	Sandrine:	Chì facianu [fajianu] d'inguernu?
15		**What did they do in winter?**

In these sequences, the teacher conveys the expectation to the students that they should be able to move beyond reading-as-decoding and give a coherent voice to the text. While I cannot fully develop this point here, I want to point out that the aesthetics of reading aloud is complex, since the reader must both mobilize his or her oral competencies and adapt them to textual structures and constraints that differ considerably from spoken interactional forms. What is of interest in relationship to the discussion here is that children are called upon to develop and exercise advanced skills that straddle oral and written competence in Corsican. These same skills are emphasized in the same way in French. Overall, the focus on delivery and the way that it is manifested in the teacher's evaluations put French and Corsican on equal footing in the classroom: as languages of equal importance and authority, in which the children are expected to attain equal oral competence.

Grammar and Usage

Outside of the domain of pronunciation, the teacher also corrected children's errors of grammar and usage. One illustration of this can be seen in Excerpt VII, where Sandrine uses the present of the verb "to do" on line 10. The teacher's response is to repeat her answer in the past (imperfect tense) on line 13. Sandrine acknowledges this as a correction by repeating it in line 15. In Excerpt VIII, below, Jean-Marie, the only second-grader and the youngest child in the class, reads a third person plural verb, *pudianu* [they could], as a third person singular, *pudia* [he/she could], and the teacher calls on other students to provide the correct form.

Excerpt VIII

1	Teacher:	Qualè chì face a terza dumanda? *Allez* prova o Ghjuvà.
2		**Who will do the third question?** *Go ahead*, **try it Ghjuvà.**[6]
3	Jean-Marie:	Induve...
4		Where...
5	Teacher:	'Induve,' bravu...attente. Jeanne l'astica...lasci per
6		piacè. Induve...
7		**"Where," good...look closely. Jeanne, the rubber band,**
8		**leave it alone please. Where...**
9	Jean-Marie:	Induve...
10		**Where...**
11	Teacher:	Ghjè difficiule à leghje sta parolla? Iè
12		**Is it difficult to read that word? Yes.**
13	Martin:	Pudia andà
14		**Could he/she go?**
15	Teacher:	Pudia? Ghjè "pudia"? Sò dui, i ghjatti. Induve....
16		**Could he/she? It's "pudia"? The cats—there are two of**
17		**them. Where...?**
18	Kids:	Pudianu
19		**Could they**
20	Martin:	Pudimu
21		**Could we**
22	Teacher:	'Pudimu,' no.
23		**'Could we,' no.**
24	Pierre	Pudianu
25		**Could they**
26	Martin:	Pudianu andà?
27		**Could they go?**
28	Teacher:	Ripete ò ciù.
29		**(to Jean-Marie) Repeat it little guy.**
30	Jean-Marie:	Induve pudianu andà?
31		**Where could they go?**

Jean-Marie's performance is carefully monitored by the teacher, who frames it, with two supportive comments on lines 5 and 11, as being a good effort on a difficult task. Interestingly, her affirmation of the difficulty of "reading that word" on line 11 seems to obscure the corrective purpose of her comment, since the next student who volunteers, Martin, does not alter the tense of the verb in his contribution but, by simply reading further than Jean-Marie (line 13), construes previous interaction as being about the smaller boy getting stuck in the process of decoding a sentence. This leads the teacher to address the issue of verb number (albeit indirectly) by asking if it could be *pudia* when there are *two* cats (line 15). This elicits a correct, choral answer from several children and yet another incorrect verb form from Martin on line 20. After the teacher tells him that he is wrong, the correct verb is supplied by another child and repeated by Martin. The teacher then turns back to Jean-Marie, the original reader, and asks him to repeat the phrase (line 28). The teacher thus creates a collaborative interaction, which makes it possible for Jean-Marie, supported by the collective knowledge of his peers, to close this question-and-answer sequence by uttering the correct words.

In the twenty-five minutes of class captured in the transcript from which these excerpts are taken, there were two other corrections of verb tense, two corrections that had to do with subject-verb agreement, and one correction of a preposition. These corrections are, on the one hand, another domain of symbolic parity with French, for they are done in much the same way as corrections of children's French grammatical errors. If we look at these oral corrections in Corsican in the context of patterns of literacy instruction across the two languages, however, we find that they are not backed up with the same amount of explicit grammatical instruction as in French. This is not to say that this does not go on in Corsican; in fact, in the week after this lesson, the teacher responded to some of the conjugation problems she had encountered by doing an in-class exercise and providing a worksheet dealing exclusively with the singular and plural forms of third person verbs from all three groups. Yet this grammatical lesson was one of only three or four that I witnessed in a year of classroom observation, compared to weekly French grammar lessons. In summary, Excerpt VIII shows evaluative practice surrounding grammar filling the same functions as it did in pronunciation and delivery: working in the service of French-Corsican political parity at the same time as it carves out a special niche for Corsican, by engaging children in a collective rather than individual relationship with performance standards in that language.

Excerpt IX illustrates the way the teacher deals with the children's use of French words or adaptations of French words into Corsican. The issue of French language influence on Corsican is significant because it is a concrete linguistic manifestation of language shift and the dominance of French at both the individual and the societal levels. French influences in Corsican, like mispronunciations of the *cambiarine*, can brand the speaker as "inauthentic."[7] And, seen through a dominant language ideological lens, the incursion of French into Corsican is also a challenge to the minority language's status as a discrete and bounded code (Jaffe, 2000). Thus the treatment of these linguistic phenomena in the classroom implicitly addresses the issue of linguistic identity: the identity of Corsican as a code, and the identity of teachers and children as authentic speakers. The format of this particular lesson foregrounds both the use of French and French influence because, unlike many other discussions in this class, it explicitly calls for responses in Corsican: Corsican questions are read from a Corsican handout in preparation for the writing of a Corsican summary. In the following sequence, Pierre and Martin try to transpose the noun phrase *une pelote de laine* [a ball of wool] from French into Corsican in order to answer a question.

Excerpt IX

1	**Teacher:**	Allora chì facianu?
2		**So what did they do?**
3	**Pierre:**	Ghjuccavanu.
4		**They played.**
5	**Teacher:**	Eccu! Ghjuccavanu...
6		**Right, they played**...
7	**Pierre:**	À corre ind'è e scale appresu à una castagna.
8		**Running down the stairs after a chestnut.**
9	**Teacher:**	Eccu, o à ghjuccà cù?
10		**Right, or with?**
11	**Martin:**	Una pela di [pela di]
12		**A pela di [pela di]**
13	**Teacher:**	Una? Una chè? una pela [pela]?
14		**A? A what? A pela [pela]?**
15	**Pierre:**	Una pala, una pala di pela. [pala i bela]
16		**A 'pala', a 'pala di pela.' [pala i bela]**
17	**Teacher:**	Una pala di pele di polo, hein! heu! A ghjuccà cùn chè, ùn
18		aghju micca intesu Martin? Caccia, fatela finita, Iè?
19		**A pala di pele di polo (ball of hide of polo: nonsense play**
20		**with sounds) eh? To play with what, I didn't hear Martin.**
21		**Remove, stop [playing with something], Yes?**
22	**Martin:**	Una pela di lena. [pela di lena]
23		**A pela di lena. [pela i lena]**
24	**Teacher:**	Di 'lena,' una 'pela di lena'?
25		**Of 'lena,' a 'pela di lena'?**
26	**Martin:**	*Oui!*
27		*Yes!*
28	**Teacher:**	Chì vole dì? *Tu veux dire une pelote de laine, je ne le crois pas!*
29		Una pala di lena. O ghjè un ghjumellu, di lana o di canapu.
30		Un ghjumellu, eh? di lana, và bè? Allora d'inguernu, i
31		dui ghjatti ùn sortenu micca. Un sortenu ghjoccanu, allora
32		ghjucavanu, eh, postu chè ghjucavanu...
33		**What does that mean?** *You are trying to say a ball of wool.*
34		*I don't believe it.* **A "pela" of wool, or it is a ball of wool**
35		**or of string. A ball of wool, that's fine. So in winter, the**
36		**two cats don't go out, they play, they played since...**
37	**Jean-Marie:**	A fallà e scale dopu à una castagna.
38		**Running down the stairs after a chestnut.**
39	**Teacher:**	A fallà e scale dopu à una castagna, o un ghjumellu di...
40		**Running down the stairs after a chestnut or a ball of...**
41	**Children:**	canapu...lana
42		**String...wool**

43	Teacher:	Di canapu, eiu aghju dettu di canapu eh, o pò esse di lana,
44		perchè nò? Vi piace à ghjuccà cùn un ghjumellu di lana.
45		A i ghjatti li piacce assai, à i ghjattucci dinò manca à
46		i ghjatti maiò, và bè, allora, heu ! Ghjulia a dumanda
47		chì vene dopu.
48		**Of string, I had said of string, but it could be of wool,**
49		**why not? You like playing with a ball of wool. Cats like it**
50		**too, little cats and not just big ones. Ok, now, eh. Maria,**
51		**the next question.**
52	Maria:	Induve durmianu? [durmi'anu]
53		**Where did they sleep?**
54	Teacher:	Induve durmianu? [durm'ianu]
55		**Where did they sleep? (correction of syllabic stress)**

This transcript shows a complex exchange in which Martin, followed by Pierre, is trying to say "a ball of wool." Martin has obviously forgotten the Corsican phrase that was used in the story, "un ghjumellu di canapu" [a ball of string]. He tries to adapt the French "une pelote de laine" beginning on line 11, where he takes the French word "pelote" [wool ball], and produces "pela" [pela] in Corsican. This is indeed a word in Corsican, meaning "skin" or "hide," but it is not the word he is looking for. Perhaps momentarily thrown off by the fact that "pela" means something in Corsican, the teacher questions him (on line 13) by asking "a what?" and repeating the word "pela." A second child, Pierre, intervenes on line 15, proposing "pala," which means "ball." This makes sense, but Pierre continues with Martin's original formulation: "di pela," saying in effect, "a ball of hide, " which is not intelligible. This leads the teacher to good-humoredly play with the vowel sounds floating about in this sequence ("pala di pela di polo" on line 17), thus establishing what has been said so far as "non-language." This is reinforced by the fact that she repeats the question, saying "she didn't hear," a move that invites Martin to reformulate his answer, taking care not to say what has already been said. Martin retains Pierre's suggestion of "pala" and then transforms another French word, "laine," into Corsican, as "lena" (line 22). Here the teacher finally understands, or finally acknowledges, what has been said as close enough to warrant a show of understanding.

The way that the teacher handles this particular transfer from French beginning on line 28 is double-sided. First, there is the way she characterizes its intelligibility. On the one hand, she correctly interprets what Martin and Pierre have been trying to say as "a ball of wool." She signals this to the boys by *reinterpreting in French* what they have been struggling with in Corsican. This switch to French in the middle of a sequence in which she has been using Corsican exclusively is a comprehension check that shows that she assumes that French is the language of content in the boys' utterances. Yet she rhetorically construes the boys' utterances as unintelligible by prefacing her correct French interpretation with "What does that mean?" (spoken in Corsican) and following it with the comment in French that she "doesn't believe" that they would use a phrase like "una pala di lena" (line 34). This comment is also double-sided, for while it delegitimizes the boys' utterances, it also implies that they could have done better—that she can't believe that they are not mobilizing knowledge she believes they have.

Although she insists, in these lines, on the use of the word "ghjumellu" that was used in the story, she does accept the boys' choice of "wool" instead of the "string" described in the text. She provides them with the correct Corsican word for wool ("lana"), which she incoporates into the phrase "ghjumellu di lana." This is established, in her next turn, as being an acceptable substitute for "ghjumellu di canapu"—"why not?" she says (line 44). That is, she rejects "pala" on the grounds that it is simply not an authentic Corsican term for the object in question, but does not hold the boys rigidly to reproducing words from the original story when a close semantic variant does not impinge on the plot. Meanwhile, Pierre resumes the narrative by recapitulating a point he has successfully made before (about the cats playing on the stairs) and the teacher remarks that cats—and even children—like to play with wool. This comment in an informal key shifts the emphasis in the interaction away from teacher evaluation of the *form* of student utterances to a shared appreciation of story *content*.

The teacher's handling of what is ostensibly a problem of competence in Corsican is multifaceted. At the same time as she identifies "error" and "unintelligibility," and thus casts what the boys say as "not Corsican," she also incorporates the intent and content of their utterances into her own discourse. This is a form of what O'Connor and Michaels (1993) call teacher "revoicing" of student utterances, which functions to give credit to students for desired formulations while aligning their speech with school-valued formats and pedagogical goals. Martin and Pierre become, through her words, the authors of a descriptive phrase—a ball of wool—that was not in the original story but that is accepted as part of the classroom reformulation of the story through question-and-answer sequences. This authorial role legitimizes the children as speakers of Corsican and participants in Corsican literacy. The teacher also balances attention to form with attention to content, which validates the children's ability to understand and respond to Corsican texts, even if they do not have native speaker productive competence. It also legitimizes the collaboratively produced Corsican text—the summary that will be written based on the children's answers to the questions.

Excerpts X and XI (and their alternative representation as "strips" of discourse in Figures 6-1 and 6-2) also deal in complex ways with the attribution of competence and collaboration. What I have attempted to highlight in the two figures is the way that sequential utterances are interlocked, and the sense in which they can be seen, at least at certain moments in the interaction, as components of a single or a joint utterance.

Excerpt X

1	**Lisa:**	Assai robba da manghjà.
2		**Lots of things to eat.**
3	**Teacher:**	Ie, vale à dì?
4		**Yes, such as?**
5	**Lisa:**	A noce
6		**A nut**
7	**Teacher:**	Una noce
8		**One nut**
9	**Lisa:**	No, e noce
10		**No, nuts.**
11	**Teacher:**	E noce cusì, ci n'era assai=
12		**Nuts, that's it, there were many=**
13	**Lisa:**	noce=
14		**walnuts=**
15	**Teacher:**	noce=
16		**walnuts=**
17	**Lisa:**	castagne=
18		**chestnuts=**
19	**Teacher:**	castagne=
20		**chestnuts=**
21	**Lisa:**	amandule=
22		**almonds=**
23	**Teacher:**	amandule è perchè=
24		**almonds and because=**
25	**Martin:**	*et du mais*
26		*and corn*
27	**Teacher:**	è cum'avemu dettu avà? tu si scappatu à tempu, l'aghju
28		dettu, cumu si dice allora,
29		**and how did we say, you who just ran off a minute ago,**
30		**I said it, how is it said then,**
31		o—l'aghju dettu avà.
32		**oh, I said it now.**
33	**Martin:**	*je sais pas.*
34		*I don't know.*
35	**Teacher:**	l'aghju dettu avà, he!
36		**I just said it, eh!**
37	**Child:**	granone
38		**ears of corn**

39	Teacher:	Spighe di granone, e spighe di granone.
40		**Ears of corn, the ears of corn.**
41	Child:	*Mais il y était!*
42		***But he was there!***
43	Teacher:	Iè, aghju capitu, *tu avais cerné le problème,* và bè.
44		**Yes, I have understood,** ***you've identified the problem,***
45		**that's it.**

Excerpt XI

1	Pierre:	Vede chì=
2		**He sees that=**
3	Maria:	a scala=
4		**the ladder=**
5	Pierre:	chì a scala pe cullà in granaghju era=
6		**that the ladder leading up to the attic had been=**
7	Teacher:	era firmata=
8		**had been left=**
9	Pierre:	era firmata=
10		**had been left=**
11	Teacher:	Ai dettu dunque era fermata appughjata contra à u muru=
12		**You said therefore that it had been left leaning up against**
13		**the wall=**
14	Pierre:	contra à u muru=
15		**against the wall=**
16	Teacher:	E chì anu fattu i dui ghjatti dopu?
17		**And what did the two cats do after that?**
18	Pierre:	Sò cullati=
19		**They climbed**
20	Teacher:	Sò cullati tramindui=
21		**The two of them climbed=**
22	Pierre:	In granaghju=
23		**Up into the attic=**
24	Teacher:	Allora ch'ella era=
25		**While that was=**
26	Pierre:	*interdit*=
27		**forbidden=**
28	Teacher:	difesa; era *"interdit,"* avemu capitu allora ch'ella era difesa.
29		**forbidden; it was** ***"forbidden,"*** **we have understood that it**
30		**was forbidden.**

Now, the jointness here does not mean that there is no communicative hierarchy. The teacher clearly plays a defining, sometimes
overtly directive, role in shaping the linguistic outcome. This is
particularly evident in the first and last parts of Excerpt X (and Figure
6-1). But there are sequences in which her interventions have a more
collaborative than corrective character. For example, in Excerpt XI,
line 18 (and in the second strip of Figure 6-2), Pierre begins a sentence,

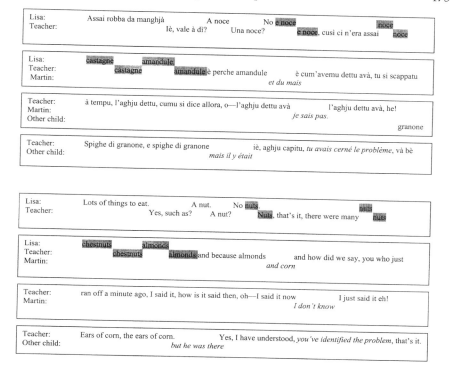

| Lisa: | Assai robba da manghjà | A noce | No e noce | noce |
| Teacher: | | Iè, vale à dì? | Una noce? | e noce, cusì ci n'era assai | noce |

Lisa:	castagne	amandule
Teacher:	castagne	amandule è perche amandule	è cum'avemu dettu avà, tu si scappatu
Martin:		*et du mais*

Teacher:	à tempu, l'aghju dettu, cumu si dice allora, o—l'aghju dettu avà	l'aghju dettu avà, he!
Martin:	*je sais pas.*
Other child:	granone

| Teacher: | Spighe di granone, e spighe di granone | iè, aghju capitu, *tu avais cerné le problème*, và bè |
| Other child: | *mais il y était* |

| Lisa: | Lots of things to eat. | A nut. | No nuts. | nuts |
| Teacher: | | Yes, such as? | A nut? | Nuts, that's it, there were many | nuts |

Lisa:	chestnuts	almonds
Teacher:	chestnuts	almonds and because almonds	and how did we say, you who just
Martin:		*and corn*

| Teacher: | ran off a minute ago, I said it, how is it said then, oh—I said it now | I just said it eh! |
| Martin: | *I don't know* |

| Teacher: | Ears of corn, the ears of corn. | Yes, I have understood, *you've identified the problem*, that's it. |
| Other child: | *but he was there* |

Figure 6-1.

"They climbed," and the teacher repeats and expands it with "tramindui"[both]. This is not a correction; in fact, it is almost as though the teacher were talking out loud with Pierre. Pierre does not miss his stride and continues with the next word of the sentence. Similarly, in lines 13-24 of Excerpt X (and in the first strip of Figure 6-1), we see the teacher echoing the names of the foods (nuts, chestnuts, almonds) enumerated by Lisa; it is Lisa's sequence and voice that leads. Moreover, the teacher is not the only person who intervenes: Maria provides the word "ladder" for Pierre on line 4 of Excerpt XI (and at the beginning of the first strip of Figure 6-2).

Another facet of this collaborative character involves acts of teacher incorporation of student utterances (which we have seen in the analysis of the ball of wool sequence in Excerpt IX). We find an interesting example of this in Excerpt XI (first strip of Figure 6-2), where the teacher interrupts Pierre (line 12), and finishes his sentence while saying "So you said that . . . ." This both anticipates her words and retroactively constructs them as Pierre's in a preemptive form of "revoicing." The teacher also aligns student speech with her own in Excerpt XI by incorporating

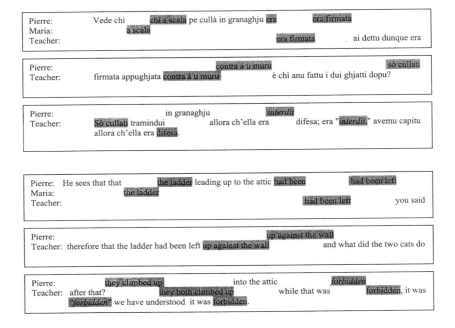

Figure 6-2.

Martin's interjection in French, "interdit" [forbidden], first in Corsican translation ("difesa"), then in its original language, and finally (prefaced by "we understand that") again in Corsican. On the one hand, her translation into the target language, Corsican, makes linguistic form (in this case, code choice) salient (see Arthur, 2001, p. 68). But the fact that she immediately follows with the French ("interdit"), and the incorporative "we understand that" to preface her second use of the Corsican "difesa," symbolically identifies the teacher and the children with a *bilingual* voice and a dual set of linguistic competencies. Here, we see how an ideological stance that concerns the preferred relationship between speakers and a language is interactionally constructed.

There is a breakdown, however, of the collaborative mode in Excerpt X (and second strip of Figure 6-1). At first glance, it is difficult to understand why Martin's interjection of the French word "maïs" [corn] on line 26 is not validated and incorporated in the way that his use of "interdit" [forbidden] is in Excerpt XI. But closer examination shows that his use of "corn" in French is rejected because, only five minutes earlier, there had been a long discussion of how "ears of corn" was said in Corsican. On line 27, the teacher accuses Martin of having left the room (she implies, without permission) and thus being responsible for having missed this discussion. When another child claims that Martin was not actually absent (line 41), the teacher comments, "yes, you've identified the problem." This comment frames the problem as one of attention and involvement: if Martin was there, he was not being the kind of active listener the teacher values. The teacher's comment thus embodies a stance toward the relationship between community and language in which linguistic incorporation hinges on social incorporation. Social incorporation is based on criteria of individual responsibility and collaborative engagement in the collectivity of the class.

This notion of collective responsibility is not just an implicit value displayed in discourse patterns; it is also a central feature of the explicit organization of the school on a "cooperative model." This model is part of the Freinet model of "new education," which emphasizes cooperative and inquiry-based learning in which student interests and student textual productions play a central role in the curriculum. Both teachers in this bilingual school belonged to the French Freinet association (la Fédération Internationale du Movement de l'Ecole Moderne) (Schlemminger, 1997). Each year, they had the children elect officers in a cooperative structure. Cooperative meetings were conducted almost every Monday morning. In principle, these meetings were to be student-run, and the students were supposed to play an active role in defining, prioritizing, and following through on classroom projects and other school activities.

To return to the question of language and cultural ownership, I believe that the image or ideal of the collectivity is particularly important in this bilingual classroom because it allows the texts created orally and in writing to belong to all of the people who are in the class, differences in their levels of input and competence notwithstanding. Martin is not taken to task because he doesn't know a word but rather because his social disengagement undermines a model in which collective competence can symbolically compensate for individual weaknesses (see also Berry & Weibe, 2001; Mets & Van den Hauwe, 2000). As we have seen, compensating for such weaknesses is important identity work in the context of Corsican language teaching and its goals of revitalizing the minority language.

COMPARISON AND CONTRAST WITH FRENCH LITERACY WORK

Shared Practice: Equivalence and Parity

When we compare and contrast French and Corsican literacy work, we also find evidence of dual pedagogical emphases: on creating political parity for Corsican and French and on differentiating Corsican as a language of privileged cultural identity. There are many similarities in the ways in which the children in this class do literacy work in Corsican and French. In both languages, children do a great deal of collective oral preparation for writing. Texts produced in the classroom are also often read out loud, and during these oral performances of texts the teacher carefully monitors the children's pronunciation, delivery, and grammar. Collective oral preparation for writing is almost always followed by collective composition of a text. Either the teacher or a student secretary writes on the blackboard the sentences that have been composed out loud by the group. This written text is subject to further editing based on teacher (and sometimes student) input. When there is a student secretary, the teacher makes on-the-spot corrections to spelling and grammar. There is also a premium placed on graphic representation (handwriting, visual arrangement, cutting and pasting). This attention contributes to the "wholeness" and authoritativeness of the texts that are produced and reproduced. This wholeness and correctness are also emphasized by reading out loud and through the act of copying; texts become embodied through these practices.

Differentiation from French: Texts, Independent Work and Evaluation

Yet there are subtle differences in the status of French versus Corsican texts and the literacy work done around them. Almost all Corsican texts used in the class come to the children as this one did—orally. In the year that I observed the class, only one professionally printed Corsican language book was handed out to the children, and this was only after it had been read aloud first. The children never encounter a Corsican text first as a written product, and they do almost no silent or individual reading of such texts. In contrast, they are regularly assigned French language books. These are read at home, and they have to write book reports on them, in French. French texts and worksheets are also given out in class for individual, rather than collective work.

As we have seen in some of the preceding excerpts, there are also differences in the way that individual competence is judged in French as compared to Corsican. Despite the fact that the teacher does a great deal of correcting of Corsican oral and written production at all stages of the process, this correction is done on volunteers during group exercise. They are almost never forced to volunteer. When the teacher does force participation by calling on an individual student, she lowers the bar of linguistic performance, often only requiring the children to repeat a Corsican sentence that either has just been spoken or has been worked and reworked many times (see Sandrine at the end of Excerpt III). This is a form of what Chick has labeled "safetalk": school language practices that allow students (and teachers) to avoid the loss of face associated with being wrong in public (Hornberger & Chick, 2001; see also Arthur, 2001; Mets & Van den Hauwe, 2000). While it is true that the self-selection norm also operates in French, and shy or weak students can avoid heavy participation in that language as well, they are far more regularly forced to demonstrate their individual knowledge in French than in Corsican. This is also reflected in the examination system. At the end of the year, they have to pass written tests in French, but are assigned a grade in Corsican based on the teacher's global evaluation of their ability.

Despite a shared attention to form in French and Corsican, there are also differences in the way that spelling and grammar are treated in one language versus the other. Points of Corsican spelling and grammar—like the *cambiarine* that appear in this lesson—are taught formally and explicitly, much like French. Yet, as I have mentioned, this formalization is done less frequently than in French, and it is usually closely tied to work being done on a particular text (as in the case of the third person plural worksheet that was developed in response to the lesson described here). But overall, Corsican grammar has a much less visible role than French grammar as an autonomous subject. This can be seen by looking in the children's class notebooks, where the volume of French grammar worksheets, exercises, and tables is three times greater than similar exercises in Corsican.

These differences in French versus Corsican literacy practices help to explain children's responses to an interview I conducted about Corsican versus French spelling. All of the children reported that French spelling was "easier" and that they had greater difficulty writing in Corsican. This is in fact not entirely borne out by their written production, where I see more similarities than differences in the volume and nature of their spelling mistakes in both languages. They also told me that they "did more" reading and writing in French. Again, this contrasts with my observations of the class, where there is virtual parity in the classroom hours spent dealing with texts in Corsican and in French. But the children's perceptions are shaped by a number of other factors: (1) their homework, that is, the time they spend outside of class reading and writing reports on French books; (2) the fact that they are put to the test more regularly in French in the class; and (3) the differences in formal language teaching previously described. In other words, the children have learned to associate formal models of learning and testing with the acquisition of competence and may tend to "misrecognize" skills that they have acquired through repeated practice that is not always accompanied by formal explication. There is also no doubt that outside of the classroom, the children have no opportunity to practice Corsican literacy skills and that parents, if they intervene in this domain, do so in French.

CONCLUSIONS

Symbolically, the bilingualism of the classroom is about parity—equivalence—between Corsican and French. There are many ways in which teaching practices in this classroom and in this school are oriented toward that parity. Children work with Corsican texts and work in Corsican at least as much as they work in French. Their oral and written work is evaluated, shaped, and corrected by the teacher with reference to authoritative models of "good usage." In this respect, we can see the classroom as having its own microculture, in which language identity and linguistic authority are constructed in classroom interaction.

But the fact remains that the two languages do not have parity in the wider society, and the school is not insulated from that wider context. The presence of the "outside" within the classroom walls involves the teacher in the constant management of difference. The first kind of difference she must manage is difference-as-a-problem. The wide variation in children's competencies in Corsican and the fact that they are almost all less competent in Corsican than in French pose a problem both for the functioning of the classroom (where 50% of the content is done in Corsican) and for the ideological validation of authentic ownership of the language. We have seen this on the micro-interactional level, in the nuanced way that the teacher handles children's errors in Corsican. In some respect, the accomplishment of the bilingual classroom requires that the children have, and have attributed to them, linguistic competence in Corsican. When the teacher incorporates the children's French or French-influenced utterances into her Corsican discourse, she symbolically validates the high listening comprehension that allows the children to do the bilingualism of the class, that is, to follow lessons in all academic subjects in Corsican. In doing so, she capitalizes on a competence that they all have individually at the same time as she symbolically confers a competence that they only have collectively.

We have also seen that the discursive attribution of oral competence takes place at a collective, rather than at an individual level. That is, it is the ability of the whole class to answer questions or to create oral and written texts that "counts as" competence and allows the lesson to move forward. On the one hand, the kind of "safetalk" facilitated through the teacher's incorporations and emphasis on collective work does insulate the weaker speakers in the class from criticism, and the strongest speakers end up "carrying" the class. Yet in contrast to the school contexts described by Hornberger and Chick (2001), Arthur (2001), and Mets and Van den Hauwe (2000), safetalk in the Corsican classroom does not just disguise a lack of learning taking place. Rather, it is a particular kind of learning involving language and emphasizing linguistic identity. To return to a theme raised in the introduction, the collective ownership of Corsican texts that is created through these patterns of literacy practice is a way of de-emphasizing the stratifying properties of literacy. Taken as a whole, the oral work done around texts in this classroom stands in opposition to an "essentialist" model of language and cultural identity, by defining the relationship between the two as a set of socially situated practices and not as an innate quality or ability. Classroom practices in Corsican create conditions for students to become "legitimate peripheral participants" (Lave & Wenger, 1991) in a community of linguistic practice. The teacher's scaffolding of Corsican literacy work allows the children to work as linguistic apprentices who have legitimate relationships with the language in question and to contribute meaningfully to a final product (e.g., a text, a dramatic reading of a text) without being fully responsible for that final product.

Other pedagogical strategies that differentiate the literacy work done around Corsican from French are oriented toward "giving" the children an authentic Corsican voice. This is the explicit rationale given by the teacher for not giving the children Corsican texts before they have been spoken out loud, and it is the function of the oral repetition of correct answers and completed texts. Through these practices, the "right" words and the "right" pronunciations are put into the children's mouths. I think that this impulse can be related to the status of Corsican as a language of culture. The project of the bilingual schools is not just teaching Corsican to children who don't know it, but also teaching a Corsican that will be recognized as authentic by the society at large. This makes "learner's Corsican" highly problematic, particularly with regard to pronunciation. Pronunciation is key to the linguistic identity work that is part of the implicit curriculum of this bilingual school.

But difference between Corsican and French language pedagogies also enters the classroom through another path, which has to do with the philosophical and institutional status of bilingual education. Teaching in Corsican—doing bilingual education—is always, implicitly, about differentiation from dominant, monolingual models of pedagogy and, by extension, identity. This is partly because bilingual education is so new on Corsica, and the teaching of Corsican takes place outside a highly regimented institutional structure. There are no detailed, standardized evaluation criteria for bilingual classes, and there is certainly no enforcement of the general standards in the one existing document published by the Academy (in fact, not every bilingual teacher even has it). Although this lack of criteria is perceived as a problem by many teachers in bilingual schools, it also gives the teachers a measure of freedom that they do not have (or do not perceive themselves to have) with respect to the teaching of French. So, when I commented to the teacher in this class that she did less formalized grammar/spelling teaching in Corsican than in French, she said that yes, it was true. Rather than saying that she ought to do more in Corsican, she said that she regretted the extent to which she taught grammar and spelling for their own sake in French. She would rather, she said, that all of this formal instruction flow out of the exigencies of meaningful literacy activities: reading a text, writing a story, or sending a letter. These comments identify her pedagogical practices in Corsican as the most satisfactory expression of her teaching philosophy, with values centered around cooperative learning, multiculturalism, and student-initiated and driven projects. While these values also shaped how she worked in French, her teaching in that language was highly constrained by standards of evaluation in the French school system. She knew that parents and future teachers of her students (at the junior high level) would measure her children's aptitude and her teaching by how well they read and wrote in French. She also knew that people who were not particularly sympathetic to bilingual education would use any "failures" or shortcomings of her students in spelling or grammar to discredit the entire bilingual project. And, finally, conversations I have had with her revealed something else: she too has misgivings about the efficacy of her methods when she compares her students' mastery of French with her own at their age. So even though bilingual education has been part of her questioning of the educational status quo and traditional French language education based heavily on formal spelling and grammar instruction, she is not fully able to extract herself, practically or psychologically, from its linguistic ideologies and hierarchies.

So the bilingual classroom is also structurally and intermittently in pedagogical practice a place where these dominant ideologies surface and structure the way that both Corsican and French are taught and the way that language competence is imagined. It is a place where the recognition of the socially enacted dimension of linguistic identity cohabits with the popular, essentialist models that naturalize the connection between language and identity and which structure most popular language attitudes, much historical and current educational practice and policy, and the contemporaneous sociopolitical context of bilingual education on Corsica.

NOTES

This research was supported by grants from the National Science Foundation and the Spencer Foundation.

1. See Woolard and Schieffelin (1994) for an overview of theoretical and methodological approaches to language ideology.
2. Transcription conventions: In the original, Corsican is in regular type and French in italics. In the translation, Corsican is translated in regular boldface and French in italicized boldface. Phonetic representations of pronunciation are in brackets.
3. See Arthur (2001, p. 68) for similar discursive indices of teacher's attention to form over content.
4. These can be seen, by and large, as phonemes, though there is some debate among Corsican linguists about the phonemic status of certain orthographic conventions.
5. The diminutive suffix -ucciu on "Martin" creates an affectionate tone.
6. The vocative "Ghjuvà" is a shortened form of the full name Ghjuvan-Maria, the Corsican version of Jean-Marie's name. It has a familiar, affectionate inflection.
7. This is complicated by the fact that there are many influences from French that have been incorporated in the language for so long that they are no longer perceived as French by older native speakers, but may be branded "impure" by language activists.

REFERENCES

Arthur, J. (2001). Codeswitching and collusion: Classroom interaction in Botswana primary schools. In M. Heller & M. Martin-Jones (Eds.), *Voices of Authority: Education and Linguistic Difference* (pp. 57–76). Westport, CT: Ablex.

Berry, R., & Weibe, A. (2001). Large-group lessons in two inclusion classrooms: Providing access to the general education curriculum for students with learning disabilities. Paper presented at the 22d Annual Ethnography in Education Research Forum, University of Pennsylvania, Philadelphia.

Cazden, C. (1988). *Classroom Discourse: The Language of Teaching and Learning.* Portsmouth, NH: Heinemann.

Collins, J. (1991). Hegemonic practice: Literacy and standard language in educational practice in public education. In C. Mitchell & K. Weiler (Eds.), *Rewriting Literacy* (pp. 229–253). New York: Bergin and Garvey.

Gee, J. (1991). What is literacy? In Candace Mitchell & Kathleen Weiler (Eds.), *Rewriting Literacy* (pp. 3-8). New York: Bergin and Garvey.

Heath, S. B. (1983). *Ways with Words.* New York: Cambridge University Press.

Heller, M. (1999). *Linguistic Minorities and Modernity.* Paramus, NJ: Prentice-Hall.

Henze, R., & Davis, K. (1999). Authenticity and identity: Lessons from indigenous language education. *Anthropology and Education Quarterly, 30*(1), 3–21.

Hornberger, N., & Chick, J. K. (2001). Co-constructing school safetime: Safetalk practices in Peruvian and South African classrooms. In M. Heller & M. Martin-Jones (Eds.), *Voices of Authority: Education and Linguistic Difference* (pp. 31–55). Westport, CT: Ablex.

184 Linguistic Anthropology of Education

Jaffe, A. (1999) *Ideologies in Action: Language Politics on Corsica*. Berlin: Mouton de Gruyter.

Jaffe, A. (2000). Comic performance and the articulation of hybrid identity. *Pragmatics*, 10(1), 39–60.

Jaffe, A. (2001). Authority and authenticity: Corsican discourse on bilingual education. In M. Heller & M. Martin-Jones (Eds.), *Voices of Authority: Education and Linguistic Difference* (pp. 269–296). Westport, CT: Ablex.

Lave, J., & Wenger, E. (1991). *Situated Learning: Legitimate Peripheral Participation*. New York: Cambridge University Press.

Mets, B., & Van den Hauwe, J. (2000). Masked heterogeneity in a multilingual classroom. Manuscript.

Michaels, S. (1991). Hearing the connections between children's oral and written discourse. In C. Mitchell & K. Weiler (Eds.), *Rewriting Literacy* (pp. 103–121). New York: Bergin and Garvey.

O'Connor, M. C., & Michaels, S. (1993). Aligning academic task and participation status through revoicing: Analysis of a classroom discourse strategy. *Anthropology and Education Quarterly*, 24(4), 318–335.

Rampton, B. (1995). *Crossing*. New York: Longman.

Schlemminger, G. (1997). History of Freinet pedagogy. Actes du séminaire international de la pédagogie Freinet. Online: http://freinet.org/icem/history.htm

Street, B. (1995). *Social Literacies*. New York: Longman.

7

"Ellos se comen las eses/heces"

The Perceived Language Differences of Matambú

Karen Stocker

As Kathryn Woolard asserts, "we look to social facts to explain linguistic facts" (1989, p. 3). In the case of Matambú, a small Chorotega indigenous reservation in Northwestern Costa Rica, the fact of the social inferiority ascribed to Indians within this self-proclaimed European-like nation leads to a perception of their lesser linguistic capacity. In turn, this perceived language difference serves to anchor these residents in a stigmatized social position. While social facts do, in this case, explain linguistic facts, the reverse is also true. What are taken to be linguistic facts—although oftentimes these are fictions—index, explain, justify, and rationalize the inferior treatment of indigenous residents by dominant society, who see the former both as diverging from the national linguistic norm and "choosing" a lesser position in society.

This chapter describes a particular case of indexicality, as the use of a particular dialect is perceived to identify a given group of speakers as intellectually inferior. It describes processes of regimentation, as language ideology (which privileges standard language and values its speakers) is taught directly in the classroom, and as teachers use this to rationalize their treatment of students from the reservation. The chapter also describes linguistic creativity and the poetic function of language, as students draw attention to and parody types of speech. Furthermore, this chapter examines the ways in which speakers' performance of a standard language or their divergence from it may be related to their social location as national subjects.

Benedict Anderson draws attention to the way tools of the colonial state such as the census, map, and museum have created sharp categories characterized by an "intolerance of multiple, politically 'transvestite,' blurred, or changing identifications" (1983, p. 166). In the context I address here, the seemingly impermeable (though arbitrarily placed) boundary of the reservation artificially-yet-authoritatively drawn on the national map differentiates standard speakers from non-standard speakers.

In the absence of traditional markers of difference (such as a distinct worldview, style of dress, foodways, religion, or a stark difference in physical appearance) available to distinguish Matambugueños (as those from the reservation of Matambú are known) from those not from there, outsiders have invented, and to a great degree come to believe in, the existence of such essential differences. The perception of language difference, in particular, has proven persistent. Firmly in place, this perceived language difference has had serious repercussions for students from the reservation who attend high school outside it, where they meet with discrimination from teachers and peers on a daily basis. The idea that Matambugueños are not only culturally distinct, but also inferior, hinges in part on this perception of linguistic difference.

My argument consists of several points. Matambú's perceived ethnic difference as "indigenous" is tied to its inhabitants' residence within an arbitrarily placed political boundary. This imposed identity is a stigmatized one. While it is common for outsiders to project the social value of an ethnic group onto that group's linguistic practices, the reverse happens in Matambú. As a result of their ascribed Indian identity, Matambugueños are viewed as speaking an Indian dialect, although their language use is phonetically, morphologically, and lexically indistinguishable from that of other individuals from the same province. I argue that people from surrounding communities imagine this linguistic difference in order to view an arbitrary political boundary as a cultural one. Thus, they envision a traditional ethnic boundary marker, in this case language, where it does not exist. The language deemed inferior that is seen as unique to Matambugueños does exist inside the reservation, but it is also common to surrounding areas throughout the province of Guanacaste. The perceived correlation between ethnic and linguistic difference, however, results in the popular perception that this dialect is used on the reservation only.

Thus I observe a particular sort of regimentation or framing of verbal interactions in and around the reservation. Speakers known or suspected to be from the reservation are heard to be speaking a stigmatized dialect, and this often places them in a subordinate position. Schools reinforce this type of regimentation. Though at times teachers explicitly argue against stereotyping, the overall effect of schooling on language ideology is to support the stereotypes of indigenous speakers. Thus, I also argue that regimentation takes place through public schooling, is spreading to the reservation itself, and that it may inhibit the school success of students from Matambú. Language ideology is key to this situation, because the attitudes surrounding differential language use—attitudes learned in part through schooling—shape people's interpretations of speakers perceived to be from the reservation.

DEVELOPMENT OF THE RESEARCH QUESTION AND METHODOLOGY

My focus on the ascribed Indian identity of Matambugueños represents the culmination of several years of research. When I began my studies in Matambú in 1993, my research focus had nothing to do with ethnic identity, and Matambú was only one of four communities in my comparative study on machismo. Its status as a reservation was incidental; I chose it as a study site due to its geographical location. However, the issue of ethnic identity soon took precedence over my initial topic of study, as it proved to be a more salient issue in the community itself. I continued to study issues related to ethnic identity and language throughout six years after that initial study. My stints of fieldwork have varied in duration from two years to ten days, between 1993 and 1999. They have involved hundreds of interviews and conversations and thousands of hours of participant observation. My interviews encompassed a wide spectrum of issues, including identity, the history of the reservation and its effects on ethnic identity, and narrative practices.

During that time, it became clear that the high school experience, in which some Matambugueños come into prolonged contact, for the first time, with those who will impose an indigenous identity upon them, was a key site to examine identity formation. Thus, most recently, I returned to Matambú in 1999 to spend one year living on the reservation, but also attending the local high school outside the reservation on a daily basis.

During that year, I conducted 1,125 hours of observation in the school, I interviewed all twenty-eight high school students from Matambú in depth, and I interviewed twenty-four former high school students from the reservation as well as several Matambugueños of high school age who never attended. I interviewed all thirty-seven teachers and administrators from the high school as well as ten promi-nent community members and leaders from Hojancha, the neighboring town in which the high school is located. I held meetings with Matambugueño parents, as well as less formal interviews with non-Matambugueño students. I followed fourteen homeroom classes for one week each (a total of 346 students) and interviewed three to four students from each of these classes in depth. I observed classes taught by all teachers, covering all subjects taught in the school. Among these were the classes of two Spanish teachers (one teaching certain grades, and the other the remaining grades) whose lessons addressed literature from Costa Rica and Spain and grammar lessons in Castilian and Costa Rican Spanish.

My focus was on discrimination in high school—prejudices and dis-criminatory actions that take a variety of forms, have manifestations too numerous to address in the context of this chapter, and have various targets, but which most often affect students from the reservation. While this discrimination is talked about in terms of "race," it has more to do with Indianness as defined by place of residence within the reser-vation, given that the vast majority of students in the high school are physically similar to the students from the reservation. However, an-other axis of difference is social class. All of these attributes—class, place, and color—intermingle in complex ways. While, in fact, they may not be attributes that clearly distinguish inhabitants of the reservation from others, they do, in their perceived existence, constitute the domi-nant lines of division. Thus, a dark child not from the reservation might be discriminated against more than a whiter child from the reservation. A poor student from the dominant town might also find himself or her-self the target of discrimination. Most often, however, Matambugueños are viewed as being darker, poorer, and of a different ethnic category than others, so they are the students most often discriminated against.

The examples offered in the present chapter come from the 1999 high school–based study. However, to begin to address the more recent findings of my study—those related to the linguistic questions ad-dressed here—I begin with a brief history of the reservation.

HISTORICAL CONTEXT AND SOCIAL SITUATION

Externally imposed changes in affiliation are not new to the town of Matambú. In 1825, the entire province of Guanacaste was annexed to Costa Rica from neighboring Nicaragua (Quesada Pacheco, 1991, p. 33). Thus, former Nicaraguans instantly became Costa Rican. In 1979, the town of Matambú, located in the province of Guanacaste, was arbitrar-ily named the Chorotega indigenous reservation. This was done despite the fact that official Costa Rican history claims that the country's indigenous populations were rendered extinct in the colonial era, four centuries earlier (Arroyo, 1972; Gagini, 1917, p. 72; Monge Alfaro, 1960; Peralta, 1893). Matambú was one of twenty-three reservations that were demarcated where peoples self-identified as indigenous or where indigenous peoples were known to have lived at the time of colonization. Matambú fit the latter criterion. Though all of Guanacaste, the northern-most province of Costa Rica, is considered Chorotega territory, just one small area was selected to become the Chorotega reservation.[1] This labeling did not have the effect of making Matambú's inhabitants suddenly Indian—a stigmatized identity in a country that projects an image of whiteness.[2] Instead, it effectively absolved all those people outside the reservation of this stigmatized label in spite of their identical cultural heritage. With the exception of a small white settler population dominating the neighboring town of Hojancha, those people living in the towns surrounding the reservation share the same cultural heritage of those inside its borders. According to those I interviewed on the matter, this issue was not disputed before to the 1970s, when the reservation was demarcated.

There are no significant differences in language, religion, or worldview between people inside and outside the reservation. Thus, the defining factor for Indian identity—at least ascribed Indian identity—is place of residence. If two siblings live on either side of the reservation's boundary, only one will be recognized as Indian. A 16-year-old commented on this when he noted that "It's not because of the race, but more because of the name [of the reservation which marks its inhabitants as Indian]. I'm from the indigenous reservation and for that reason they discriminate against me."

Aside from difference in place of residence, however, the usual markers of cultural difference are conspicuously absent from the border between Matambú and its surrounding communities. Linguistic difference, however, is noted as a cultural attribute that sets Matambugueños apart from those who are, for all practical purposes, indistinguishable from them if place of residence is overlooked, despite the fact that I have been unable to document systematic linguistic differences between the reservation and the surrounding areas.

In the absence of a legal definition of Indianness in Costa Rica, the term has come to be synonymous with residence within one of the nation's twenty-three reservations (as only Indians may own reservation land). However, a secondary lay interpretation of the label "indigenous" holds that "official" Indians are those who speak an indigenous language. In some cases, scholars discuss "remaining" aboriginal tribes in Costa Rica and list those who have maintained or recuperated an indigenous language (Arroyo, 1972, p. 13; Barrientos et al., 1982, p. 251; Bozzoli de Wille, 1986; Guevara Berger & Chacón, 1992, p. 38). One set

of scholars of Costa Rican indigenous groups states explicitly, in defining what it means to be indigenous in Costa Rica, that "Indigenous
people speak their own languages" (Palmer, Sánchez, & Mayorga, 1993,
p. 27). This correlation between ethnic identity and linguistic difference
is a key theoretical underpinning of this chapter. It is this and other
theoretical concerns to which I now turn.

THEORETICAL FRAMEWORK

My analysis uses the concept of language ideology, which, according
to Woolard and Schieffelin, "relates the microculture of communicative
action to political economic considerations of power and social inequality, confronting macrosocial constraints on language behavior" (1994,
p. 72). It is the goal of this chapter to demonstrate how perceived
language use and social status are inextricably linked in the
Matambugueño/Guanacastecan context. Woolard and Schieffelin note
that "language varieties that are regularly associated with (and thus
index) particular speakers are often revalorized—or misrecognized—
not just as symbols of group identity, but as emblems of political
allegiance or of social, intellectual, or moral worth" (1994, p. 61). Furthermore, such "symbolic revalorization often makes discrimination on
linguistic grounds publicly acceptable" (1994, p. 62). I argue that, indeed, discrimination is made acceptable through linguistic "proof" in
the context of Matambú, but that the perceived language difference of
Matambugueños hinges on the common perception that language is a
key marker of ethnic difference (and, in this case, the perception that
"ethnic" difference is a marker of linguistic difference).

Adams notes that "Perhaps the most commonly cited ethnic marker
is language and there is no question that the loss of language signals
not only the loss of basic tools of self-expression, but also much of the
cognitive framework [i.e., indigenous beliefs and cultural differences
also assumed to exist in the Matambugueño case] that depends on the
persistence of these forms" (1991, p. 199). This tie between language and
ethnic groups' distinctiveness is so strong that one scholar refers to the
"equation of language and culture" (Abercrombie, 1991, p. 98). Thus it
is not uncommon for a given language to stand for a people, and a
people for a language. This is particularly expected of indigenous
peoples, although most of these now either live within diglossic contexts or have adopted the language of the colonizer.

Greg Urban speaks to these situations and their consequences:

> Due to the semipermeable membrane phenomenon, the language of the
> dominant group tends to spread to the dominated group, while the dom-
> inated language recedes. However, de-ideologized elements of culture are
> not subjected to the same pressure. Consequently, they tend to persist even

after the language with which they were originally associated has disap-
peared. (Urban, 1991, pp. 318-19)

Although the inhabitants of the reservation speak only Spanish, they
are still associated with an Indian language deemed socially inferior.
Urban asserts that "linguistic relationships between European and
Amerindian languages congealed into symbolically meaningful and
manipulable signs" in various parts of Latin America, and that these
"meanings can be traced to the relational indexical characteristics of the
languages as signs that took shape during the early years of contact"
(1991, p. 321). This may explain why the expectation that indigenous
peoples maintain indigenous language persists so strongly and why, in
spite of linguistic change, they may still be considered representative
of, or represented by, a given language.

Yet this equation of language and ethnicity is most problematic in the
geographic region in which I work. First, as Renan states, "[l]anguage
invites people to unite, but it does not force them to do so" (Renan, 1990,
p. 16). Bonfil Batalla, in a similar line of argument, asserts that

the problem [with using language as a definitive ethnic marker] consists
of [the fact that] speaking an indigenous language, while it is an important
fact, does not permit the conclusion that all of the speakers and only the
speakers of aboriginal languages constitute the total indigenous population. (Bonfil Batalla, 1989, p. 46; translation mine)

Bonfil Batalla further notes that language is an inadequate (and misleading) ethnic marker given that in all countries "there is a sector of
Indians that does not speak the aboriginal language, just as there is a
number of speakers of these languages [such as non-indigenous
Guaraní speakers in Paraguay and academics who have studied indigenous languages] that are not defined as indigenous" (Bonfil Batalla,
1972, p. 106; translation mine). In spite of the problems inherent in
viewing language as an index of ethnic difference, this occurs in the case
at hand. Indeed, there is a "tendency to project a one language/one
social group interpretation" (Urban, 1991, p. 309).

However, the situation that I examine takes this one step further. As
I show later in the chapter, it is not that linguistic difference leads people
to conclude that inhabitants of the reservation are ethnically different,
but the reverse. As a result of Matambugueños' geopolitical separation
from the rest of society, through their town's reservation status, outsiders perceive linguistic variation in speakers from the reservation. Le
Page and Tabouret-Keller assert that "Language is frequently used as a
defining characteristic of ethnic groups and genetic inferences are made
on the basis of those groups" (1985, p. 44). However, I argue that the

opposite is the case in the township of Hojancha and in the town of the same name. In that area, a form of speech is defined as "Indian" because those who speak it live within an arbitrarily placed political boundary.

As several linguists note, where there exists linguistic variation, there are often prejudicial attitudes toward varieties which deviate from the standard speech. According to Gordon Allport, "especially in a culture where uniformity is prized, the name of *any* deviant carries with it *ipso facto* a negative value-judgment" (1974, p. 112). In similar fashion, Labov asserts that "if a certain group of speakers uses a particular variant, then the social values attributed to that group will be transferred to that linguistic variant" (1972b, p. 251). Thus, perceived linguistic deviance carries with it social consequences. I will argue that perhaps in response to the need of Hojancheños or non-Matambugueño Guanacastecos to view an arbitrary political boundary as a cultural one, they perceive a traditional boundary marker such as language where it does not exist.

Douglas Foley's explanations are useful in exposing the logic behind such a practice. Though Foley's insights come from an entirely different geographical area, they are relevant to the case at hand as well. In the line of thought Foley refers to, "the white outsider [tries] to find traditional Mesquaki culture in essential material cultural objects and practices. . . . The logic of this approach goes like this: If these people have some obvious traditional traits and objects, surely they are still Indian" (1995, p. 94). By analogy, in the case of Matambú, if it can be proven (through remaining cultural practices) that Matambugueños are truly Indian, they can be more easily differentiated from the larger society. Thus, perhaps, outsiders can rationalize their differential—and prejudicial—treatment of Matambugueños. Gal and Woolard suggest that "the standard language . . . defines (and legitimates) a political territory, sometimes precisely because it is not spoken by any actual group" (1995, p. 135). For Matambú, the perception that Guanacastecan Spanish is spoken only in Matambú legitimates the political creation of a reservation and the mistreatment of its residents.

Public education also has a role in this identification of Matambugueños as essentially different. Both directly and indirectly, schools are principal sites of the inculcation of language ideologies. Le Page and Tabouret-Keller point out that "there is a tendency in a number of modern nation-states to wish to make ethnic consciousness synonymous with national consciousness, and language is frequently seen as a major tool for this purpose, via the education system" (1985, p. 249). My own data support both this and Ferguson's assertion that in a diglossic context, "the actual learning of H [the prestige variety] is chiefly accomplished by the means of formal education" (1972, p. 239). Schools are key actors in the perpetuation of attitudes that identify the use of particular dialects as indexes of social rankings. Susan Gal affirms Bourdieu's suggestion that "linguistic forms have no power in themselves, they only reflect the power of the groups they index. But [Bourdieu] adds that the educational system succeeds in legitimating a particular linguistic variant . . . [and] presenting it instead as an inherently better form" (Gal, 1989, pp. 353-54). Thus, schools are linked to what Collins refers to as "the ideological core of prescriptivism . . .— that 'correcting language' leads to social betterment" (1996, pp. 208–9).

Yet while indexicality links linguistic practices to essentialized beliefs about types of people, people are also capable of recognizing and reacting to the ways their language use marks them. Those who navigate two dialectical forms in a diglossic situation know how to employ different ones depending on the context. As Giles and Powesland note, "It is possible, in the case of an individual who lives near an 'accent border' (a somewhat arbitrary geographical boundary between regions with identifiable accents) for a speaker to possess more than one regional 'branch' " (1975, p. 171). Such an individual will select linguistic forms based on the demands of the situation. "The speaker is motivated, consciously or sub-consciously, to conform to the behaviours that are overtly or covertly prescribed for the situation in question" (Coupland, 1985, p. 155). Basso comments on this phenomenon when he notes that:

> Sociolinguists have observed repeatedly that the languages and language varieties of multilingual speech communities typically exhibit *functional differentiation*. This is a convenient but overly abbreviated way of noting that when members of such communities engage in verbal interaction they do not alternate randomly between distinct linguistic codes but choose systematically among them and put them to specialized uses. (Basso, 1979, pp. 7-8; emphasis in original)

The speakers central to this chapter employ accommodation to diminish the negative stigmas attached to particular linguistic varieties. In the case at hand, accommodation is used to eschew the discriminatory treatment accorded to speakers of the non-prestige variant. Thus, as Giles and Powesland point out, "accommodation through speech can be regarded as an attempt on the part of a speaker to modify or disguise his persona in order to make it more acceptable to the person addressed" (Giles & Powesland, 1975, p. 158).

Sometimes speakers do not accommodate to a higher-status dialect because they cannot speak it. But sometimes non-accommodation may be employed pointedly as a strategy of calling attention to usually unrecognized linguistic competence in more than one dialect. Basso argues that "if it is useful to understand that language alternations convey messages about what is 'present' in social situations, it is equally important to recognize that they may also convey messages about what is 'absent' from them as well" (1979, p. 11). I will show how selective non-accommodation draws attention to the differential values given to different dialects. Giles and Powesland note that accommodation "seems to depend for its effectiveness upon its *not* being recognized as such by the receiver" as "detection by the listener of accommodation in this category would possibly tend to discredit the speaker" (1975, pp. 169-170; emphasis in original). However, in cases where its non-use is employed to call attention to linguistic expectations, the purposeful recognition of one's ability to accommodate effectively signals speakers' linguistic creativity.

In spite of the realities of individuals' linguistic competence in more than one dialect, however, at times perception is stronger than reality, where linguistic expectations are concerned. The equation of language and culture is so strong that sometimes people will conflate linguistic difference with cultural, racial, or ethnic difference even when there is no linguistic difference in existence. Williams, Whitehead, and Miller found that although a child may come to speak the prestige code to perfection, he or she "might still be perceived as speaking in a nonstandard way" (1971, p. 109). Williams, Whitehead, and Miller demonstrated this by superimposing white children's speech on videotaped images of African-American children and having viewers evaluate the child's speech as standard or non-standard. In many cases, viewers evaluated what they thought was African-American children's speech (by virtue of the image they saw) as non-standard, although they may have judged that same speech as standard when it was played along with the visual image of a white child.

> In general, findings indicated that the videotape image showing the child's ethnicity affects ratings of his language in the direction of racial stereotyping expectations. For black children the bias was in the direction of expecting them to sound more nonstandard and ethnic than their white peers. (Williams et al., 1971, p. 170)

This finding of perceived linguistic difference on the basis of racial or ethnic difference has serious repercussions for schooling. "A teacher in a classroom situation is likely to expect less of a child with a nonstandard accent than of one with a standard accent" (Giles & Powesland, 1975, p. 107).

INDEXICALITY, REGIMENTATION, AND CREATIVITY IN MATAMBÚ AND HOJANCHA

In the case of Matambú, the linguistic relationship between Spanish speakers and speakers of Amerindian languages is no longer in existence, given that Spanish is the language spoken by both Indians (as defined by their residence on the reservation) and non-Indians (all others) in this region. However, the correlative social relationship is still apparent in the dominant belief that the language difference continues to underlie and justify the unequal treatment of "Indians." While in many cases ethnic groups are deemed distinct due to their linguistic difference, as described previously, the reverse occurs in Matambú. Based on the arbitrary geopolitical boundary which identifies Matambú as a distinct ethnic aggregate, it is assumed that Matambugueños speak a language other than Spanish. This belief is prevalent on the local level (but not on a national level).

On national and academic levels, Matambú is considered insufficiently Indian to merit reservation status. Locally, however, its inhabitants are viewed as Indian enough for them to be the recipients of near constant prejudice.[3] The language situation parallels this phenomenon. Similarly, on a national scale the absence of an indigenous language[4] marks Matambugueños as not legitimately Indian. But on the local level, the powerful perception that Matambugueños do speak differently proves their difference and justifies discrimination against them.

Similarly, if one recalls that Matambú's sudden reservation status did not result in the immediate Indianness of its inhabitants, but rather absolved those outside the reservation of stigmatized Indian status, the perception of linguistic difference makes sense. There is, indeed, a dialect associated with the Province of Guanacaste, in which Matambú is located, which differs from the standard Spanish spoken in Costa Rica—identified with the speech style of those who live in the Central Plateau and capitol city. On a local level, where individuals draw lines of division between themselves and the "Indians" (who are considered to reside in Matambú only), this dialect gets reduced from being a variant characteristic of all of Guanacaste to one spoken uniquely in Matambú. It is not acknowledged locally that it is a dialect common to the entire region. In other words, Matambugueños are, indeed, capable of speaking a dialect not common to the whole of the nation. However, this is not a capability unique to inhabitants of the reservation. Rather, it is common to all individuals from the province of Guanacaste. However, given that Matambugueños are singled out as the "Indian" inhabitants of the province, the dialect is commonly attributed to them alone. Not coincidentally, there are several stark similarities of this dialect to that dialect of Spanish spoken in Nicaragua by other individuals with stigmatized identities (given common Costa Rican prejudices against Nicaraguans). The relative value placed on this stigmatized dialect is transferred to its speakers, and vice versa. Language, then, reflects social standing.

Characteristics of Guanacastecan Spanish

The dialect recognized (if only erroneously so) as "Matambugueño" is considered poorly spoken by dominant Costa Rican society (which calls it Guanacastecan speech, alluding to the whole province for which it is characteristic) and is very similar phonetically, morphologically, and lexically to Nicaraguan Spanish (Lipski, 1994, p. 291). With regard to phonetics, Guanacastecan Spanish includes the following characteristics: the elision of the intervocalic /d/; the pronunciation of the posterior fricative [x] as a weakly aspirated [h] or the elision of this fricative altogether; the weakening of the intervocalic /y/, the hypercorrection effectuated by the insertion of a [y] in the hiatus combinations, which begin with /i/; the velarization [nasalization] of word-final /n/; the alveolar articulation of /tr/ (resulting in a very slight difference between the pronunciation of the word "otro" and "ocho," for example), and the reduction of word-final and syllable-final /s/ (Lipski, 1994, pp. 222, 290–291).

With regard to morphology, the use of the informal second person pronoun *vos* predominates in personal and familiar interactions. Lipski suggests that Nicaraguans (and my own observations corroborate that this is true for many Guanacastecans) are criticized by urban Costa Ricans for assuming "too much confidence" (an excessive closeness) in their frequent use of *vos* (Lipski, 1994, p. 313). With regard to the Guanacastecan lexicon, many Nahuatl words exist; however, these are not recognized as anything other than rural Spanish by their speakers.

To Lipski's list of characteristics of Nicaraguan and Guanacastecan speech, I would add some that were evident in my observations from 1993 to 1999. Among the narratives that I recorded and in local everyday speech (in environments such as Matambú's general store in which Guanacastecan speech is far less stigmatized than in the neighboring town of Hojancha), I frequently heard the pluralization of already plural words (such as "pieses" for "pies," which one could translate as the use of "feets" in place of "feet"), the disappearance of word-final and syllable-final /s/ in morphological redundancies (such as "los gatos" pronounced as "lo gato"), and an uncommon pronunciation of several verbs.

The xenophobia common in Costa Rica and the nationalist prejudice against Nicaraguans and their speech, in particular, contribute to the stigma Costa Ricans place on this dialect. One could argue that what Gal and Woolard (1995) refer to as a "policing of correctness in national standards" (p. 129) is, at once, a policing of the boundary between those deserving of Costa Rican citizenship and persons viewed as detrimental to its sharply mapped national boundaries.

In a study described by Quesada Pacheco (1991; but carried out by Majorie Arrieta, Carla Jara, and Covadonga Pendones in 1986), the investigators interviewed Costa Ricans to examine how speech from the Central Plateau (widely considered standard speech or "typical" Costa Rican Spanish) and Guanacastecan speech were perceived (Lipski, 1994, p. 138). The results of this research indicate that Guanacastecan speakers considered the form of Spanish spoken in the Central Plateau to be of greater prestige than Guanacastecan speech (Quesada Pacheco, 1991, p. 25). In fact, Fernando Ferraz notes that "Costa Rican Spanish contains fewer Nahuatl elements than in Central American nations to the north" (in Lipski, 1994, p. 225). This indicates that the form of Spanish considered standard Costa Rican Spanish does not include Guanacastecan speech. I experienced this ideology when I published a collection of narratives written phonetically so as to preserve the dialect in which they had been told (Stocker, 1995). The publisher requested that I change this Guanacastecan Spanish "to sound more Costa Rican"—to more closely approximate standard Costa Rican Spanish and thus diminish the similarity to Nicaraguan Spanish.

These examples illustrate the truth of Lipski's affirmation that "although regional varieties cut across national boundaries, the sociolinguistic consciousness of individual countries is still tightly bound up with nationalist sentiments" (1994, p. 139). This attitude is evident through the use of a derogatory phrase, used on the national level, to characterize Guanacastecan speech. Because Hojancheño society mirrors dominant Costa Rican society's treatment of Guanacastecans, in its dealings with Matambugueños, I heard this criticism of Matambugueño speech in Hojancha, as well. The phrase, used in the title of this chapter, is "ellos se comen las eses." The phrase literally means "they eat their s's," referring to the tendency to aspirate or delete the word-final /s/. However, the pronunciation of this phrase is identical to that of the phrase "se comen las heces," meaning "They eat their own feces." Thus, Matambugueños (and Guanacastecans) are judged as socially inept and inferior on the basis of their language usage.

The stigmatization of Guanacastecan speech reflects or demonstrates this speech community's location within a racial and social hierarchy on the national level. In the contact zones, it is considered that the "Indians" speak strangely and the "Cartagos"[5] speak the prestige variety. Furthermore, the relative status of both groups is, in part, due to their form of speech. Conversely, each group's form of speech is perceived as an ethnic legacy. In other words, it is considered that Matambugueños, as many Hojancheños pointed out to me, "speak Indian." While most of the theories regarding the equation of language and culture consider that distinct languages signal particular cultures as different, the opposite is the case in the township of Hojancha. In this context, a form of speech is defined as "Indian" by the fact that those who speak it are identified in this manner as a result of their residence within an arbitrarily placed political boundary.

Given that the inhabitants of Hojancha (as dominated by "Cartagos," who identify themselves as white and Spanish) express pride in the fact that they originate from the Central Plateau, and given their perception that Matambugueños speak the stigmatized dialect known as Guanacastecan Spanish, it makes sense that in contact between Hojancheños and Guanacastecans there arises, at times, a certain linguistic clash that corresponds to the ethnic conflict that also exists. Sometimes this linguistic conflict is evident in the manner in which Hojancheños ridicule Matambugueño speech.

Numerous individuals in the high school—among them, both teachers and students—spoke to me of the different way that Matambugueños talk. These individuals spoke with an unquestioning tone, suggesting that anyone would consider the linguistic difference a fact. Jaime, a self-defined "racist" seventh-grader, cited the way they speak and the accent Matambugueños have as one of the major differences between Matambugueño and Hojancheño culture. He could not, however, give me any examples. His cousin, who also participated in the discussion, suggested that the linguistic difference lay in the fact that Matambugueños do not use certain phrases of courtesy, such as "with your permission," when they are in others' houses. She based this conclusion on her observations of the actions of one woman from Matambú in her mother's house.

A teacher justified his making fun of a Matambugueña girl in front of her peers by noting that the students present were already ridiculing the way she spoke. He added, "you know the strange way they have of talking." He could not give me examples either. A student from Matambú, white enough to pass for non-Matambugueña, noted that her classmates joke about her way of speaking as "Indian." She could give me no examples of how her speech is different.

An eighth grade girl from Hojancha who physically resembles most Matambugueños explained to me that the difference between Hojancheños and Matambugueños is racial (and she pulled up her pant legs to exemplify her own perceived whiteness to me). She also identified linguistic difference as one of the main ways in which Matambugueños differ from Hojancheños. The example she gave me of this was that they do not pronounce their s's (though she did not use the derogatory phrase that serves as the title of this chapter). She gave the example of the word "pues," which, she said, Matambugueños pronounce as "pueh." Thus, her example of Matambugueño speech was one of Guanacastecan speech. I pointed out to her that I have heard Hojancheños speak the same way. A Guanacastecan teacher present at that moment explained (to both of us, perhaps) that the pronunciation "pueh" was neither uniquely Matambugueño nor Guanacastecan. She said that it was Nicaraguan Spanish. This comment supports my assertion that dominant Hojancheño society reduces Guanacastecan speech to Matambú only.

Indeed, Guanacasteco Spanish can define the province as a speech community (if only loosely; here, too, the provincial border will by no means correlate directly with Guanacastecan speakers). By fitting the image of a speech community different from the national standard, Guanacastecan Spanish speakers thus call into question their own belonging to the nation. Indeed, residents of this province are often referred to by the derogatory phrase "Nicas regala'os," which, roughly, means "leftover Nicaraguans." The label alludes to the annexation of the province of Guanacaste to Costa Rica from Nicaragua in relatively recent national history. This name applied to Guanacastecans at once calls into question their citizenship and links this shaky national loyalty to their linguistic patterns, as the very label imitates the elided intervocalic /d/ considered characteristic of stigmatized Guanacastecan speech.

However, perhaps due to the need to differentiate Matambugueños (as Indians) from all others in the province of Guanacaste (as non-Indians), the speech community gets reduced to the otherized community alone: Matambú. As an ethnically different, indigenous identity is imposed upon Matambugueños, so is the erroneous perception of different monolingual language use. The perception of language difference in Matambú serves to set that community off as an entirely different entity from those around it. Its perceived language difference seemingly traps the reservation in time and space.

Role of the Educational System in Regimentation

Interestingly, the dominant assumption that Matambugueño Spanish is a dialect different from that spoken by inhabitants of the surrounding communities appears unaffected by contrary, explicit teachings in Spanish grammar classes in the high school, which label as Guanacastecan Spanish those stigmatized speech elements often assumed to be limited to inhabitants of the reservation. In this case, the education system serves to support the language ideology that associates nonstandard (Guanacastecan) speech with inferior speech. But then teachers, students, and other Hojancheños limit the stigmatized variety to Matambugueños.

I observed numerous lessons regarding Spanish grammar and the dialects of it spoken within Costa Rica in classes taught by two teachers to students in grades seven to eleven. In lessons given to eighth graders, in particular, numerous linguistic facts were discussed that are relevant to this chapter. Some of these lessons, however, appear contradictory. The first of these (as documented in a student's notebook) began with a discussion of why Spanish is the official language of Costa Rica. It was explained (by either the teacher or the text from which the student drew notes) that this is due to political invasions of the Americas by the Spaniards (resulting in the destruction of culture and language and the replacement of these by those of the invaders), and later due to a law that decreed it thus, and because all of the laws of the country are written in this language. Article 76, line 7 of the Costa Rican constitution declares that Spanish is the official language of the nation.

The lesson went on to teach that languages change for a variety of reasons, and urged students to consider that "when we possess a language we should take care of it because it not only signifies the form of speaking but also the form of being as well as the national history and identity" (my translation, from a student's notebook where this was taken as dictation; it was likely a mix of text read aloud from the book by the teacher with her own comments interjected). Even in a dry text, the link between identity and language is made clear.

The text further explains that Costa Rican Spanish is distinct from other variants such as those spoken in Argentina and Nicaragua. It listed variants within Costa Rica as related to dialects spoken in Guanacaste, San José (the capitol city), Heredia (a city near the capital), and Limón (a province largely inhabited by an Afro-Caribbean population with apparent English linguistic influence). Specifically, the text states that with regard to variants within Costa Rica, "we can mention the Spanish of Guanacaste or of Limón without underestimating either, given that a language is perfect if it permits the communication of its speakers" (Varela Barboza and Sandino Argulo, 1998, p. 4). It is interesting to note that these are perhaps the two most socially stigmatized regions of the country. The reasons behind these and other variants, the text explains, are geographic, social, gendered, and professional.

Furthermore, the text explains several different kinds of Spanish. These include "educated Spanish" (*el español culto*), "Popular Spanish" (*el español popular*), jargon, and argot. "Educated Spanish" is "distinguished by its *correct* pronunciation, the paused tone, and adequate accentuation. If it is written, by the spelling and the respect of syntax" (emphasis added, translation mine). "Popular Spanish," on the other hand, "is constituted by everyday conversations, is characterized by the use of regional vocabulary, expressions, sayings, and popular intonation and pronunciation" (translation mine). While the text does not pass judgment on popular Spanish as inferior, note the use of the word "correct" in correlation with Educated Spanish, thus implying that Popular Spanish is less so.

Jargon is explained as language appropriate to certain professional groups, while argot is explained as pertaining to a small group "generally of low social constitution and without education, for example, the way of speaking of *chapulines* [urban adolescent gang members]." Note that this last definition combines issues of language and class or social status and, again, implies social "wrongness." The text then goes on to discuss linguistic registers as different forms of speech that an individual adopts according to his or her circumstances. A revealing phrase, in the eighth-grader's notebook, explained: "An educated person changes idiomatic registers. [He/she] is uneducated if he/she only possesses one way of speaking."

It is here that the tables are turned with regard to Matambugueño speakers. Up to this point, the characterizations of popular Spanish correlated with dominant opinions surrounding speakers from the reservation and their relative level of culture and education. According to local popular opinion, Matambugueños speak a dialect (with the same characteristics as Guanacastecan Spanish) different from that spoken by individuals living outside the reservation's borders. What is not considered is that Matambugueño students in high school, knowing they will be chided for Guanacastecan speech, are perhaps the most adept at changing registers of any students. The simultaneous options of Guanacastecan Spanish and Standard Spanish contribute to a diglossic situation in which Guanacastecan Spanish (erroneously viewed as limited to Matambugueño speakers) is the low language and Standard Spanish is the prestige variant.

One of the Spanish grammar teachers, allying her views with the claims of the text, acknowledged this diglossia when she told her class of eighth graders (this time in a lesson I observed directly) that "in colloquial speech, we use one terminology, but we change it according to the situation." She added, in a telling phrase, that "the goal [of such discussions of language in class] is to better the language." This contradicts the point of the lesson that I heard her make on more than one occasion—that no language is worth any less than another as long as it is used to communicate effectively. In other words (also hers), "Any language is worthy as long as it communicates." Other aspects of her lessons, however, suggested otherwise.

In a lesson on the characteristics of Guanacastecan speech, she reviewed students' homework, in which they had been asked to come up with fifteen examples of "popular language use" heard in each student's community.[6] The teacher criticized students' answers, noting that they lacked an example of the *voseo* (the second personal familiar verb form employed in Costa Rica, generally, and in Guanacaste, in particular). She then reviewed the characteristics of Guanacastecan speech (naming it as such) as follows:

1. The *voseo*
2. Alteration of diphthongs (*higénico* instead of *higiénico*)
3. Replacement of the hiatus with a diphthong (*león* changed to *lión*)
4. Pronunciation of the /g/ for /h/ (as in *güesped* instead of *huesped*)
5. Morphological distortion
6. Loss of word-final /d/

She concluded that "we Guanacastecans" have a different form of speaking. She told students that in Cartago (where the "cartagos"—the speakers of the prestige variety, on the local level—are said to have originated), "they *also* speak badly," and she cited the example of the africated /r/ (emphasis added). This teacher later acknowledged, to me alone, that Guanacasteco speech is characteristic of the whole province—not just Matambú. This message does not seem to have been picked up on by her students, however.

The other Spanish teacher did not focus on Guanacastecan speech in any of the lessons I observed or heard about. In fact, the Spanish she taught presented and revolved around masculine forms of Castillian Spanish—the prestige form used in Spain. This form is used in Hojancha only by the priest, who is, himself, a Spaniard and whose vocation requires it. It is distinct from the standard form spoken in Hojancha with regard to phonology and morphology. The principal morphological difference lies in the use of *tú* as the second person singular familiar form (in Castillian Spanish) as opposed to *vos* employed in Costa Rica. The use of *vosotros* for the second person plural familiar form in Castillian Spanish is generally not used in Costa Rica, where *ustedes* is used, thus not distinguishing between a formal and an informal second person plural in the Costa Rican dialect.

The only times the *vosotros* form is used in Costa Rica is in Biblical quotations, in speech by Catholic religious leaders, and in spoken legal documents such as oaths. Interestingly, in the case of legal documents, this Castillian form gives the speech event an air of importance and formality in spite of the informal character of the verb form in its original Castillian context. Indeed, the value placed on Castillian Spanish in Costa Rica reflects such an air. In discussing my own use of Spanish (called "correct" by locals due to my use of the subjunctive form increasingly uncommon to rural speech in Costa Rica), an eighth grade girl commented on the fact that in different places, Spanish is spoken differently. She gave the example of the variety spoken in the Central Plateau of Costa Rica (as opposed to Guanacastecan Spanish) and added that she was not sure which was "the most correct Spanish." A boy seated nearby replied that Spain's is "the most correct" dialect.

I should note, in fairness to these teachers, that it was not their personal decision to teach the Castillian form. Rather, the Ministry of

Education gives national examinations to ninth and eleventh graders each year. These examinations, greatly feared by students, include testing of Spanish grammar and verb forms, including the *vosotros* form used in Spain. In fact, one of the Spanish teachers commented to me that "The *vosotros* form is not within our form of being. And unfortunately, we have to read *Don Quixote*, the vosotros form is there, and in the Bible, there it is, too. And the priest will always use *vosotros* because that is his way." However, it was her opinion that "we should definitely not use the *vosotros* form."

Thus, students were made aware of dialectical differences—regional and national—through formal Spanish grammar classes. A social studies teacher also broached the issue of dialectical differences on a different day, with a class of ninth graders, when he addressed stereotypes. He imitated stereotypical speech from a beach town relatively near school (which included English loan words and an accent associated with a higher economic class), Nicaraguan Spanish, Guanacastecan Spanish (similar to his version of Nicaraguan Spanish, but with less accentuated elision of word-final /s/), and the standard Costa Spanish from Central Plateau. He then performed the stereotypical Indian war cry produced by emitting sound while intermittently covering and uncovering the mouth with his hand. He noted that stereotypes hold that this is Matambugueño speech.

His point, as he made clear subsequent to the demonstration, was that these stereotypes were not true of many speakers from those regions. However, one could argue that his imitation of all varieties except that attributed to Matambú did, at least, involve linguistic elements true of *some* speakers of those regions. In the case of Matambú, however, the "dialect" to which he alluded is true for no speakers whatsoever, outside of those imitating Hollywood westerns' stereotypical representations of North American Indians. Thus, in effect, he was teaching that this particular stereotype of Matambugueño "speech" was equally valid or invalid as stereotypes of other regional dialects.

In short, classrooms were filled with numerous discussions of linguistic "competence" (as the dialects studied were value-laden even when teachers alluded to a contrary truth), which, I argue, contributes to the regimentation of non-standard speech as indicative of both lesser-valued speech forms and lesser-valued speakers. As I shall demonstrate shortly, it is clear that students, in their own informal conversations outside of class, have internalized the value systems presented by their teachers with regard to language use. In the stereotypes learned and circulated by students, those lesser-valued speakers associated with non-standard speech were almost invariably Matambugueño. So the school teaches students to make judgments of value and character based on different types of language use. And local beliefs teach students to apply those stigmatizing judgments to Matambugueños in particular. These stereotypes, however, failed to note that Matambugueños may be the most skilled at switching dialects according to the social environment at hand.

Creativity in the Subversion of Stereotyped Linguistic Difference

As mentioned previously, speakers who live near accent borders often speak more than one dialect. This is readily observable in the linguistic behavior of inhabitants of the reservation, where the geographic barrier at hand was extremely arbitrary at its inception. I observed different situational uses of dialect and register by Matambugueños, and teachers commented on changes in Matambugueños' speech over time. One teacher of vocational classes, in my interview of her, remarked upon linguistic change by Matambugueños. She did not acknowledge the use of different registers by individual speakers from Matambú, but she did note a change over time toward the standard variety, in general terms, by students from the reservation. One of the Spanish teachers—the one who frequently remarked on the perfection of any language capable of communicating ideas—had commented that "Matambugueños couldn't speak [in years past]. They could, but when they spoke, the others laughed at their accent. Then they tried to imitate them."

A teacher of vocational classes noted that there had been a decrease in discrimination against Matambugueño students due to a change over time in their manner of speaking. She added that it was lamentable that Matambugueño students had "lost" their form of speech (referring to Guanacastecan speech, as she described it in this same interview) because she, personally, felt pity at this loss.

> I think one should maintain certain customs. They have lost their form of speaking, they have bettered it, relatively. Now they speak better than those before. I have spoken and worked here a long time and I see this. They [Matambugueños], upon interacting with the people . . . [pause] from here, they have become equal in this sense.

There are several noteworthy elements in this comment. First, it is interesting that while she considers that change of dialect was instrumental to the decrease in discrimination against Matambugueños, she laments that shift. Second, until adding the words "from here," after a considerable pause, "the people" seemed to be equated with those residing in Hojancha. Finally, her use of the concept of "betterment" with regard to linguistic change from Guanacastecan speech to the standard form used in Hojancha reveals the underlying and common perception that Guanacastecan speech is inferior to the standard variety. Thus, teachers (perhaps unconsciously) rationalize their treatment of students on the basis of the ideology activated in the curriculum.

It is more likely that what this teacher has observed is not so much a general change in speech among Matambugueños from Guanacastecan speech to standard speech in all situations, but an increase in Matambugueños' negotiation of social situations through speech (a phenomenon I often observed). Individuals do, indeed, select from a speech repertoire the forms most suitable for a given social context. It is probable that this vocational teacher has observed an increased use of situational selection over time by Matambugueño students who, like her, have noted the correlation between speech style and discrimination.

Change over time in Matambugueño speech (from a predominance of Guanacastecan speech to that of the standard) was not something I observed throughout my six years of experience in the region. I did, however, note shifts in register by Matambugueños in varying social situations. Perhaps the most striking example of this was enacted by an eighth grader from Matambú whom I will call Juan Pablo. After the Spanish lesson for which students were asked to bring examples of Guanacastecan (regional) Spanish as homework, Juan Pablo and his classmates headed for their English class. Another student asked if the English classroom was open yet. Rather than replying with the standard Spanish reply, "*Está abierto*" ("It's open"), Juan Pablo, between grins, remarked, "*Está abri[d]o*" with a heavy Guanacastecan accent (thus employing what his textbook called "morphological distortion" as well as the elision of an intervocalic /d/, reportedly typical of Guanacastecan speech) and, simultaneously, skillfully employing speech divergence. Through this act, Juan Pablo parodied parodies of what was assumed to be his form of speech: he imitated imitations of the stereotypical speech form attributed to him. In this case, one could see Juan Pablo's comment as a ritual of inversion. I argue that Juan Pablo's response displays creativity, as it drew attention to the direct teaching of standard language and the lesser value placed on those presumed to be non-standard speakers.

In spite of the lesson stating that uneducated speakers—usually a term equated with speakers of the stigmatized Guanacastecan dialect— were capable of speaking only one register, Juan Pablo demonstrated that he is able to speak the dialect expected of him and, at the same time, tacitly proved that he normally does not do so in the school setting. Although non-accommodation is often attributed to a limited repertoire on the part of the speaker (Giles & Powesland, 1975, p. 166), Juan Pablo not only debunked the view of non-standard speakers' competence in only one register, he also challenged the common perception that Matambugueños speaking in the Guanacastecan dialect have such a limited repertoire. He effectively demonstrated his ability to use different dialects depending on the situation at hand by purposely "failing" to use the dialect he would normally use in the school setting.

Although calling attention to one's ability to speak the lesser-valued variant in a diglossic situation is not usual, Juan Pablo's utterance is one example of doing just that in a context in which this individual would normally use the High variety. If Giles and Powesland are correct in their suggestion that accommodation is a means to disguise one's persona, we may view Juan Pablo's pointed speech divergence as a deliberate attempt to draw the everyday acts of speech convergence or accommodation into focus. Furthermore, Giles and Powesland suggest that the success of accommodation depends upon its not being recognized as such. In Juan Pablo's example, however, he was perhaps identifying himself as *not* a monodialectal speaker.

Language Variation Outside of the School Setting

Standard speech (Hojancheño-style) is that most commonly used by Matambugueños in the school setting. Guanacastecan speech is common inside the reservation among speakers from Matambú. I heard examples of this frequently in narrative and everyday conversation. In my earlier years of research, I did not hear Guanacastecan speech ridiculed inside Matambú. It is unclear to me now if my notice of such chiding in the past year is due to change in language use or to my increased attention to such matters in more recent years. In earlier years of research (1993-1998), however, I did not notice a middle ground between the use of the prestige variety and the stigmatized variety in which the use of one or the other was called into question by a speaker. In my most recent research (2000), however, I frequently noted that phenomenon.

In particular, I detected this in speech situations in the general store/pool hall where I frequently worked during the evenings. This is a setting where men gather in the evenings to play pool, dominoes, and checkers and to smoke in the company of other adolescent to middle-aged men. Occasionally, women came to the general store part of the structure (separated from the pool hall by a thin wall perforated by large windows) to make purchases or use the town's one telephone. In that setting, I heard men order basic products (cigarettes, soft drinks served "to go" and poured into small plastic bags with straws, and snack foods). At times, they would do so using Guanacastecan speech, then look around, imitate their own speech with a thicker accent or more obviously elided /s/, or omitted intervocalic /d/, and add on the phrase, *"Dijo el nica"* ("Said the [derogatory term for] Nicaraguan").

In this manner, they called attention to their own usage of Guanacastecan speech as a stigmatized dialect, then seemingly tried to pass it off as an intentional imitation of a group deemed inferior. In such cases (as performed by adolescents and men in their late thirties to early forties, but not by the older generation of pool-hall-goers), speakers seemed to call attention to the diglossic situation that Silverstein describes as follows. "Every popular presentation of regional accents, especially phonological variation, portrays the defects of the accent, with respect to Standard, as the cause of 'confusion' and lack of 'clarity.' Indeed, 'clarity' of expression is foremost among the rationalizable attributes of Standard . . . and threats to that clarity come in ethnic-, regional-, gender-, and class-based deviations from it" (1987, p. 9). Thus, by attributing the "defects of the accent" performed, perhaps unwittingly, in the general store and pool hall, Guanacastecan speakers tried subsequently to attribute their display to a clever imitation of those foreign linguistic deviants. In so doing, they obscured their own "threat" to a homogenous national whole.

While the situational selection of speech styles and accommodation are commonly noted phenomena, generally speaking, it is only in recent times that I have noted a change in the settings in which linguistic accommodation to the standard variety takes place. It is common to hear Matambugueños—even those who narrate traditional oral histories routinely in Guanacastecan Spanish—use speech accommodation while in Hojancha, perhaps unconsciously.

Frequently Matambugueños change their form of speech by omitting or diminishing the stigmatized Guanacastecan elements to avoid discrimination by "Cartagos" on account of their speech. Thus Matambugueños both deny an imposed identity and conform to the non-stigmatized form of speech. Just as Williams, Whitehead, and Miller (1971) found to be the case for non-standard speakers, Matambugueños change their manner of speech to avoid the lower status that Hojancheños and others ascribe to speakers of Guanacastecan Spanish.

Nevertheless, sometimes perception is stronger than reality, as the study carried out by Williams, Whitehead, and Miller demonstrated. My own studies support this tendency of people's linguistic expectations for a person to supersede that person's actual linguistic patterns. This has serious repercussions in the educational setting. As with Black English vernacular and other nonstandard dialects in the United States (see Labov, 1972a), the nonstandard variety in Costa Rica gets labeled "uneducated." Similarly, in classrooms in Hojancha, the Guanacastecan speech stereotypically associated with students from the reservation is considered a mark of lacking education, while the standard variety connotes a more complete education.

Teachers' lower expectations for nonstandard-speaking students can affect the students' relative school success. This affects students in Matambú—whether they perform Guanacastecan speech competence (viewed by many as linguistic *in*competence) or not, they are perceived to do so by teachers and peers. These individuals' expectation is that Matambugueños speak differently, in accordance with the dominant ideology that regiments their interactions with "Indians." Indeed, many teachers who spoke of Matambugueños' supposed linguistic difference noted that they have not had good students from the reservation. Teachers spoke to me of Matambugueños' "strange" manner of speaking as if this were a fact I would not question. Students not from Matambú chided their Matambugueño peers for poor speech when other markers of inferiority were absent. As in the case of other traditional cultural markers, language is perceived as a difference that differentiates Matambugueños from Hojancheños.

CONCLUSION

In spite of the existence of Guanacastecan speech outside of Matambú, throughout the province of Guanacaste among "non-Cartago" speakers, the perception exists that only those who inhabit the reservation speak "worse" (or in a more "Indian" manner) than the rest. I maintain that this is the result of the commonly held correlation between ethnic identity and language use, despite its objective absence, in a place where the desire to create difference is great. This created difference, in turn, serves to separate those "deserving" of prejudice from those who dish it out.

The perception that Matambugueños *se comen las eses* (elide their word-final /s/) allows powerful outsiders to treat them as if it were the case that they *se comen las heces* (eat their own feces). Their perceived linguistic difference serves to mark them as distinctly inferior to standard speakers—even if the monolingual use of standard speech among Hojancheños is equally a mere perception. Language ideology, as Woolard and Schieffelin assert, points to larger social relations. By using a linguistic anthropological approach to study schools, I have been able to show the school's influence over student identity both within the educational context and after their departure from it. I argue that Matambugueños' perceived language difference is perpetuated in the high school, both explicitly and implicitly, in spite of Matambugueño students' skillful accommodation tactics. Furthermore, I maintain that this has potentially detrimental effects on the school success of students from the reservation. However, the implications of perceived language difference do not stop there.

In the case of Matambú, the ideology of perceived language difference places Matambugueños in an inferior position in the social hierarchy of the high school, specifically, and calls into question their legitimacy as national citizens, more generally. The interrelation of perceived language difference and ascribed social rank anchor Matambugueños in the lower rungs of society, both national and local, as their social inferiority both fuels and feeds on the (mis)perception of their linguistic difference.

NOTES

1. The reasons for this and the repercussions of this decree are too numerous to be addressed here. For further information, see Stocker, 2000.

2. Costa Rica is commonly discussed as the "Switzerland of Central America." This phrase at once alludes to its declared pacifism and its European descent (though not from Switzerland itself). Numerous individuals spoke to me of the lack of indigenous influences in Costa Rica and the resulting European flavor of the nation. Some did so directly, in those terms. Others chose less explicit avenues. On more than one occasion (in different parts of the country and social spheres), people who heard I was an anthropologist suggested that my studies would be more fruitful if carried out in Guatemala or some part of Central America other than Costa Rica. The logic behind their arguments rested on the assumption that anthropologists study Indians, first of all, and, second, upon the assumption that there are no indigenous peoples in Costa Rica. Dominant historical and civics texts from this region support the view that Costa Rica is a more European nation than its neighbors.

3. This near-constant prejudice faced by individuals from the reservation is the focal topic of a larger project, and its intricacies are beyond the scope of this chapter. Such prejudice takes a variety of forms, including name-calling, poor treatment, and differential access to public services, including public education. The interpretations of and reactions to this discrimination are too varied to address here.

4. The Chorotegas are known to have spoken Mangue at the time of Conquest. This Oto-Manguean language was later replaced by Nahuatl as Spaniards encouraged its use as a *lingua franca*. Though this double language shift was likely due (in both events) to political dominance, it is often discussed as a result of poor choice or rejection of identity on the part of Matambugeuños by local outsiders.

5. Those non-Indian Costa Ricans in this region who identify as white and of European descent are known as "Cartagos," after the city in the Central Plateau by this name from which many of the white inhabitants of Hojancha migrated.

6. Examples included *humildá* (*humildad*), *lión* (*león*), *pión* (*peón*), *agastar* (*gastar*), *agüelo* (*abuelo*), *pelúo* (*peludo*), *parao* (*parado*), and *interesao* (*interesado*).

REFERENCES

Abercrombie, T. (1991). To be Indian, to be Bolivian: "Ethnic" and national discourses of identity. In G. Urban & J. Sherzer (Eds.), *Nation-States and Indians in Latin America* (pp. 95–130). Austin: University of Texas Press.

Adams, R. M. (1991). Strategies of ethnic survival in Central America. In G. Urban & J. Sherzer (Eds.), *Nation-States and Indians in Latin America* (pp. 181–206). Austin: University of Texas Press.

Allport, G. (1974). Linguistic factors in prejudice. In P. A. Eschholz et al. (Eds.), *Language Awareness* (pp. 107–119). New York: St. Martin's Press.

Anderson, B. *Imagined Communities: Reflections on the Origin and Spread of Nationalism*. London, New York: Verso, 1983.

Arroyo, V. M. (1972). *Lenguas Indígenas Costarricenses*. Costa Rica: Editorial Centroamericana, EDUCA.

Barrientos, G., Borge, C., Gudiño, P., Soto, C., Rodríguez, G., & Swaby, A. (1982). El caso de los Bribris, indígenas talamanqueños. Costa Rica. In G. B. Batalla et al. (Eds.), *América Latina: Etnodesarrollo y etnodicio* (pp. 249–55). San José: Ediciones FLASCO.

Basso, K. H. (1979). *Portraits of "the Whiteman."* Cambridge: Cambridge University Press.

Bonfil Batalla, G. (1972). El concepto del indio en América: Una categoría de la situación colonial. *Anales de Antropología, 9*, 105–124.

Bonfil Batalla, G. (1989). *México Profundo: Una Civilización Negada*. México, D.F.: Grijalbo.

Bozzoli de Wille, M. E. (1986). *El Indígena Costarricense y su Ambiente Natural*. San José: Editorial Porvenir.

Collins, J. (1996). Socialization to text: Structure and contradiction in schooled literacy. In M. Silverstein & G. Urban (Eds.), *Natural Histories of Social Discourse* (pp. 203–228). Chicago: University of Chicago Press.

Coupland, N. (1985). "Hark, hark, the lark": Social motivations for phonological style-shifting. *Language and Communication, 5*(3), 153–171.

Ferguson, C. A. (1972). Diglossia. In P. P. Giglioli (Ed.), *Language and Social Context* (pp. 232–251). Baltimore: Penguin.

Foley, D. (1995). *The Heartland Chronicles*. Philadelphia: University of Pennsylvania Press.

Gagini, C. (1917). *Los Aborígenes de Costa Rica*. San José: Trejos Hermanos.

Gal, S. (1989). Language and political economy. *Annual Review of Anthropology, 18*, 345–367.

Gal, S., & Woolard, K. A. (1995). Constructing languages and publics: Authority and representation. *Pragmatics, 5*(2), 129–138.

Giles, H., & Powesland, P. F. (1975). *Speech Style and Social Evaluation*. New York: Academic Press.

Guevara Berger, M., & Chacón, R. (1992). *Territorios Indios en Costa Rica: Orígenes, Situación Actual y Perspectivas*. San José: García Hermanos, S.A.

Labov, W. (1972a). *Language in the Inner City*. Philadelphia: University of Pennsylvania Press.

Labov, W. (1972b). *Sociological Patterns*. Philadelphia: University of Pennsylvania Press.

Le Page, R. B., & Tabouret-Keller, A. (1985). *Acts of Identity: Creole-Based Approaches to Language and Ethnicity*. Cambridge: Cambridge University Press.

Lipski, J. M. (1994). *Latin American Spanish*. London, New York: Longman.

Monge Alfaro, C. (1960). *Historia de Costa Rica*. San José: Trejos.

Palmer, P., Sánchez, J., & Mayorga, G. (1993). *Taking Care of Sibö's Gifts: An Environmental Treatise from Costa Rica's KéköLdi Reserve*. San José: Asociación Integral de Desarrollo de la Reserva Indígena Cocles/KéköLdi.

Peralta, Manuel M. de. (1893). *Etnología Centro-Americana: Catálogo razonado de los objetosarqueológicos de la República de Costa Rica*. Madrid: Hijos de M. Gines Hernandez.

Quesada Pacheco, M. A. (1990). *El Español Colonial de Costa Rica*. San José: Editorial de la Universidad de Costa Rica.

Quesada Pacheco, M. A. (1991). *El Español de Guanacaste*. San José: Editorial de la Universidad de Costa Rica.

Renan, E. (1990). What is a nation? In H. K. Bhabha (Ed.), *Nation and Narration* (pp. 8–22). London and New York: Routledge.

Silverstein, M. (1987). Monoglot "standard" in America: Standardization and metaphors of linguistic hegemony. *Working Papers and Proceedings of the Center for Psychosocial Studies, 13*, 1–25.

Stocker, K. (1995). *Historias Matambugueñas*. Heredia: EUNA.

Stocker, K. (2000). *No somos nada: Ethnicity and three dominant and contradictory indigenist discourses in Costa Rica*. The University of New Mexico Latin American Institute Research Paper Series No. 35.

Urban, G. (1991). The semiotics of State-Indian linguistic relationships: Peru, Paraguay, and Brazil. In G. Urban & J. Sherzer (Eds.), *Nation-States and Indians in Latin America* (pp. 307–330). Austin: University of Texas Press.

Varela Barboza, M., & Argulo, W. S. (1998). *Español 8° Año*. Heredia: Ediciones Marwal de Heredia.

Williams, F., Whitehead, J. L., & Miller, L. M. (1971). Ethnic stereotyping and judgments of children's speech. *Speech Monographs 38*, 166-170.

Woolard, K. A. (1989). *Double Talk: Bilingualism and the Politics of Ethnicity in Catalonia*. Stanford: Stanford University Press.

Woolard, K. A., & Schieffelin, B. B. (1994). Language ideology. *Annual Review of Anthropology, 23*, 55–82.

8

Voices of the Children

Language and Literacy Ideologies in a Dual Language Immersion Program

Norma González and Elizabeth Arnot-Hopffer

Although this volume highlights the mutual influence that linguistic anthropology and educational research can have on each other, this chapter argues that another important element should cut across work in both anthropology and education, and that is a focus on children. As Marjorie Harness Goodwin has emphasized:

> We need to move children from the margins to the center of anthropological inquiry. It is time we take children seriously and use the distinctive practices of anthropology to give voice to their social worlds and concerns. . . . Through language, children of diverse ethnicities, social classes, ages, abilities, and genders orchestrate their social organization and socialize one another across a range of activities. Without longitudinal ethnographic studies of children from different ethnic backgrounds in diverse structural settings, we will not know how children's lives are shaped by their encounters with family, peers, adults, and others expressing various language ideologies, in neighborhoods, schools and after school, or how children change developmentally over time. (1997, p. 5)

Terry Eagleton, the critical theorist, also argues that children "make the best theorists":

> Children make the best theorists since they have not yet been educated into accepting our routine social practices as "natural," and so insist on posing to those practices the most embarrassingly general and fundamental questions, regarding them with wonderful estrangement which we adults have long forgotten. . . . It is those children who remain discontent with this shabby parental response who tend to grow up to be emancipatory theorists, unable to conquer their amazement at what everyone else seems to take for granted. (1990, p. 34)

This chapter investigates children's language ideologies and their relationship to biliteracy and school success. It is based on a three-year study that is examining the relationship between language ideologies and biliteracy development in a dual language (DL) program, i.e., a school where all children are taught to read and write in two languages. The study is investigating three research questions, but for the purposes of this chapter the following two will be addressed:

1. How do language ideologies influence the implementation of this dual language program?
2. How do children transform biliteracy into a personal tool for thinking?

Although our initial research questions went beyond the formation and transformation of children's language ideologies (Moll & González, 2000), we found that this topic has captured us both theoretically and methodologically. This chapter examines the multiple layers of language practices of children, and the complex relations between larger language ideologies and particular instances of school language use within a DL setting.

THEORETICAL BACKGROUND

Language Ideologies

Our first challenge was to differentiate how various traditions of language study and social theory use the term *ideology*. Woolard (1992, 1998; Woolard & Schieffelin, 1994) provides a useful interpretive framework tracing "ideology" and its conceptual underpinnings. Despite different conceptualizations, as Woolard notes, "what most researchers share, and what makes the term useful in spite of its problems, is a view of ideology as rooted in or responsive to the experience of a particular social position" (Woolard & Schieffelin, 1994, p. 58). An ideology is a set of beliefs that are tied to a certain social position.

From an Althusserian (1971) perspective, ideology "interpellates" or "hails" individuals within social structure. This type of ideology is unconscious, but it functions to maintain social stratification as it operates in particular speech practices. But not all accounts of ideology refer solely to pre-existing social stratification and the reproduction of group privilege (Woolard, Schieffelin & Kroskrity, 1998). From a more Durkheimian perspective, ideology can refer to any body of assumed notions, expressed through implicit or explicit metalinguistic discourse. Although we recognize the value of Durkheimian accounts, in this chapter we argue that "ideology" implicates power, the exercise of power, and the reproduction of dominant/subordinate relations.

The concept of language ideology is also related to the concept of "regimentation." Regimentation refers to the fact that utterances do not have their meanings easily available for decoding, but are regimented or framed by what Collins and Wortham (this volume) refer to as larger "metadiscourses" or ideologies. The articulation between micro-level interaction and macro-level patterns can be studied in schools by examining, on the one hand, what children say, who they say it to, and under what circumstances and, on the other hand, circulating metadiscourses about language, the purpose and use of language, about learning about language, and about learning through language.

Literacy and Language Ideologies

We frame literacy as a social practice, not a cognitive or psychological phenomenon that happens in the head of the reader, but a set of intertextual resources that connect children's lived experiences to texts. As Gee notes, "Literacy is seen as a set of discourse practices, that is, as ways of using language and making sense both in speech and writing" (1986, p. 719). In this way, biliteracy involves participation in at least two different sets of discourse practices habitually associated with different linguistic codes.

In our study, we have linked language ideologies to the development of biliteracy because this linkage highlights the process of constructing critical literacies. We concur with Luke and Freebody, who remind us that "reading is a social practice using written text as a means for the construction and reconstruction of statements, messages and meanings. . . . Reading is tied up in the politics and power relations of everyday life in literate cultures" (Luke & Freebody, 1997, p. 185). The "materials and interactive practices of reading education are best seen as key sites, where cultural discourses, political ideologies and economic interests are transmitted, transformed and can be contested" (p. 192). This per-spective on literacy has direct implications for the link between the study between language ideologies and biliteracy development. As Hornberger and Skilton-Sylvester (2000) have proposed, to understand biliterate contexts, media, and content, one must take into account the power relations embedded within biliteracy development.

Language Ideologies and Biliteracy Development in Dual Language Programs

The research on the promotion of biliteracy through schooling is somewhat limited because the research agendas of bilingualism and literacy have developed separately. Linguists interested in bilingual-ism have tended to focus on oral proficiency, and relatively few studies of literacy have focused on language minority students. Even as the literature on DL programs continues to grow, research coming from within school contexts continues to be sparse. Two areas of research that are underrepresented in the literature are children's perspectives on DL programs in general and, more specifically, children's perspec-tives on the development of biliteracy through schooling in DL programs.

Our project brings together theories of language ideology, the study of children's perspectives, and the process of biliteracy development within DL programs. In doing so, we operate within a Vygotskian paradigm that affirms the social and historical essence of childhood (Andrade Rosi & Moll, 1993). The tight connection between literacy and the broader ideologies of our respective communities is critical in researching children's formation of language ideologies and their biliteracy development. As Moll notes, "It is by controlling literacy that we develop the disposition to access the broader resources (funds of knowledge) of the (proximal or distal) communities in which we live" (Moll, 1999, pp. 5–6).

Biliteracy Development as Learning Language, Learning About Language, Learning Through Language

From this sociopolitical perspective, children are never simply learn-ing language in a vacuum. They are always simultaneously learning about language and *through* language (Halliday, 1985, in Short, 1999, p. 131). This is a complex experience in a biliterate environment in which students are learning about language and literacy by talking and listen-ing to others, by exploring how both Spanish and English function, and by using both languages to get things done (Short, 1999). Students are also inevitably learning, through two languages, the language ideologies circulating around each and, generally, which language is valued in a given context. Research has shown that the more equal the status of the two languages involved, the more likely it is that students will develop high proficiency in both languages (Cloud, Genesee, & Hamayan, 2000). Accordingly, this DL program is also engaged in the complex task of boosting the legitimacy of a language that is delegitimized in other U.S. contexts. Our study examines how the process of biliteracy development in this DL program shapes and is shaped by language ideologies circulating within the school context and also in the larger political context within which the school is situated.

CONTEXT OF THE STUDY: DESCRIPTION OF THE SCHOOL SITE

The school site we have chosen is a focal point (one might even say a lightning rod) for the coming together of layers of sociohistorically laden language use. Founded in 1901 in the heart of one of Tucson's oldest Mexican-American barrios, the school has served families of the surrounding neighborhoods, most of whom have been speakers of minority languages, mainly Spanish, but also Chinese, Tohono O'odham, and Yaqui. Despite the multilingual nature of the population, and in keeping with Arizona law, the school was a monolingual English school for the first eight decades of its existence. It was also one of the poorest schools in the Tucson Unified School District (Smith, Arnot-Hopffer, Carmichael, Murphy, Valle, González, & Poveda, 2002).

In 1981, through the efforts of both the neighborhood residents and bilingual educators and administrators, it became the district's first bilingual magnet school. As such, the school receives monies that other schools do not receive. This status as a magnet school provides funds for music and art specialists, a counselor, librarian, curriculum specialist, as well as a fully staffed extended-day program. The music program is particularly stellar, producing the *Guitarristas*, first through fifth grade guitar players, and the *Mariachi Aguilitas*, both polished musical performing groups. Currently, magnet students make up approximately 65% of the student population, and most of these students are English dominant; 70% of the student population is Latino, coming in as both barrio and magnet students. However, language dominance does not equal ethnicity. A significant percentage of the Latino students at the school are third or fourth generation Mexican-origin students. These students are enrolled at the school for a variety of reasons, including its strong ancillary programs, but many families cite a desire for their children to recapture the Spanish language that has often been erased through English-only instruction.

Dual Language Instruction

The program at the elementary school was not initiated as a heritage language program, although it could be argued that it has become one. Instead, the DL program at the school developed as a direct result of research conducted by a faculty well grounded in both theory and practice (Smith, 2000). Between 1981 and 1993, a maintenance bilingual education program was in place in which teachers were expected to use Spanish as a vehicle for instruction 50% of the time and English 50% of the time. By the mid 1980s the school began to question this model as it became obvious that students who entered the program dominant in Spanish exited in fifth grade bilingual and biliterate, but that students who entered the program dominant in English made little progress toward becoming productive bilinguals, although most had good receptive skills. In the late 1980s, under the direction of a teacher leader and the curriculum specialist, a teacher study group was formed to examine different bilingual education program models and goals (Murphy, 1999). During the 1993-1994 academic year the school decided to implement a new model currently referred to as the DL immersion program, *El Programa de Inmersión en Dos Idiomas*. This DL program is one in which all students, regardless of language background, receive instruction through Spanish during their first two years (K-1), with an increase in English as the language of instruction in subsequent years, but never going below 70% Spanish, as shown in Table 8-1. All students are immersed in literacy experiences in Spanish first.

Exito Bilingüe

In the spring of 1997, during the teacher study group meetings, teachers began to express frustration with the wide range of Spanish literacy skills reflected in each classroom. In first grade, for example, some students were still learning color words in Spanish while others were reading Spanish chapter books. Another problem identified by

TABLE 8-1. Distribution of Minority and Majority Languages

Grade	DL Program Spanish/English %
K	100-0
1	100-0
2	85-15
3	70-30
4	70-30
5	70-30

teachers was the placement of English-dominant "newcomers," students without previous bilingual education or Spanish literacy, who entered the program in the intermediate grades. A third issue involved coordination with district-wide plans for a new "balanced literacy" approach to reading and writing instruction. Teachers asked to what extent and how this magnet school, as the only DL school in the district, would incorporate an approach to literacy instruction designed for children reading in their first language.

Together, the faculty began to develop ways to deal more effectively with the variety of strengths and needs in Spanish reading and writing at each grade level. Teachers decided to create a school-wide multiage interactive literacy program in Spanish to better meet the needs of students at all levels of Spanish literacy development. Support from the district was critical to this effort, as faculty were paid to participate in a week-long training during the summer of 1997 aimed at understanding the components of a balanced literacy program and the implementation of interactive literacy strategies. Thus Exito Bilingüe, a non-scripted, negotiated curriculum that integrates the professional expertise of faculty and the interests and strengths of students, was born. It is important to emphasize that this is a school-wide program designed for all students from first through fifth grade. Kindergarten teachers decided that their students would be included in Exito Bilingüe on an individual basis so that reading and writing did not become the overriding focus of the kindergarten experience. Exceptional education students participate, as does the faculty, including instructional aides and specialists. Exito Bilingüe began in the fall of 1998 and is implemented three days a week for seventy-five-minute periods (see Smith & Arnot-Hopffer, 1998).

METHODOLOGY

The operationalization of the term *language ideology* in this context, and its relationship to biliteracy, presented us with methodological dilemmas. One area of tension in studies of language ideology concerns the problem of the alternate sitings of ideologies (Woolard, 1998, p. 9). Are ideologies discoverable in language practices themselves? Is metapragmatic discourse—talk about how language is used—the window to how we think about language? Or must studies of language ideologies focus on what is unsaid, that is, the implicit framing of texts that do not always rise to discursive consciousness? We have assumed that language ideologies both constitute and are embedded in social practices, that is, in actual activity. Thus, they can be observed, recorded, and subjected to analysis. They can also be connected to an array of semiotic systems at work within the institution of the school and within the larger community. Thus, in order to capture the breadth and depth of possible ideological sitings and to read across multiple layers of language use, both explicit and implicit, we have concentrated on multiple sites of data collection.

Another area of tension between our theories of ideology and the context of our study was the relevance of such theory to the language ideologies of children. Locating sites of children's language ideologies can be a complex research endeavor. Are theoretical constructs that have emerged in studies of adults transferable to children? Are children "interpellated," by ideologies or influenced by metadiscourses, in the same way as adults? What is the effect of public discourses on children in a DL program? How can we capture children's words and worlds and frame them within adult conceptualizations? Children are exposed to an array of overt and covert language ideologies through media, politics, parents, peers, and schooling. They must engage with what even adults are not able to untangle: contradictions and ambiguities about who typically and normatively speaks what language to whom and under what circumstances.

Theoretically, we consider children's utterances concerning language use as a kind of cognitive apprenticeship, a trying out and trying on of language ideologies. This theoretical orientation has led us to investigate a variety of data sources, triangulating household interviews, classroom observations, and children's own utterances. While we cannot pretend to freeze the shifting social landscapes upon which children's linguistic formations erupt, we have attempted to carve out a space where we might grasp the multidimensional phenomenon by gathering data from multiple sources:

1. Interviews: The students and their parents have been interviewed by the authors and by colleagues participating in the aforementioned longitudinal study. These interviews have been recorded and the tapes have been transcribed and translated.
2. Observations: The participants have been observed in their Spanish literacy groups and in their classrooms. They were observed in the cafeteria by one of the authors. The goal of these observations is to understand better how these students are becoming biliterate.
3. Assessments and artifacts: Running records (reading assessments, see Smith & Arnot-Hopffer, 1998, for a detailed explanation) in both Spanish and English were collected. These reading assessments are administered by teachers and provide tools for coding, scoring, and analyzing reading behaviors. Running records, first developed by Marie Clay (1975, 1993), document a reader's actual reading of a target text, "providing quantitative and qualitative

information" (Fountas & Pinnell, 1996, p. 78). At this school, the levels range from a pre-primer level to level 44, the highest possible score. Writing samples in both Spanish and English were also collected. Oral language proficiency scores were measured on the Pre-IPT and the IPT (an oral language proficiency test). The IPT tests four basic areas of oral language proficiency: vocabulary, comprehension, syntax, and verbal expression. In addition, the school site developed its own version of the Student Oral Language Observation Matrix for both teacher assessment and student self-assessment.

4. Literature circles: The students and the researcher have participated in three literature circle discussions using children's literature in Spanish, including *El Libro de los Cerdos* by Anthony Browne, *Rosa Caramelo* by Adela Turin and Nella Bosnia, and *La Mariposa* by Francisco Jimenez. These discussions were audio taped, transcribed, and translated.

The researchers in the longitudinal study, including the authors, are analyzing these data with support from the classroom teachers, the students, and their families. Interview transcripts and field notes have been entered into a qualitative data management program (NUD*IST) to facilitate quick retrieval and categorization of data.

Our initial results indicate that our methods, which were designed to study multiple arenas of ideology, can also be successful in documenting aspects of children's ideologies of language as well as their developing critical biliteracy.

RESULTS

Circulating Language Ideologies

Even though we knew that the linguistic borderlands, like the contexts of this dual language school, would be a fertile landscape for examining language ideologies, when we first conceptualized the study we had not counted on a series of events that crystallized language ideologies within media and public discourses. These events led to Arizona's version of California's anti–bilingual education initiative, voted on as Proposition 203 in the November 2000 election. This proposition provides that "Children in Arizona Public Schools *shall be taught English by being taught in English* and all children shall be placed in English Language Classrooms. Children who are English Language Learners shall be educated through Sheltered English Immersion during a temporary transition period not normally intended to exceed one year." The Arizona proposition further stipulates that "Any school board member or other elected official or administrator who willfully and repeatedly refuses to implement the terms of this statute may be held personally liable for fees and actual and compensatory damages by the child's parents or legal guardian, and cannot be subsequently indemnified for such assessed damages by any public or private third party." Spearheaded in Arizona as in California by Ron Unz, the Silicon Valley millionaire entrepreneur, under the auspices of the group "English for the Children of Arizona," Proposition 203 passed by a margin of 30%, underscoring again how ideologies can impact classroom practice.

The public media debate over the proposition highlighted some predictable types of language ideology and others that are more multi-layered. One camp proposed the isomorphism of nationhood with monolingualism. The trope of *disunification* is also a clarion call for some proponents of Proposition 203, who view a single language as foundation for nationhood and multilingualism as anti-American. In a letter to the editor of the *Arizona Daily Star* (24 March 2000), a reader reiterates this assumption: "the purpose of a common language and culture is to unite a nation made up of peoples from many parts of the world" (Buran, 2000, p. A18).

A second camp coalesced around the claim about "caring" and "concern " for the future of English learners, freeing them, as one advocate claimed, from the "shackles of bilingual education."[1] This camp also addressed literacy specifically, promoting the mantra of Ron Unz that "lack of literacy in English is a crippling, almost fatal disadvantage in our global economy" (1997), and assuming that literacy is a zero-sum game in which literacy in another language precludes literacy in English. Parents at the school site echoed this concern about English literacy. Even though parents may be comfortable with the oral language proficiency of their children in both English and Spanish, when it came to literacy they were often more concerned about English than Spanish. The curriculum specialist of the school, one of the authors (EAH), comments: "I wish I had kept track of the number of times that parents have come to see me because they are very pleased that their child is learning Spanish but they want to know when she/he will be reading in English."

This concern resonates within a third language ideology, one that emphasizes economic and social stratification, wherein language, rather than political hegemony, is seen as the barrier to economic security. Children are brought into this volatile and contentious mix of viewpoints, often through mass media. For instance, in Spanish language television programming, which many Latino families watch, advertising for *Inglés Sin Barreras* (English Without Barriers), a pricey English language instruction program, promises success and riches as a consequence of learning English. English is "a jewel that no one can take away from you" and "the passport that no one can rescind," claim the ads. Children are sometimes portrayed in the ads overhearing their parents' struggles over lack of employment opportunities and advancement due to lack of English, as the commercials claim that "every day that goes by without speaking English is money that is lost." Interestingly, Euro-American parents whose children are enrolled at the school cited an instrumental reason for learning *Spanish*: that of increased marketability in a global marketplace, exactly the argument that Unz used for the learning of English.

Positions toward and against Proposition 203 were not coherent across communities, and xenophobia was not the only operative motive. Indeed, the segmentation of language ideologies *within* the Latino community was a pivotal factor in the debate, although apparently not in the vote. Although few Latinos are given a high profile in the media, local data from school districts continue to show overwhelming support for bilingual education among Latino parents.

Three Case Study Students: *Las Tres Amigas*

As these multiple ideologies about language were circulating in the broader school context, particular students were making sense of themselves as English and Spanish speakers. This section presents case studies of three students, Jessica, Amy, and Augusta (self-selected pseudonyms). The analysis shows layers of complexity in how language ideologies get taken up by particular children.

The three participants in this focus group session, conducted by one of the authors (EAH), were chosen from a larger pool of twenty-one case study students being monitored. Initial selection was based on several factors, including age, gender, and language dominance. Our selection of three female students in the second grade does not provide opportunities for comparisons based on gender or age, but it does allow for the richness of detail that gives qualitative data its salience. When EAH suggested that we invite a boy to join our group, the participants were clear that they perceive themselves as a cohort: *las tres amigas*, as indicated in the following segment.[2] (Within these excerpts, transcriptions are as spoken, and translations follow.)

EAH: *¿Quieren incluír un niño en nuestro trabajo este semestre? Tal vez sería interesante aprender lo que piensan los niños sobre el proceso de aprender a leer y escribir en dos idiomas?*
JESSICA: No way, Miss.
AUGUSTA: *Somos las tres amigas.*

EAH: Would you like to include a boy in our work this semester? Perhaps it would be interesting to learn what the boys think

about the process of learning to read and write in two
languages?

JESSICA: No way, Miss.

AUGUSTA:We are the three girlfriends.

Language dominance was also considered in the initial selection of
these participants. One of the girls, Jessica, comes from a Spanish-dominant home, while another, Amy, comes from an English-dominant
home, and the third, Augusta, comes from a home in which both English
and Spanish are spoken. Language dominance and cultural identity
were also a topic of discussion in the focus groups, and each participant
defined herself distinctly through her own language dominance and
cultural identity. These characteristics and the background of each of
the participants are discussed next and are summarized in Table 8-2.

AMY

Background

Amy was nine years old and living in Barrio Anita with three older
siblings and her mother at the time of the study. She was in fourth grade
in fall, 2001. Amy's mom worked in the school cafeteria when Amy was
in second grade, and she is active in the Barrio Anita Neighborhood
Association. Amy's older sister graduated from the DL program in May
2000. Amy studies guitar and art in the after-school program, and has

TABLE 8-2. The Participants

Name	AMY		AUGUSTA		JESSICA	
Home Language	English		Spanish & English		Spanish	
Age and Grade	9 - Fourth (8/01)		9 - Fourth (8/01)		9 - Fourth (8/01)	
Teacher Assessments of Language Dominance, Grades 2 and 3	*Grade 2* Bilingual - English Dominant	*Grade 3* Bilingual- English Dominant	*Grade 2* Bilingual	*Grade 3* Bilingual- English Dominant	*Grade 2* Spanish Dominant	*Grade 3* Spanish Dominant
After School Activities	Art	Guitar	Violin	Ballet Folklórico	Violin	Art
School SOLOM Self-Assessment Score, 4/00 & 10/00	*4/00* 24/25-Spn 25/25-Eng	*10/00* 21/25-Spn 25/25-Eng	*4/00* 20/25-Spn 23/25-Eng	*10/00* 23/25-Spn 24/25-Eng	*4/00* 24/25-Spn 17/25-Eng	*10/00* 25/25-Spn 8/25-Eng
School SOLOM Teacher Assessment Score, 5/01	22/25-Spn 25/25-Eng		23/25-Spn 25/25-Eng		25/25-Spn 17/25-Eng	
Running Records Results of 5/01	44-Spn 44- Eng		44-Spn 44-Eng		40-Spn 16-Eng	
Cultural Identity	American		Mexican-American		*Grade 2* Mexican	*Grade 3* Mexican-American

taken piano lessons outside the school with a private tutor. She has also been active in the School After Dark Program, participating two evenings a week for much of her second-grade year to help write and illustrate a bilingual children's book about the historic connections between Barrio Anita and the Santa Cruz River (Camino al Rio Press, 2000). Amy qualifies for the free/reduced lunch program.

Language Dominance
Amy began the DL program in kindergarten as a monolingual English speaker, and in interviews she also explains that English is her home language.

> EAH: *Amy, ¿cuándo usas inglés y español tú?*
> AMY: *En Exito Bilingüe yo hablo español. Y también en música porque Sr. Valenzuela habla mucho español y un poquito de inglés.*
> EAH: *¿Con quién más hablas español?*
> AMY: *Tú, y hablo inglés con mi familia y mis otros amigos.*

> EAH: Amy, when do you use English and Spanish?
> AMY: In Exito Bilingüe I speak Spanish. And also in music because Mr. Valenzuela (music teacher) speaks a lot of Spanish and a little bit of English.
> EAH: Who else do you speak Spanish with?
> AMY: With you, and I speak English with my family and my other friends.

Still, despite her English dominance, Amy participates in Exito Bilingüe at level 44. She attributes her success in acquiring Spanish as a second language, and in learning to read and write in Spanish, to her own personal effort and commitment to Exito Bilingüe. Indeed, our awareness of Amy's determination to speak Spanish has made it awkward to conduct interviews with her in English.

> EAH: *¿Qué has hecho tú para subir de niveles en Exito Bilingüe?*
> AMY: *Hablo mucho español.*

> EAH: Is that how you learned so much Spanish so fast, from trying very hard?
> AMY: From trying my best and from Exito Bilingüe.
> EAH: What have you done to go up in the Exito Bilingüe levels?
> AMY: I speak a lot of Spanish.

In November of her kindergarten year, Amy's English dominance was reflected in her classification as a "Non-Spanish speaker" and "Fluent English speaker" on the Pre-IPT test. Her third grade teacher

identified Amy as "Bilingual/English dominant" when asked to identify the students in her class as English dominant, Spanish dominant,
or bilingual. In October of 2000 using the school SOLOM student
self-assessment of oral language proficiency, Amy gave herself a composite score of 21 in Spanish and 25 in English out of a total score of 50.
In December of 2000, halfway through her third grade year, Amy tested
at level 44 in reading in English based on running record results. (See
Figure 8-1 for an explanation of levels.[3])

Cultural Identity

Throughout the study, despite her commitment to learning Spanish
and her participation in bilingual extracurricular projects, Amy consistently identified herself as American in response to questions about her
cultural identity.

EAH: *Y tú Amy,¿de cuál cultura eres?*
AMY: *Americana.*

EAH: And you, Amy, what culture are you?
AMY: American.

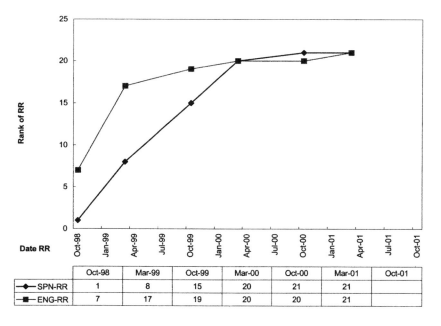

	Oct-98	Mar-99	Oct-99	Mar-00	Oct-00	Mar-01	Oct-01
SPN-RR	1	8	15	20	21	21	
ENG-RR	7	17	19	20	20	21	

Figure 8-1. Amy.-English Dominant Student.

However, as the following excerpt suggests, Amy's commitment to learning and speaking Spanish begins to temper her cultural identification.

EAH:	*¿Y tú, Amy?*
AMY:	*Um, yo no sé.*
JESSICA:	(in English) Were you born right here or in Mexico?
AMY:	*Aquí, pero mi mamá...yo soy americana pero hablo un poco de español.*
EAH:	And you, Amy?
AMY:	Um, I don't know.
JESSICA:	(in English) Were you born right here or in Mexico?
AMY:	Here, but my mom . . . I am American, but I speak a little Spanish.

AUGUSTA

Background

Augusta was nine years old at the time of the study and began fourth grade in fall 2001. She has three younger siblings, a half sister with whom she lives at her mother's home and a half-sister and baby half-brother with whom she lives when she is at her father's home. Augusta qualifies for the free/reduced lunch program. Like Jessica and Amy, Augusta began the DL program as a kindergartner.

Augusta is student of violin and *ballet folklórico* in the after-school program, as well as a member of the school's performing mariachi group, *Las Aguilitas*. Along with three older students on trumpet and guitar, Augusta often greets faculty, students, and visitors with a mariachi jam session as they arrive at school. Augusta was the second place winner in a school-wide English spelling bee in the fall of second grade. Four months later, she won the statewide Spanish spelling competition in her age group.

Language Dominance

Augusta is one of relatively few magnet students who began the DL program as a fluent speaker of Spanish and English, according to a home language survey. She discussed this home bilingualism in the interviews:

AUGUSTA: *Yo uso español con mi tata de Magdalena o cuando vamos allá. Porque él no más sabe español y está aprendiendo inglés. Yo hablo español y inglés con mi mamá porque ella quiere que aprendo más español para ser más bilingüe. Con la esposa de mi papá yo hablo inglés porque ella no sabe español.*

AUGUSTA: I speak Spanish with my Grandpa from Magdalena or when we go there. Because he only speaks Spanish and he is learning English. I speak Spanish and English with my mom because she wants me to learn more Spanish so I can be more bilingual. With my dad's wife I speak English because she doesn't know Spanish.

Like Amy, Augusta's oral bilingualism is matched by her strong biliteracy. She participates in Exito Bilingüe at level 44 and credits her mother with teaching her to read in Spanish.

> AUGUSTA: *Cuando mi mamá me estaba enseñando a leer en español, ella me dijo que había algunas palabras que se dicen en inglés un poquito igual como en español. Entonces fue más fácil para mi aprender a leer en Español.*

> AUGUSTA: When my mom was teaching me to read in Spanish she told me that there were some words in English that are a little bit like the words in Spanish. So it was easier for me to learn to read in Spanish.

Augusta also named Jessica as a friend with whom she speaks Spanish.

Augusta's dual language abilities were revealed in the kindergarten oral language assessments (Pre-IPT) in both languages. Her third grade teacher identified her as Bilingual/English dominant when asked to identify the students in her class as Spanish dominant, English dominant, or bilingual. In October of 2000, using the school SOLOM student self-assessment of oral language proficiency, Augusta gave herself a composite score of 23 in Spanish and 24 in English out of a total score of 50. Near the beginning of her second grade year, she was assessed at level 44 in English and at the same level in Spanish reading. Level 44 is the highest level of running record assessment at the school.

Cultural Identity

Mariachi music is one aspect of Augusta's self-identification as a Mexican American, and this was a cultural identity that she stressed consistently in the focus group interviews.

> EAH: *Y tú Augusta, ¿eres de cuál cultura?*
> AUGUSTA: *Mexicana-Americana.*

> EAH: And you Augusta, what culture are you?
> AUGUSTA: Mexican-American.

She consistently repeated this at other such interviews, such as the one a year later:

> EAH: *Y tú, ¿qué eres?*
> AUGUSTA: *Mexicana-Americana también (igual que Jessica).*

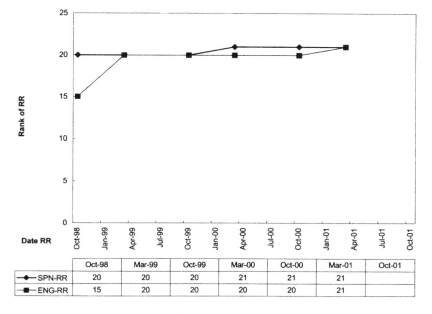

	Oct-98	Mar-99	Oct-99	Mar-00	Oct-00	Mar-01	Oct-01
SPN-RR	20	20	20	21	21	21	
ENG-RR	15	20	20	20	20	21	

Figure 8-2. Augusta.-Bilingual Student.

EAH: And you, what are you?
AUGUSTA: Mexican American also (the same as Jessica).

JESSICA

Background
Jessica is nine years old and entered fourth grade in fall 2001. She is the eldest of four children in an extended Latino family with a long history of residence in Barrio Anita. Her cousins are also students in the DL program at the school. Jessica began the DL program in kindergarten; at that time her family lived in Barrio Anita. The family has since moved out of the school neighborhood and Jessica's mother provides transportation to and from school for Jessica and her younger sister, who will be in second grade. Both children participate in the after school program in which Jessica studies violin and art. Jessica qualifies for the free/reduced lunch program.

Language Dominance
Jessica's primary language is Spanish. She lives in a Spanish dominant home and, in interviews, she identifies herself as being "born into Spanish":

JESSICA: *Yo uso español en mi casa y con mi familia porque yo nací en español. En Exito Bilingüe también. Uso inglés cuando hay personas quien hablan inglés no más.*

JESSICA: I use Spanish at my house and with my family because I was born into Spanish. In Exito Bilingüe also. I use English when there are people who only speak English.

She also prefers reading and writing in Spanish:

> EAH: *¿Te gusta escribir más en inglés o en español?*
> JESSICA: *En español.*
> EAH: *¿Por qué?*
> JESSICA: *Porque es mi idioma*
>
> EAH: Do you like to write in Spanish or in English?
> JESSICA: In Spanish
> EAH: Why?
> JESSICA: Because it is my language.

Early oral language assessments also found Jessica to be a "Fluent Spanish Speaker." In kindergarten she was also classified as a "Non-English Speaker" on the Pre-IPT, unable to respond non-verbally to contextualized commands (Carmichael, 1998). Her third grade teacher identified Jessica as "Spanish dominant" when asked to identify the students in her class as Spanish dominant, English dominant, or bilingual in April 2001.

In October 2000, using the school SOLOM student self-assessment of oral language proficiency, Jessica gave herself a composite score of 25 in Spanish and 8 in English. In May 2001, at the end of Jessica's third grade year, her Spanish running record reached level 40, and her English running record score was level 16 (see Figure 8-3).

Cultural Identity

When asked about her cultural identity in second grade, Jessica identified herself as *blanco,* then *mexicana* when spontaneously coached by Augusta.

> EAH: *¿Tú eres de cuál cultura entonces, Jessica?*
> JESSICA: *Blanco.*
> AUGUSTA: (whispering) *Mexicana.*
> JESSICA: *Mexicana.*
> EAH: *La cultura blanca o ¿eres de la cultura mexicana, Jessica?*
> JESSICA: *Mexicana.*
>
> EAH: What culture are you then, Jessica?
> JESSICA: White.

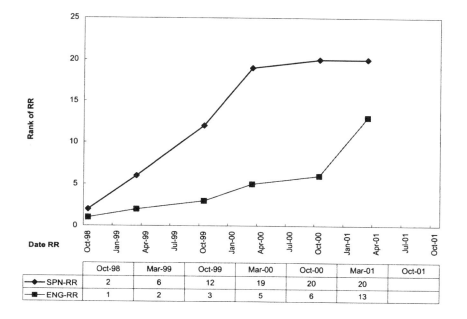

Date RR	Oct-98	Mar-99	Oct-99	Mar-00	Oct-00	Mar-01	Oct-01
◆ SPN-RR	2	6	12	19	20	20	
■ ENG-RR	1	2	3	5	6	13	

Figure 8-3. Jessica.-Spanish Dominant Student.

AUGUSTA:	(whispering) Mexican.
JESSICA:	Mexican.
EAH:	The white culture or are you from the Mexican culture, Jessica?
JESSICA:	Mexican.

In third grade, again coached by Augusta, she identified herself as *mexicana-americana*.

AMY:	*Jessica es mexicana y ella puede escribir en español.*
EAH:	*¿Quién?*
AMY:	*Jessica, porque ella es mexicana y*
JESSICA:	(interrupts and switches codes from Spanish to English – *I'm not a Mexican. I was born right here.*
AUGUSTA:	*Right here? Aquí en esta clase?*
JESSICA:	No, in this state.
EAH:	*¿Tú no eres mexicana?*
JESSICA:	*No.*
EAH:	*No, ¿qué eres?*
JESSICA:	*¿Yo? Yo no soy nada. Ni mexicana ni…es que nací aquí.*
EAH:	*Yo ya sé que naciste aquí, pero ¿qué eres entonces?*

JESSICA:	*Yo no sé.*
AMY:	Irish.
AUGUSTA:	(whispering to Jessica) *Mexicana-Americana.*
JESSICA:	*Mexicana-Americana.*
AMY:	Jessica is Mexican and she can write in Spanish.
EAH:	Who?
AMY:	Jessica, because she is Mexican and
JESSICA:	(interrupts and switches codes from Spanish to English) – I'm not a Mexican. I was born right here.
AUGUSTA:	Right here? Here in this class?
JESSICA:	No, in this state.
EAH:	You aren't Mexican?
JESSICA:	No.
EAH:	No, what are you?
JESSICA:	Me? I'm nothing. Not Mexican and not . . . it's because I was born here.
EAH:	I know that you were born here, but what are you then?
JESSICA:	I don't know.
AMY:	Irish.
AUGUSTA:	(whispering to Jessica) Mexican American.
JESSICA:	Mexican American.

Perhaps the most interesting and telling insight from this interview is the change that has occurred in Jessica's language ideologies. As a kindergarten student, Jessica claimed that she "didn't much like Spanish." Illustrating how beliefs about language and identity can shift quickly among children, Jessica now says that Spanish "*es mi idioma*" (is my language). In the three-year span between these two statements, Jessica has stopped voicing her previous antipathy to Spanish, though her conflict over cultural identity is still evident in the interview. Her interpellation by metadiscourses has apparently been intercepted through a process of language socialization and the influence of her peers—*las otras amigas*. These processes have entered into dialogue with the hegemony of English, as can be witnessed in the preceding excerpts as Jessica changes her claim to cultural identity from *Mexicana* to *Nada* to *Mexicana-Americana*.

The complex dynamics of context, identity, language, and literacy are demonstrated through the experiences of Amy and Augusta with the SOLOM (measure of oral proficiency) self-assessment. Amy, described by her teacher as Bilingual/English Dominant, and who began the DL program monolingual in English, gave herself a higher composite score in Spanish (24) than did Augusta (composite score in Spanish = 20), who started the DL program speaking both Spanish and English and whom the teacher identified as Bilingual/Biliterate.

The contexts in which Amy and Augusta are assessing their abilities in Spanish are, as Duranti and Goodwin suggest, a "socially constituted, interactively sustained, time-bound phenomenon" (1992, p. 6). Amy identifies herself as very bilingual because in the context of her home, compared to her mother and siblings, she is. Augusta's rating of her Spanish proficiency is probably more accurate because in the context of her world, she has access to more bilingual models with whom to compare her proficiency.

It is not clear what it means to label children as monolingual or bilingual, given their different language histories, social contexts, peer relations, family arrangements, and so on. When we asked teachers to identify children in their classes as "Spanish dominant," "English dominant," or "bilingual," a second-grade teacher responded by asking the researchers to clarify their criteria for bilingualism. What labels, she asked, should be given to those students who, although clearly dominant in one language, demonstrate that they are capable of learning via written and spoken Spanish and English? Consistent with their understanding of learner proficiency in two languages, several teachers created separate categories for students whom they regard as bilingual but dominant in one language or the other, like Amy. Other teachers distinguished between oral and written proficiency and receptive versus productive competencies in Spanish and English. These are issues at the heart of DL education and the promotion of biliteracy through schooling (Smith & Arnot-Hopffer, 1998).

Learning About Language *Through* Language: Paths to Critical Biliteracy

By learning about language *through language* and its associated contexts, children in this dual language program develop critical biliteracy. In what follows we examine the biliteracy experiences of these three girls and others in the DL program, and the relationship between these experiences and larger ideologies or "regimes of language" (Kroskrity, 2000).

Learning about language through language

As Jessica, Amy, and Augusta participate in the DL program, they are learning about language and literacy by talking and listening in Spanish and English, by switching languages according to the task at hand, and by gradually acquiring awareness as to the appropriate purposes for English and Spanish. Pivotal to the development of this awareness has been their experience in Exito Bilingüe. This is important for two reasons: first, in the current climate of growing public support for commercially prepared and sometimes highly scripted reading programs, Exito Bilingüe demonstrates that schools and teachers are capable of researching, designing, and implementing effective literacy programs that meet district and state guidelines without imposing packaged curriculum materials or invasive evaluation procedures that devalue what learners and teachers know (Smith & Arnot-Hopffer, 1998). Second, Exito Bilingüe illustrates the need to mark certain domains as Spanish-Only as a way to privilege the minority language (cf., Fishman 1976, in Edelsky, 1996). Augusta provides a student perspective supporting the claim that students mark Exito Bilingüe as a Spanish-only context.

> EAH: *Augusta,¿cómo es diferente tu clase a tu clase de Exito Bilingüe?*
> AUGUSTA: *Es mucho diferente porque . . ., nuestra clase es bilingüe pero en Exito Bilingüe es no más español.*

> EAH: Augusta, how is your classroom different from your Exito Bilingüe class?
> AUGUSTA: It is very different . . . our class is bilingual but in Exito Bilingüe it is only Spanish.

The fact that English continues to be the language of choice among students on the playground and in the lunchroom demonstrates the need to keep Exito Bilingüe an all-Spanish domain. Although Exito Bilingüe is designed exclusively for promoting literacy in Spanish, it is necessary because the two languages do not have the same status in the larger society. English is the language of power and it predominates in the society at large. Since English literacy is omnipresent, Exito Bilingüe is one way educators at the school have chosen to tilt the balance in favor of Spanish literacy by consciously elevating its status, at least within the boundaries of the school. And, as Augusta's comment suggests, students are aware of this emphasis.

Multiple paths to biliteracy

To claim one developmental path to biliteracy would be to underestimate the contextual dynamics of language acquisition and literacy development. This study suggests that children follow different paths to biliteracy, growing at different speeds through diverse experiences along the continua of biliteracy (Hornberger, 1989). Multiple paths to biliteracy demand programs like Exito Bilingüe where, through multi-age grouping, students are challenged to work at their cognitive maximum.

Amy's biliteracy development, in particular, illustrates how Exito Bilingüe affords multiple paths to biliteracy. Amy, the student who demonstrated the greatest quantitative success in Exito Bilingüe (she started second grade at level 6 and finished the year at level 40), credits Exito Bilingüe and "trying her best" for her success in Spanish literacy. She also mentions speaking lots of Spanish when asked what she has done to increase Spanish reading levels in Exito Bilingüe. And Amy reports reading often and (nearly) everywhere in both languages:

EAH: *¿Dónde te gusta leer?*
AMY: *En mi casa, en la escuela, en el carro, en mi cama, en todos lados menos el swimming pool.*

EAH: Where do you like to read?
AMY: At my house, at school, in the car, in my bed, everywhere except in the swimming pool.

This child's identity is caught up in the promotion of biliteracy through schooling.

In Amy's case, as in the cases of Jessica and Augusta, the ideological dimensions of a purposeful and deliberate school language policy are directly implicated in the development of biliteracy skills. Each of these three girls was able to scaffold from their native language (or two languages, in the case of Augusta) up to higher levels of proficiency in a second language. Literacy practices valued by the school were built on the linguistic and cultural funds of knowledge of each child.

The development of critical biliteracy: Children's counter-discourses
Becoming biliterate in the DL context also involved the reading of discourses of power, as students became aware of competing ideologies of languages. They thus became involved in what Freire and Macedo (1987) refer to as "reading the word and the world." Meacham and Buendía (1999) affirm that:

Literacy instruction within this framework becomes a mechanism for teaching students how to exercise their "voice" (Aronowitz & Giroux, 1992, p. 100) within this intertextual network of power and meaning. Through the exercise of voice, students learn how to read amidst the networks of text and power, identifying possibilities for personal growth and strategies for social change. (p. 515)

The children in this study have developed literacy within multiple discourses, and thus demonstrate a heightened awareness of the representation of ideologies and discourses in texts. Indeed, we have found in these children the emancipatory theorists that Terry Eagleton (1990) affirms: children who have not conquered their amazement at what others take for granted. These children actively pick and choose among circulating ideologies, whether they are those expressed by their parents or circulating more widely in society at large, to develop their own critical counter-discourses.

Children do not necessarily mirror their parents' language concerns and ideologies, and often articulate their own ideas about language and language use, sometimes in direct contrast to that of their own households. In fact, in some of our interviews and interactions, children might articulate opinions about language use that are completely incongruent with both household and school discourses. Jessica, in an interview with a teacher-researcher (Carmichael, 1998), claimed that when she is an adult, she would no longer be speaking Spanish, because she "doesn't like Spanish much" (1998, p. 7). She further claimed that if a child doesn't learn to speak English, s/he would wind up begging in the street for food. Not learning English, according to Jessica, is a reflection of your inability to listen and learn at school (1998, p. 10).

The interview in her home, in stark contrast, revealed her mother's strong and consistent support for maintaining Spanish. Jessica's mother affirms, "I am Mexican and I like my own language best . . . with that language I grew up"(p. 13). As the researcher wrote at the time, "Unlike her daughter, (Jessica's mother) views English as important to speak only when necessary" (p. 14). Like Jessica's home environment, the school environment is overwhelmingly positive and nurturing of Spanish language maintenance. We can see in this case that children are hardly driven to reproduce parental and school ideologies, and that they are quite capable of formulating their own judgments. Jessica has not simply been socialized into a prefabricated adult role. She is an active agent in a dialogical process of forming her own language ideology by piecing together and transforming ideologies that circulate in the school, the media, and the home.

Students also developed counter-discourses to language ideologies circulating in the larger society. Despite the language wars, their own occasional resistance, and their own parents occasionally wavering as to the advisability of immersing their children in Spanish, children have organized counter-discourses to Proposition 203 in generative and surprising ways. The members of a second grade class wrote letters to the editor and to a local newspaper and expressed their dismay at the possibility of their way of schooling being taken away from them. Fourth graders scripted a radio broadcast for a local Spanish language radio station, affirming their desire to be educated in two languages. Parents have reported that children have a keen and insightful understanding of the issue. "Why," asked one second grader, "do they want to take our choice away?" Another first-grader answered the phone with "No on 203. Hello." They have participated in marches and carried placards, and in the process have brought a conscious awareness of the contested nature of language and language use.

Through the overt ideological dimensions of the "English for the Children" initiative, students at this school have constructed critical literacies through their own critical readings of public signs and symbols. Intertextual meaning-making processes within their own writing, and within classroom talk, captured the centrality of schools, government, and media in the social construction of literacy. They and their teachers took up questions about local textual practices that were forged as counter-discourses and counter-stories to the dispute over representations of language. Children marshaled their own literacy practices to contest whose representations of whom are to count. In this way, the linking of language ideologies to biliteracy development has helped us to conceptualize textual production as the essence of teaching and learning.

Children have also taken for granted what adults have viewed with amazement. In the 2000 Arizona standardized tests that are currently being piloted throughout the state to third and fifth graders, the Arizona Instrument to Measure Standards test, 100% of the third graders at the school met or exceeded the state standard in English reading, and 96% of fifth graders at the school met or exceeded state standards in English reading. Why is this amazing to adults? Because these are children whose early literacy instruction has been completely in Spanish. They were never "taught" to read English. The interplay of their skills and strategies between two languages resulted in measurable successful outcomes that the children take for granted. In a description of a DL classroom in Phoenix, one newspaper reporter writes, "whereas adults may learn hesitantly, these kids just 'go for it.'" In other words, they have no fears about another language. To them, it's just another way to learn. And the reporter laments: "If only the English-only folks were as perceptive" (Pimentel, 2000).

Yet, in the aftermath of the vote, the children have been demoralized that their efforts did not result in the desired effect. They saw the tremendous effort put forth by their parents, their teachers, and themselves rejected by a 2-to-1 margin. Some students came to school in tears the day after the election, fearful that their teachers would be put in jail if they spoke to them in Spanish. They asked, "Will we still be able to sing in Spanish in mariachi?" "Can we keep our books in Spanish?" The deep emotional impact on many of the children was so marked that the school organized an assembly two days after the election, so that they could talk about their disillusionment and address their confusion. Many children learned early in their lives the deep and painful price that language ideologies can extract.

An Illustrative Example of Critical Biliteracy in Practice

Yet, as we considered the relationship between adult ideologies and children's ideologies, it was again the children who made us quite aware that they were perfectly capable of marshalling their literate resources in their own defense. One telling example concerns a letter to the editor written by one of the main proponents of Proposition 203, Hector Ayala, after its passage. The letter refers to a newspaper article that featured students returning to class the day after the election and expressing their concerns. The text of the letter is as follows:

Teachers' Influence

Regarding the report on the service held for the passing of bilingual education at XXXX Elementary School: As if that weren't absurd enough, didn't it strike everyone as unfortunate that all the children in that school seemed to be exhibiting certain suspiciously preconditioned responses to the passing of 203?

Where would children of elementary school age create reactions to 203 in the manner that they did? These children have no capacity to do that by themselves; obviously they were conditioned by their teachers, including Caroline Vega, who, by the way, has written us a couple of embarrassingly rude and nasty letters.

We can only imagine how long these children had been scared about 203 by the time it passed. Still these "adults" dare parade themselves in front of the community as saintly victims of some oppressive, racist group.

That story by the principal about a child who asked her teacher if she was going to jail for speaking Spanish: Doesn't that sound at least a little suspect? Where in the world would a child have learned to ask that question?

These teachers have been guilty of something immoral if they have scared their students that way. They claim they have the best interests of their students in mind, yet they shamelessly scare them witless for their own political attention.

                                                            HECTOR AYALA

Although individual faculty members, and we as researchers, wrote letters to the editor refuting Ayala's claims, the most convincing letter came from one of our third grade case study students. The text of her letter is on the following page.

This child is no unwitting pawn of suspect teachers. Here is a budding emancipatory theorist, invoking her own theories of language and identity ("Why do you want to take Spanish away if you're from Nogales?") and intertextual connections ("You are like Cruela DeVil from 101 and 102 Dalmations."). This student began the DL program as

12-1-00   español

Querido Sr. H. Ayala.
        Unos días pasados yo estaba en
el radio, y las maestras. no mes
dijeron, "Jennie dí que somos muy buenos
maestras! Eres como la Ecuela Devil de
101 y los Dalmacions. Tengo una pregunta,
¿Porque quieres quitar Español Sí tú
eres de Nogales?

                                Sinceramente,

Dear mr. H Ayale?
        A couple of days ago, I was on
the radio and the teachers never
Said, "Jennie tell them that we
are very good teachers" You're like
Cruela Devil from 101 and 102 Dalmations
I have a question for you, Why
do you want to take Spanish away if
you're from Nogales?

                                from,

an English monolingual speaker and, as the above text indicates, is able
to marshal her biliteracy skills in public as well as school domains. Yet,
it is clearly linguistic ideologies circulating in the school that have
served as the catalyst for her biliteracy development. Without the
explicit affirmation of biliteracy and bilingualism, it is unlikely that this
child would have penned this incisive missive.

Along with the current theoretical emphasis on the "practices" of
literacy and on the intellectual consequences associated with different
practices, the social and ideological circumstances of those practices are

a necessary component of analysis. These broader social and ideological factors mediate the nature of schooling for children in this program. We can see in this excerpt how children can transform literacy into a personal tool for thinking, and we see the mediating factor of language ideologies in creating additive instructional conditions. This student used whatever literacy tools were at her disposal; because her repertoire includes biliteracy, she expanded her sphere of influence and her capacity to impact larger audiences, thus extending her own intellectual trajectory.

CONCLUSIONS

The conceptual tool of language ideology is an analytical lens that helps us to perceive that words, in written or oral form, have no unambiguous inherent meaning, but are framed through circulating, often competing, metadiscourses and ideologies. These children are not passive receptacles for teachers' or parents' ideas about language and literacy, and they are not interpellated in a predictable or even a coherent fashion. We are able to glimpse the processes of languages in contested grounds in this school site, where children are keenly aware that language choice signals not only a referential code, but also a social statement.

One fifth-grade boy encapsulates the regimentation of language as social process. In the assembly following the passage of Proposition 203, when students were asked to voice their concerns, he asked: "Will we have to do square dancing now instead of *folklórico*?" Although the comment elicited a laugh from the audience, the comment reveals a deep understanding of the interpenetrations of language, self, and expressive culture in the formation of children's ideologies. Here is another emancipatory theorist in the making: a child who has understood the power of language to constitute other social formations and the contested and contesting regimes of language.

So as we contemplate the analytical power that educational research can gain from linguistic anthropology, we should be mindful that in addition to anthropological linguistics, we might also consider what Ana Celia Zentella (1997) terms an "anthro*political*" linguistics, that is, an approach that connects language to complex issues of political economy and social identities. Schools are not neutral sites, and they are impacted by larger semiotic and discursive practices that can produce, reproduce, or interrogate language practices.

We might argue that a Linguistic Anthropology of Education is *inevitably* an "anthropolitical" linguistics, since whenever microphenomena are examined carefully, implicit ideologies are revealed. To extend Althusser's interpellation, we are "hailed" and implicated by the very conceptualization of the field of a Linguistic Anthropology of Education, embedded as it is in circulating political and educational discourses. While other methods of inquiry have examined DL programs and bilingual education, a paradigm based on a Linguistic Anthropology of Education requires an articulation of micro and macro phenomena. As anthropologists interested in public policy issues, we can no longer be content only to paint the portrait. We are obligated to work within an engaged anthropology that extends into domains that impact educational policy, that recognizes the "voices" of children, and that recognizes that ultimately they are the ones who will pay the full price for the language wars.

NOTES

The research reported in this chapter was made possible by a grant from the Spencer Foundation, Luis Moll and Norma González, Principal Investigators.

1. This concern over the future of English learners implies that the proponents of the proposition care more about the future of these children than the parents of the children themselves, and that the right to choose the option of bilingual education must be eliminated for parents.
2. In the excerpts, the actual transcript is given first, then a translation.
3. Running record levels range from 2 to 44, but levels at times are combined. To facilitate a graphic representation, a rank (1-20) corresponding to the consecutive levels has been assigned. The highest rank (20) corresponds to the highest levels (40 to 44).

REFERENCES

Althusser, L. (1971). Ideology and ideological state apparatuses. In L. Althusser (Ed.), *Lenin and Philosophy and Other Essays* (pp. 127–186). New York: Monthly Review Press.
Andrade Rosi, A. C., & Moll, L. C. (1993). The social worlds of children: An emic view. *Journal of the Society for Accelerative Learning and Teaching, 18*(1&2), 81–125.
Aronowitz, S., & Giroux, H. (1992). *Postmodern Education: Politics, Culture and Social Criticism.* Minneapolis: University of Minnesota Press.
Buran, D. (2000). Bilingualism a bad idea. *Arizona Daily Star*, March 24, A18.
Carmichael, C. (1998). Hablar dos veces: Talking twice: Language ideologies in a dual-language kindergarten. Unpublished manuscript, University of Arizona.
Children and Neighbors from Barrio Anita. (2000). *A Path to the River: Memories of the Santa Cruz River and Barrio Anita.* Tuscon: Camino al Rio Press.
Clay, M. M. (1975). *What Did I Write?* Portsmouth, NH: Heinemann.
Clay, M. M. (1993). An observation survey of early literacy achievement. *Reading Teacher, 45*, 264–273.
Cloud, N., Genesee, F., & Hamayan, E. (2000). *Dual Language Instruction: A Handbook for Enriched Education.* Boston: Heinle & Heinle.

Duranti, A., & Goodwin, C. (1992). *Rethinking Context*. Cambridge, MA: Cambridge University Press.

Eagleton, T. (1990). *The Significance of Theory*. Oxford: Basil Blackwell.

Edelsky, C. (1996). *With Literacy and Justice for All: Rethinking the Social in Language and Education*. London: Taylor & Francis.

Fountas, I. C., & Pinnell, G. S. (1996). *Guided Reading: Good First Teaching for All Children*. Portsmouth, NH: Heinemann.

Freire, P., & Macedo, D. (1987). *Literacy: Reading the Word and the World*. London: Bergin & Garvey.

Gee, J. P. (1986). Orality and literacy: From the savage mind to ways with words. *TESOL Quarterly, 20*, 719–746

Goodwin, M. H. (1997, April). Children's linguistic and social worlds. *Anthropology Newsletter, 38*(4), 1, 4–5.

Halliday, M. (1985). Three aspects of children's language development: Learn language, learn about language, learn through language. Unpublished manuscript, Department of Linguistics, University of Sydney, Australia.

Hornberger, N. H. (1989). Continua of biliteracy. *Review of Educational Research, 59*(3), 271–296.

Hornberger, N. H., & Skilton-Sylvester, E. (2000). Revisiting the continua of biliteracy: International and critical perspectives. *Language and Education: An International Journal, 14*(2), 96–122.

Kroskrity, P. (2000). *Regimes of Language: Ideologies, Politics and Identities*. Santa Fe, NM : School of American Research Press.

Luke, A., & Freebody, P. (1997). Shaping the social practices of reading. In S. Muspratt, A. Luke, & P. Freebody (Eds.), *Constructing Critical Literacies: Teaching and Learning Textual Practice*. Cresskill, NJ: Hampton Press.

Meacham, S., & Buendía, E. (1999). Modernism, postmodernism, and post-structuralism and their impact on literacy. *Language Arts, 76*(6), 510–516.

Moll, L. C. (1999). Biliteracy notes #2: Assessing biliteracy. Unpublished project paper.

Moll, L. C., & González, N. (2000). Language ideology and biliteracy development: A longitudinal analysis of learning through dual language schooling. Unpublished report. Tucson: University of Arizona.

Murphy, E. (1999). Where do we go from here? Participatory learning and action in a teacher study group. Paper presented at the annual meetings of the Society for Applied Anthropology, Tucson.

Pimentel, O. R. (2000, October 17). Why is "bilingual" a dirty word? *Arizona Republic*.

Short, K. (1999). The search for "balance" in a literature-rich curriculum. *Theory into Practice, 38*(3), 130–136.

Smith, P. (2000). Community as a resource for minority language learning: A case study of Spanish-English dual language schooling. Unpublished doctoral dissertation. College of Education, University of Arizona.

Smith, P., & Arnot-Hopffer, E. (1998). Exito Bilingüe: Promoting Spanish literacy in a dual language immersion program. *The Bilingual Research Journal, 22*(2,3,4), 261–277.

Smith, P., Arnot-Hopffer, E., Carmichael, C., Murphy, E., Valle, A., González, N., & Poveda, A. (2002). Raise a child, not a test score: Perspectives on bilingual education at Davis Bilingual Magnet School. *Bilingual Research Journal, 26*(1), 1–19.

Unz, R. (1997, October 16). Bilingualism vs. bilingual education. *Los Angeles Times*, M6.

Woolard, K. (1992). Language ideology: Issues and approaches. *Pragmatics, 2*(3), 235–250.

Woolard, K. (1998). Introduction: Language ideology as a field of inquiry. In K.A. Woolard, B. Schieffelin, & P. Kroskrity (Eds.), *Language Ideologies: Practice and Theory* (pp. 3–47). Oxford: Oxford University Press.

Woolard, K., & Schieffelin, B. (1994). Language ideology. *Annual Review of Anthropology, 23*, 55–82.

Woolard, K. A., Schieffelin, B., & Kroskrity, P. (1998). *Language Ideologies: Practice and Theory.* Oxford: Oxford University Press.

Zentella, A. C. (1997). *Growing Up Bilingual.* Malden, MA: Blackwell.

9

Linguistic Anthropology of Education (LAE) in Context

Nancy H. Hornberger

When, in 1962, a group of linguistic anthropologists gathered at the American Anthropological Association (AAA) meetings to launch an argument that the ethnographic study of language-in-use might be mutually informing to our understanding of both language and social interaction, they could not have known that it would lead to four decades of rich interdisciplinary work, still going strong (Hymes & Gumperz, 1964). The present volume is testament to the value of that vision and the robustness of its realization.

The 1962 gathering of scholars located themselves within a newly emerging interdisciplinary field known as sociolinguistics, and many of them went on to carve out particular sociolinguistic approaches that drew from anthropological premises that favor attention to cultural practices and ethnographic methods. Other sociolinguistic approaches arising during the 1960s drew from sociological and social psychological premises favoring attention to societal level phenomena, social behaviors and identities, and survey and experimental methods. Thus today there is a rich and diverse array of interdisciplinary work in sociolinguistics, ranging, for example, from sociology of language and variationist sociolinguistics, to language socialization and intercultural communication, to the ethnography of communication and interactional sociolinguistics (cf. McKay & Hornberger, 1996, p. x; see also Paulston & Tucker, 1997).

In the decades following the 1962 meeting, education became a prime arena for sociolinguistic research, and in particular for linguistic anthropologists' ethnographic study of language-in-use. Elsewhere, I have written about three overlapping and intertwining strands of what I called "sociolinguistically-informed ethnographic research in schools," work developed in large part by linguistic anthropologists in approaches that came to be known as the ethnography of communication, interactional sociolinguistics, and microethnography (Hornberger, 1995). These strands of work form part of the context for a linguistic anthropology of education (LAE) as defined in this volume; we return to this context next. First, though, we take up two related interdisciplinary fields of study that overlap and intersect with the linguistic anthropology of education, namely educational linguistics and educational anthropology.

LAE AT THE INTERSECTION OF EDUCATIONAL LINGUISTICS AND EDUCATIONAL ANTHROPOLOGY

If we are to understand the unique contributions of a linguistic anthropology of education, it may be helpful first to define some parameters of the two fields at whose intersection it lies, educational linguistics and educational anthropology. For guidance (and partly because of my first-hand familiarity with it), we can look to the University of Pennsylvania's Graduate School of Education (Penn GSE), where Dell Hymes, co-chair of the 1962 AAA session just cited, served as dean from 1975 to 1987, during which time he was able to instill deeply embedded emphases on language, culture, and ethnographic research, which endure to the present and which to a large degree have set the directions for these fields nationwide (Hornberger, 2001).

At Hymes's very first meeting with the University of Pennsylvania's Faculty of Education in the spring of 1975, he announced his intention to develop two academic emphases under his deanship, namely educational linguistics and educational anthropology (or ethnography) (Erling Boe, personal communication, September 9, 1998). In the ensuing years at Penn GSE, there emerged, in Hymes's own words, "an environment favorable to interests in language and anthropology/ethnography, involving a variety of people, some there only for a while" (Hymes, personal communication, October 26, 1998). The educational linguistics programs were inaugurated in 1976 and housed within the newly created Language in Education Division, along with several existing programs, which eventually became unified as the Reading/Writing/Literacy program, while Hymes's goals with respect to educational anthropology were infused into the Education, Culture, and Society Division (now a program within the Educational Leadership Division) and the Center for Urban Ethnography, which hosts the annual Ethnography in Education Research Forum, first convened in 1978 and now in its twenty-third year.

Educational linguistics as practiced at Penn GSE reflects an inclusive, sociocultural view of communicative competence and communicative contexts. Communicative competence, first proposed by Hymes in 1966 (1972a) in reaction to Chomsky's (1965) use of the term competence in a much narrower sense, describes the knowledge and ability of individuals for appropriate language use in the communicative events in which they find themselves in any particular speech community. This competence is by definition variable within individuals (from event to event), across individuals, and across speech communities, and includes so-called "rules of use" as well as rules of grammar (see later).

Hymes's functional and multiple conception of language ability and use in communicative context is evident in the approach to language education practiced in the educational linguistics programs, an approach that, among other things (1) emphasizes the learning and teaching not only of linguistically defined grammatical knowledge (rules of grammar) but also of culturally embedded ways of speaking (rules of use); (2) acknowledges the role not only of the immediate interactional context but also of the historical, sociocultural, economic, and policy context surrounding language learning and teaching; (3) recognizes the value of learning and teaching not just one standard language variety, but multiple varieties and patterns of language use; and (4) perhaps most important, addresses not just language learning and teaching per se, but also the role of language in the construction and negotiation of both academic knowledge and social identity. In other words, while educational linguistics may have begun from a focus primarily on *language learning and teaching*, it has increasingly explored also *the role of language in learning and teaching*.

The proposal for a field of educational linguistics (Spolsky, 1974) was premised on the mutual relevance of linguistics and education. Two aspects of this mutual relevance present at the initial conceptualization have proven significant for the development of the field and may offer useful insight for our understanding of a linguistic anthropology of education. First, Spolsky emphasized from the outset that educational linguistics "should not be, as it often seems, the application of the latest linguistic theory to any available problem" but rather "a problem-oriented discipline, focusing on the needs of practice" (1975, p. 347). In other words, the starting point for the field is the practice of education (rather than linguistic theory), and the relationship between linguistics and education is conceived as reciprocal and dynamic, and not a simple question of applying insights one way. Second, Spolsky foresaw a highly multidisciplinary field, "drawing from available theories and principles of many relevant fields including many of the subfields of linguistics" (1975, p. 347), that is, sociolinguistics, psycholinguistics, linguistic anthropology, but also history, literature, political science, sociology, anthropology, and psychology. Thus there is a range of research topics and methodologies encompassed within educational linguistics (Hornberger, 2001, pp. 9, 13–16), of which linguistic anthropological methods and research questions addressing education are a subset (Stanton Wortham, personal communication, March 2, 2000).

Intersecting with educational linguistics to form that subset is educational anthropology. This is not the place to delve into a history or overview of the field of educational anthropology, a field about twice as old as educational linguistics and about which others are far more informed than I (Spindler & Spindler, 2000). Suffice it to say here that educational anthropology has consistently reminded us of the important role of both culture and context in the "educative process" (Spindler & Spindler, 2000, p. 26), and that schools are not the only sites where education (cultural transmission, enculturation, socialization) occurs.

Unlike educational linguistics, which started from a focus on language learning and teaching and later expanded to include the *role of language in learning and teaching*, educational anthropology can be said to have moved in the opposite direction, beginning centrally and always from a concern for *the role of culture in learning and teaching* (in both school and out-of-school settings). It has addressed only secondarily the actual learning and teaching of culture itself. Like educational linguists, however, and as pointed out by Wortham in the introduction to this volume, educational anthropologists argue that anthropological research can both benefit from and contribute to educational research and vice versa. A linguistic anthropology of education, lying at the intersection of educational linguistics and educational anthropology, certainly ought to expect a similar reciprocity; indeed, Wortham argues for exactly that and the chapters collected here demonstrate it.

The linguistic anthropology of education can be seen, then, as situated at the intersection of educational linguistics and educational anthropology. At Penn GSE, where both of these fields have a strong tradition dating from Hymes's deanship, there has been in fact space for intersection and overlap. Not only have linguistic anthropologists held appointments in both programs, but across the two programs the one emphasis has informed the other, and, indeed, a sociocultural approach to language and a linguistically informed understanding of sociocultural context have permeated other parts of the school as well.[1]

LAE As Intertwining Strands

As I noted in my opening paragraphs, education has been a prime arena for linguistic anthropologists' ethnographic study of language-in-use for the past four decades, with work developing in several overlapping and intertwining strands, three of which I highlight here: the ethnography of communication, interactional sociolinguistics, and microethnography. To understand the recent contributions of the linguistic anthropology of education as represented in the present volume, it is helpful to understand the earlier work.

All three strands focus on situated discourse, that is, language use in context, and they recognize the existence of multiple and alternative social roles and identities. Further, all three are grounded in linguistics, and in particular in the emic/etic analytical perspective, the methodological traits of using actual, naturally occurring language data and seeking out native intuition, and the analytical tool of discourse analysis (Hornberger, 1995, pp. 235–236). All these characteristics are shared in common with the research reported in the present volume, as well, hence perhaps defining some basic characteristics of a linguistic anthropology of education, in general. The three strands have their differences as well, which I will recapitulate here.

ETHNOGRAPHY OF COMMUNICATION[2]

It is now forty years since Dell Hymes introduced the ethnography of communication at the 1962 AAA session, issuing a simultaneous call for linguistics to broaden its scope to include the study of communicative interaction and for anthropology to actively pursue the study of language (Hymes, 1964). In his introduction to the collected papers from that session, Hymes suggested that such an approach must investigate directly the use of language in contexts of situation, that it cannot take linguistic form as frame of reference, but rather "must take as context a community, investigating its communicative habits as a whole, so that any given use of channel and code takes its place as but part of the resources upon which the members of the community draw" (1964, p. 3). He identified two themes that underlie the chapters in that first volume on the ethnography of communication: first, that each contribution makes use of the notion of communicative behavior, especially linguistic behavior, as situated; and second, that each one studies communicative form and function in integral relation to each other. These themes foreshadow the emphases on situated discourse and multiple and alternative social roles and identities that came to characterize the three strands, as noted previously. From its beginnings at that session and in that volume of articles, which includes such classics as

Ferguson's comparison of baby talk in six languages, Frake's account of drinking talk, Goffman on situation, and Gumperz on verbal repertoire, the ethnography of communication has become a major area of study within sociolinguistics, with innumerable book-length studies, volumes of collected papers, journal publications, conferences, and edited book series to its credit.

The basic methodological approach in all of this work is a paradigmatic one, which, as Hymes succinctly states, "requires discovering a relevant frame or context, identifying the items which contrast within it, and determining the dimensions of contrast for the items within the set so defined" (Hymes, 1968, p. 103). Hymes suggests levels of analysis for uncovering both the frames or contexts and the items within the frames, from smaller to larger: the speech act, the speech event, the speech situation, and the speech community, where, for example, a joke, told in conversation, at a party, on a university campus exemplifies the interrelationship among the levels.

Building from communicative theory and work by Jakobson, Hymes suggested an array of components that might serve as heuristic for the ethnographic study of speech events, or more generally communicative events, where such events refer to activities, or aspects of activities, that are directly governed by norms for the use of language and that consist of one or more communicative acts. This array of components, which defines the dimensions of contrast within the frame of the act, event, situation, or community, includes participants, settings, topics, etc., and was formulated by Hymes into the mnemonic SPEAKING, identified as follows (1974, pp. 53–62):

S - setting/scene: place, time, physical circumstances and cultural definition of occasion

P - participants: characteristics and role-relationships

E - ends: expected outcomes and latent goals

A - act sequence: message form and message content

K - key: tone and manner

I - instrumentalities: channels (oral, written, etc.) and forms (language, dialect, code, etc.)

N - norms: for interaction and for interpretation

G - genres: e.g., poem, myth, talk, lecture, etc.

Furthermore, Hymes suggested that ethnographers of communication need to consider the functions that communicative events may serve for participants, again suggesting an "etic grid" as heuristic: expressive, directive, poetic, contact, metalinguistic, referential, contextual, and metacommunicative functions (1964, pp. 22–23). Hymes made clear, however, that both the components and the functions of communicative events need to be identified in an ethnographic way for each speech community.

The ethnographer of communication, then, armed with a commitment to inductive discovery and using the methodological tools of participant observation/interviewing and their corollary fieldnotes/ interview transcriptions, sets out to uncover a description of the units, criteria, and patternings for the speech group or speech community under study. This is an emic description that is informed by, and in turn informs, the etic heuristic outlined previously.

The inaugural volume of the ethnography of communication as applied to education, *Functions of Language in the Classroom*, edited by Cazden, John, and Hymes, appeared ten years after the inauguration of the ethnography of communication itself, in 1972. In the introduction Hymes again called for more of this kind of study. Several of the groundbreaking studies represented there later became the basis for book-length ethnographies. For example, Philips's work on participant structures in classrooms of the Warm Springs Indian Reservation in Oregon was later published as *The Invisible Culture* (1983); Boggs's contribution on the meaning of questions and narratives to Hawaiian children presaged the later *Speaking, Relating, and Learning: A Study of Hawaiian Children at Home and at School* (1985); and Kochman, who contributed on Black American speech events and their implications for the classroom, later published *Black and White Styles in Conflict* (1981). In all these studies, ways of speaking that were different from, but equally as logical and meaningful as, those of the mainstream classroom were the focus of investigation. Implications of this work for educational practice have been clear and direct. A successful and well-known example is the development of a culturally compatible K-3 language arts program for Hawaiian children in the Kamehameha Early Education Program (KEEP). This program incorporates changes in instructional practice, classroom organization, and motivation management, based on findings from the work of Boggs and others, and resulting in improved learning for the children (Au & Jordan, 1981; Vogt, Jordan, & Tharp, 1987). Key to the successful KEEP program was the adaptation of the reading lesson in ways resembling a major speech event in Hawaiian culture, the talk-story. Specifically, the teacher establishes herself as a socially relevant figure, an adult whose approval is highly valued; and interaction is characterized by mutual participation and co-narration, features that recapitulate the themes of multiple and alternative social roles and identities and language in context that I mentioned at the outset.

Of direct relevance to the application of the ethnography of communication to education was its explicit expansion to include writing and literacy as well as speaking. While Hymes always intended to include all forms of communication, oral and written, verbal and non-verbal, vocal and non-vocal, within the notion of ethnography of communication (e.g., Hymes 1986 [1972b], pp. 62–63; cf. Saville-Troike, 1989, p. 145), his early use of the term *ethnography of speaking* and the early focus of work on spoken language misled some to believe that only spoken language was the focus of study. Basso (1974), Heath (1978), and Szwed (1981), however, early on called explicitly for ethnographies of writing and of literacy. Heath's (1983) own study of ways of speaking and writing in black and white working-class and white middle class communities of the Piedmont Carolinas and their schools has been followed by other book-length ethnographies of communication encompassing spoken and/or written language in and out of school. In addition to my own work on language use in Quechua-speaking communities of highland Peru and their schools, cited in the introduction, Guthrie (1985) studies classroom language use in a Chinese/English bilingual education program in northern California, Edelsky (1986) explores writing in a Spanish/English bilingual program in the U.S. Southwest, Shuman (1986) tells about storytelling rights among urban adolescents in Philadelphia, and McLaughlin (1992) reports on uses of Navajo literacy on a Navajo reservation in the U.S. Southwest. These studies, in turn, explore the ways in which different languages or language varieties are ratified by use in the schools, or not, and what the consequences of such uses are for the speakers of the languages, for their learning and educational opportunities, and for the future of the languages themselves.

It is perhaps not coincidental that ethnographies of communication in educational settings have often focused on bilingual or multicultural classrooms, given the complex patterns of communicative interaction that the use of multiple language varieties evokes. This same focus is true as well of work in interactional sociolinguistics and microethnography. In a recent review of the last twenty years of research on bilingual classroom interaction, Martin-Jones (1995) suggests that there has been a progression in such research from earlier studies that focused primarily on quantifying amounts of talk or communicative functions in the two languages to more recent ethnographic studies that incorporate a conversation analytic approach and take more account of learners' contributions to classroom interactions, of the sequential flow of classroom discourse, and of the negotiation of meanings moment by moment. She goes on to note that since the early 1980s when ethnographic research began to be undertaken in bilingual classrooms (see Mehan, 1981, for an early example), there has been a move toward microethnographic observation and analysis of teaching/learning events, and that this latter approach provides a means to develop the social component of research on codeswitching in the classroom.

What Martin-Jones identifies as a microethnographic approach, also referring to it as a conversational analytic approach grounded in ethnographic observation, goes as well by the name of interactional sociolinguistics (cf. Roberts et al., 1991, pp. 88–95). The conversational analytic approach (Sacks, Schegloff, & Jefferson, 1974) has its roots in ethnomethodology (Garfinkel, 1986 [1972]) and has as its focus the detailed and sequential analysis of naturally occurring conversation (looking at such phenomena as turn-taking and adjacency pairs) in order to describe the mechanisms by which people accomplish interaction in an orderly way. In the following sections, I trace some of the features and contributions of interactional sociolinguistics and microethnography, both of which draw from conversational analysis but, unlike conversational analysis, ground their analysis of conversational interaction in an understanding of the larger contexts of the interaction.

INTERACTIONAL SOCIOLINGUISTICS

As Hymes is to the ethnography of communication, so Gumperz is to interactional sociolinguistics (or, in his own phrase, interpretive sociolinguistics, cf. Gumperz, 1982, p. vii). The two have much in common. Gumperz was part of the original AAA session on the ethnography of communication; both Hymes and Gumperz are linguistic anthropologists. Together they edited the foundational sociolinguistics text, *Directions in Sociolinguistics* (1972), and they share a common assumption that the meaning, structure, and use of language are socially and culturally situated and relative. Yet, interactional sociolinguistics can be distinguished from the ethnography of communication for its focus on the actual process of communicative interaction, particularly in instances of inter-ethnic communication, as opposed to the description of the components of communicative events and the interpretation of their meaning to participants within a particular culture. One facet of this distinction is what Hymes and Gumperz themselves refer to as the difference between syntagmatic and paradigmatic dimensions of speech events: "(1) the syntagmatic, involving the temporal ordering of subunits, including allocation of rights to speaking, and (2) the paradigmatic, referring to the selection among alternates within a contextual frame" (Gumperz 1986 [1972], p. 17; see also Gumperz, 1972 [1970], p. 212; cf. Hymes, 1968, p. 103, following Jakobson & Halle, 1956). Ervin-Tripp's discussion of co-occurrence and alternation as two types of sociolinguistic rules, both worthy of further study, refers to this same distinction, as noted by Gumperz and Hymes in their introductory comments on her work (Gumperz & Hymes, 1986 [1972], pp. 213–214).

Methodologically, interactional sociolinguistics makes greater use of audio-recorded verbal interaction for analysis than does the ethnography of communication. In an increasing number of studies, an important aspect of this methodology also includes playing back the recording to the participants and eliciting a joint interpretation of what was happening in a particular interaction (cf. Roberts et al., 1991, p. 99).

One of the first fruits of Gumperz's focus on the syntagmatic dimension of communicative interaction was the recognition that codeswitching, that is, switching languages within a speech situation, was not necessarily always due to a change in the situation, for example, a change in participants or setting. It might also be due to a change in emphasis within the situation, for example, a change in topic, purpose, or salient role relationships among the participants. With this initial distinction between what he termed situational and metaphorical codeswitching (Blom & Gumperz, 1986 [1972]; Gumperz, 1972), Gumperz made clear that codeswitching is not merely mixed up language use or functional filling-in for the speaker's lack of vocabulary in one of the languages, as had often been assumed, but rather that it has social meaning. He illustrated with examples such as a Puerto Rican mother who switches from Spanish to English to convey her annoyance with her child, a Black community worker who gives emphasis to what he says by using nonstandard dialect, and an older Korean immigrant who singles out his addressee from among others present by using Korean (Gumperz, 1972).

The discovery of the social meanings embedded in codeswitching opened up whole new areas of study in two directions, one pursuing codeswitching and the other social meanings. On the one hand, there are those who have explored the multiple dimensions and meanings of codeswitching. On the other, there are those, including Gumperz, who have sought to discover and describe the whole range of means (of which codeswitching is one) by which individuals convey social and cultural meanings in the process of interaction. In both, the issues of situated language use and the recognition of multiple social roles and identities remain fundamental.

As indicated by Martin-Jones, work on codeswitching in classrooms followed a trajectory that began by identifying and quantifying communicative functions of codeswitching in the classroom and gradually moved toward a more interactional focus. Early studies in bilingual classrooms, such as those by Milk (1981) and Sapiens (1982) on Spanish/English codeswitching and by Guthrie (1983) on Chinese/English codeswitching, generally found that English predominated as the language of instruction and control. Linguistic anthropologist Zentella

(1982) looked at children's Spanish/English codeswitching during domino games played at school and found that switches were motivated by social meanings such as emphasis (Ana used English to Juan for commands and contradictions, but Spanish for caretaking functions), addressee specification (Ana used English differently with Nora and Juan), or idiomatic expressions (Juan tried out his English in formulaic expressions such as "no," "shut up," or "go away"). By taking this more ethnographic approach to her analysis of codeswitching, Zentella was able to show the children's language use in the context of their interaction and to illuminate the multiple social roles and identities they expressed through their use of codeswitching.

Martin-Jones' study of the role of bilingual Punjabi-, Gujerati-, or Urdu-speaking classroom assistants in schools in the northwest of England is another example of the move toward more interactional sociolinguistic approaches in bilingual classroom codeswitching studies. Her analysis of the participant roles of bilingual assistants revealed two dimensions of the social relations in those classrooms. On the one hand, there is a strong cultural congruence between the bilingual assistants and the learners; on the other hand, the bilingual assistants' codeswitching is a direct reflection of asymmetrical social relations in the classroom, school, and beyond, wherein the bilingual assistants find themselves acting as buffers with dual responsibility to be supportive and nurturing to the children (learner-oriented talk) and to support their learning of English (curriculum-oriented talk).

Martin-Jones ends with a plea for more of this kind of research, because

> we need to be able to show how codeswitching in bilingual discourse is shaped by the social conditions operating in different types of classrooms and how differing views about the value and purpose of bilingual education are manifested in bilingual discourse practices. We also need to take account of the fact that the main dimensions of day to day life in bilingual and multilingual classrooms—curriculum organization, pedagogy, and social relations—are crucially shaped by social and political conditions beyond the classroom. (Martin-Jones, 1995, 108)

Freeman's (1998) work at the Oyster School provides an example of a study that began by looking at patterns of language use in a bilingual school and ended by discovering that curriculum organization, pedagogy, and social relations were shaped by a larger underlying identity plan. Her original intention was to study the two-way bilingual education language plan by triangulating classroom observations, the school's bilingual education policy, and conversations with principals, teachers, and students of the school. When she began to find, however, that there was not in fact strictly equal bilingualism in the school—that codeswitching to English in Spanish class was common, but not the reverse; that there was district-wide testing in English, but not Spanish; that the English-dominant students were not as competently bilingual in Spanish as the Spanish-dominant were in English—she began a more open-ended search for "what was going on." Using an approach that draws mainly from the ethnography of communication and interactional sociolinguistics, and that she dubs ethnographic/discourse analytic, and following Carbaugh's model of cultural communication systems (1990, p. 173), Freeman shows how intertextual analysis of school policy documents, school texts, classroom interaction, and interview transcripts sheds light on the cultural identity (definitions of teachers, students, and the school), cultural frames and forms (definitions of teaching, learning, and bilingual education), and structuring norms (classroom norms and curricular content). Together they reveal Oyster as alternative to and struggling against mainstream educational discourse.

The social meanings underlying bilingual language use patterns are also present in style or dialect language use patterns, as Gumperz himself pointed out early on. Noting the contrast in teacher's language use in fast and slow reading groups in one California first grade class, Gumperz (1972) pointed out that the dialect (nonstandard Black English vernacular) speakers who made up 90% of the "slow" group were especially sensitive to the situated nature of language use and yet got the most "decontextualized" language (alphabet, spelling, grammatical concepts, pronunciation errors corrected, unsolicited remarks ignored), while the "fast" group got plenty of language in context (words in context, natural speech, no pronunciation correction despite deviant forms being used, and volunteer remarks recognized). Interactional sociolinguists argue that such a pattern of curricular organization, pedagogy, and social relations not only limits the "slow" learners' opportunities to learn, but also conveys hidden social meanings to the participants about their roles in the larger society.

Those hidden social meanings are conveyed largely by means of what Gumperz has termed contextualization cues, and the identification and interpretation of these cues have been the objective of the second area of study opened up by the discovery of the social meanings underlying codeswitching. A contextualization cue is "any feature of linguistic form that contributes to the signalling of contextual presuppositions . . . the code, dialect and style switching processes, some of the prosodic phenomena . . . as well as choice among lexical and syntactic options, formulaic expressions, conversational openings, closings and sequencing strategies . . . [and] other less readily noticed phonetic and rhythmic signs" (Gumperz, 1982, pp.

131, 140). By means of these contextualization cues, and drawing on background knowledge that they bring to the interaction (characterized as frames, schemata, or scripts, following Goffman & Bateson, Bartlett, and van Dijk, respectively; cf. Roberts et al., 1991, pp. 72-74), participants make their way moment by moment through an interaction, making situated inferences as to what is going on and what is their own role and identity as they go.

This is the kind of process that Wortham's (1995) study reveals. Ironically, experience-near examples, which ostensibly draw on participants' background knowledge and therefore ought to actively engage them, instead have the effect of flattening particulars and encouraging passivity among classroom discussants, because of the way the interaction is structured in these particular classrooms.

The discourse analysis applied in Wortham (1994, 1995), as in Freeman's (above) and Chick's (below) studies, belongs to critical discourse analysis, an approach in which language is understood and explained in terms of its key role in maintaining or challenging existing power relations (Roberts et al., 1991, p. 77). Freeman, following Fairclough (1989), sees the sociopolitical context as layers including the situational, institutional, and societal levels. He explains how Oyster's alternative educational discourse challenges the mainstream discourse.

In contrast, Chick's (1996) study of an English-medium math class for Zulu-speaking students in apartheid South Africa portrays a collusion between teacher and pupils, which appears to maintain the status quo. The students and their teacher produce a style of interaction, which he calls safe-talk, a rhythmically coordinated chorusing that maintains a façade of learning while hiding the participants' poor command of English and of the academic content of their lessons. The rhythmic nature of the interaction is not coincidental. As Chick notes, "*when* a contextualization cue occurs is as vital to successful interpretation as whether it occurs or not. Erickson shows that the verbal and non-verbal speaking and listening behavior of interlocutors engaged in successful interaction is finely synchronized" (Chick, 1996, p. xx).

MICRO-ETHNOGRAPHY

Indeed, Erickson's micro-ethnography has repeatedly shown the importance of timing and synchrony in communicative interaction. Micro-ethnography, according to Erickson, traces its intellectual roots to context analysis, the ethnography of communication and interactional sociolinguistics, work by Goffman on the social situation, ethnomethodology and conversation analysis, and continental discourse analysis (Erickson, 1996). As early as 1976, Erickson differentiated microethnography from ethnography in terms of both the scope and focus of its investigation. Whereas the scope of general ethnography is the "whole way of life of a naturally bounded social group," that of microethnography is "particular cultural scenes within key institutional settings"; whereas the analytic focus of general ethnography is the overall description of events, that of microethnography is "the processes of face-to-face interaction in the events." Essentially, this approach combines "participant observation with detailed analysis of audiovisual records of naturally occurring interaction in key scenes in people's lives" (Erickson & Mohatt, 1982, pp. 137,133). Methodologically, microethnography shares participant observation in common with the ethnography of communication; detailed sequential analysis and playback of audiorecorded interaction in common with interactional sociolinguistics; and the emic/etic perspective, the use of naturally occurring language data, the consultation of native intuition, and the tool of discourse analysis, in common with all the linguistically informed approaches to ethnography. But it differs from the rest in the use of video-recording and the focus on nonlinguistic aspects of the interaction.

As applied to education, microethnography has been particularly revealing of the more hidden cultural congruences and incongruences in inter-cultural or inter-ethnic interactions. Erickson and Shultz (1982) videotaped a series of advising sessions between students and counselors of varying ethnic backgrounds (four counselors and twenty-five students at two junior colleges); selected twenty-five all-male (with one exception) interviews as sample (p. 53); and analyzed them along the dimensions of topical content and sequencing, participation structure, contextualization cueing, timing and rhythm of speech and body motion (p. 64); constructed indices to identify instances of interactional asymmetry/asynchrony or "uncomfortable moments" in the interview (pp. 103 ff.); and found that there was a direct relationship between the indices of asynchrony and the amount of usable information that the student derived from the interview (Gumperz, 1982, p. 142). Their "finding that situationally emergent rather than normatively fixed social identity had the strongest influence on the character and outcome of the interviews" (p. 181) is consistent with the notions of situated discourse and multiple and alternative social roles and identities. These, as I said at the outset, are fundamental to all of the linguistically informed approaches to ethnography we are reviewing here.

In particular, they found that comembership, that is, an aspect of performed (or situationally emergent) social identity that involves particularistic attributes of status shared by the counselor and student (Erickson & Shultz, 1982, p. 17) was "most closely associated with levels of special help, overall behavioral smoothness, and the counselor's choices among ways of asking and explaining that were . . . supportive of the student . . . [and that] comembership [had] a powerfully overriding positive influence on the otherwise negative effects of cultural difference in communicative style" (Erickson & Shultz, 1982, pp. 180–181). In other words, the degree to which counselor and student were able, through the process of their interaction, to establish a sense of comembership based on shared attributes of their social identities was significant for the successful outcome of the interview, significant above and beyond possible culture differences in communicative style. Again, situated discourse and multiple and alternative social roles and identities are fundamental to what's going on.

Two classroom-based microethnographic studies by Erickson and others provide further evidence of the subtle ways in which proxemics, kinesics, rhythm, and non-verbal cues work together with linguistic signals in culturally specific ways to define contexts of interaction. Erickson and Mohatt (1982; see also Mohatt & Erickson, 1981) analyzed multiple hours of videotapes of two experienced first grade teachers in a northern Ontario (Odawa) reserve, one an Indian teacher who was a member of the local reserve community and the other a non-Indian teaching Indian children for the first time. Their detailed analysis of the overall timing of classroom activity; teacher movement, proxemic relationship to students, and the issuance of directives; and classroom discourse at the beginning of the school day generally showed the Indian teacher's interactional style to be more congruent with Indian interactional etiquette in the community. They are careful, however, to point out that her ways of teaching are not "pure Indian," but rather adaptive mixed forms, and that the non-Indian teacher also used mixed forms and in fact adopted some of the ways of teaching of the Indian teacher as the year progressed (Erickson & Mohatt, 1982, p. 168). A course for teachers, counselors, and administrators, designed on the basis of this research and taught by the authors, provided school personnel with a concrete definition of culture, a way to relate culture to their needs, and a way to think about solving classroom issues through an analysis of interactional events in relation to participants' cultural backgrounds (Mohatt & Erickson, 1981, p. 119).

In two Spanish/English bilingual first grade classrooms in Chicago, where all the participants were Mexican American, Erickson, Cazden, Carrasco, and Maldonado-Guzmán (1983) observed and videotaped interactions that documented not only the differences between the two teachers in their classroom organizational approach, but also the similarities in their style of classroom control. Specifically, both teachers used a personalized style—a *cariño* style—based on a close and caring relationship with their students and characterized by features such as "in-group forms of address, frequent use of diminutives, reminders to the children of norms of interpersonal respect, . . . expressions of the teacher's knowledge of her children's family life, . . . placing a child on her lap when working individually with the child, kissing the child as a reward for good work, . . . [and] codeswitching into Spanish for control" (Cazden, 1988, pp. 170-178). Again, as in the case of the Odawa teacher, nonlinguistic as well as linguistic features are combined in teachers' interactional styles in a way that contributes more or less to a strong and positive sense of community with the learners. In all of these microethnographic studies, detailed analysis of nonlinguistic and linguistic interactional behavior in an educational setting focus our attention on the situationally emergent nature of both the interaction itself and of the roles and identities of the participants in the interaction.

Whether uncovering the participant structures in mainstream and non-mainstream classrooms, documenting the patterns of language use and social relations in bilingual classrooms, comparing classroom and community ways of speaking and writing, describing the construction of an alternative educational discourse for language minority students, or exploring the dimensions of discourse that maintains the status quo in societal power relations, the three strands of linguistic anthropological research in the schools provide perspectives and methodologies that allow us to not only understand what's going on, but also to imagine and implement change. Discourse analysis, whether of the conversational analysis, critical, or another type, provides a tool by which we can analyze naturally occurring language data and measure our analyses against native (speaker) knowledge, providing a route to the emic/etic dialectic that is crucial to our understanding of the role and future of language and learning in schools.

The "New" Linguistic Anthropology of Education

The linguistic anthropology of education featured in this volume represents yet another strand (or perhaps strands), with elements both in common with and different from the earlier strands described previously. Wortham and Rymes have done a great service by foregrounding the contribution of linguistic anthropology to educational research and drawing into that spotlight lines of linguistic anthropological work that have only recently turned attention more directly to educational settings. So, for example, we have Wortham, Collins, and O'Connor drawing tools and concepts from the work of Silverstein and Urban to look at a ninth grade history class, a university literacy laboratory, and a multi-institution undergraduate engineering project, respectively. We have He and Rymes drawing from work by Ochs and Schieffelin on language socialization to explore language teaching and learning in Chinese heritage language classrooms and in two elementary public school classrooms in Georgia. And we have Jaffe, Stocker, and González and Arnot-Hopffer drawing from Woolard and Schieffelin's work on language ideologies and cultural/linguistic/social/ethnic identities to consider a bilingual Corsican classroom, a high school outside the Matambú reservation in Costa Rica, and a dual language immersion program in Tucson, Arizona. These chapters richly illustrate the continuing reciprocal contributions between linguistic anthropology and education.

In the introduction to the volume, Wortham suggests that the elements in common between this work and earlier work in linguistic anthropology of education are communicative competence, taking the native point of view, and connecting micro to macro. The differences lie in the concepts of indexicality, creativity, regimentation, and poetic structure. I am grateful to him for the clarity with which he presents these concepts from linguistic anthropological work and their relevance for education, and for his acknowledgment that this work builds on the earlier work, and would only suggest that, occasionally, I think he underestimates that earlier work. For example, that both the earlier and the new LAE study communicative competence, or language in use, that is, actual discourse or naturally occurring language data, is an acknowledged point of continuity. However, I find the earlier notion of communicative competence too narrowly interpreted here, thereby minimizing its continuity with the new work (more on this later).

Similarly, Wortham attributes the linguistic anthropologists' (then and now) emphasis on seeking to understand the native point of view only to anthropological precedents, without making the link from the etic/emic distinction in the study of human behavior to the phonetic/phonemic distinction in the study of the sound systems of language, following Pike (1967 [1954]). As a result, Wortham misses another important continuity in the earlier and newer work in LAE, namely the crucial importance of the dialectic interplay between emic and etic. The difference between the emic and the etic standpoint in the study of human behavior is that the etic standpoint is one situated outside the system studied, in which units and classifications are determined on the basis of existing knowledge of similar systems and against which the particular system is measured. The emic standpoint, on the other hand, is one situated inside the particular system studied, which views the system as an integrated whole, and in which units and classifications are determined during and not before analysis, and are discovered and not created by the researcher. Both standpoints are necessary, and it is the movement back and forth between them that takes our understanding forward. Hymes asserts that Pike's three moments, etic-1, emic, etic-2, or in other words, "the dialectic in which theoretical frameworks are employed to describe and discover systems, and such discoveries in turn change the frameworks" are fundamental to linguistics and anthropology (Hymes, 1990, p. 421) and by extension, I would argue, to linguistic anthropology.

It is good to see that Wortham brings out, as the third continuity, linguistic anthropologists' attention to the interplay between larger social processes and particular instances of language use in their educational research, a point often overlooked. In their separate chapters, Wortham and Rymes mention the classic works by Heath (1983) and Philips (1983) as examples of earlier work linking macro-level power inequities and micro-level interactional positioning (via what came to be known as the difference or cultural mismatch hypothesis). Other work, such as my own earlier study of an experimental bilingual education program in Puno, Peru (1988), and, more recently, Freeman's on the Oyster Bilingual School (1998) and Jaffe's (1999) on language politics on Corsica, explicitly seeks to link the micro level of classroom language use to the macro level of language policy and language ideology. Consistent with the two themes identified in my review of the earlier three strands of LAE, this work brings out the complexity of multiple layers of context in situated discourse (or language use) and the multiple and alternative social roles and identities that are constructed and negotiated in these contexts.

Four concepts that Wortham suggests were present in earlier LAE work, but have been elaborated more fully in contemporary work, are indexicality, creativity, regimentation, and poetic structure. He illustrates them magnificently in relation to the Maurice episode taken from his own ethnographic research in a ninth grade history class, and the several chapters in the volume further illuminate these four concepts. I offer here a few comments to more fully contextualize the new LAE in relation to the earlier work.

Indexicality refers to the fact that much of everyday speech gets its meaning indexically, from context; specifically, indexicality is the sign pointing to its object. The new LAE's concern with analyzing the specific linguistic means by which meaning gets communicated in interaction is the same concern as the interactional sociolinguists' exploration of the range of means by which individuals convey social and cultural meanings in the process of interaction, that is, contextualization cues (in fact, I cited Wortham's work as an example of interactional sociolinguistics). Yet, Wortham seems to overlook this continuity, acknowledging it only in passing later, in his discussion of mediation or "contextualization" (Silverstein, 1992).

Creativity of language-in-use, as I understand it from Wortham's discussion, refers on the one hand to the fact that speakers may violate expected norms or patterns of speaking for interactional effect and on the other to the observation that "linguistic forms can be uttered in appropriate contexts but yield unexpected results." While I concur wholeheartedly with the value of these insights, I believe they were both already present (though often overlooked by interpreters) in Hymes's notion of communicative competence. Hymes' original formulation specified four sectors of communicative competence: possibility (in terms of linguistic structure), feasibility (in terms of psycholinguistic capacity of the individual), appropriateness (in terms of context), and occurrence (referring to what does or does not occur given possibility, feasibility, appropriateness, or a lack thereof). The last sector, occurrence, has often been overlooked or misinterpreted. "It includes both what may be possible, feasible, and appropriate but nevertheless not done; and what is not possible, feasible, nor appropriate but is nevertheless done" (Hornberger, 1989, p. 218), two types of occurrence that sound to me very much like the two dimensions of creativity Wortham discusses (in reverse order).

Much of the misunderstanding seems to reside in the word "rules," though neither Hymes nor ethnographers of communication ever used the expression "rules of communicative competence" (as Wortham does). Hymes used the slogan "rules of use" as well as "rules of grammar" to extend the notion of competence beyond grammatical knowledge. Hence, the meaning of the word "rules" lies not in the normative and prescriptive sense (any more than a linguist's rules of grammar would be), but in the sense of a descriptive rule of actual language use. Hymes would never have suggested that communicative competence means there is only one appropriate type of utterance for a given context. The whole premise of the ethnography of communication is a paradigmatic one, presupposing that in any given context there are alternatives from which speakers choose to achieve the desired interactional effect (or not, as the case may be).

Paradigmatic and syntagmatic approaches within linguistic anthropology were highlighted early on (Gumperz, 1972, pp. 212–218), presaging what Wortham discusses under the notions of regimentation and emergence. In my discussion of the intertwining strands, I characterized the ethnography of communication as primarily paradigmatic and interactional sociolinguistics as primarily syntagmatic, suggesting that interactional sociolinguistics can be distinguished from the ethnography of communication for its focus on the actual process of communicative interaction, particularly in instances of inter-ethnic communication, as opposed to the description of the components of communicative events and the interpretation of their meaning to participants within a particular culture. Syntagmatic attention to the ordering of utterances and the emergence of the meaning of an utterance in relation to preceding and subsequent utterances and paradigmatic attention to the frame within which the regimentation of possible meanings is set are examples of fundamental continuities within the linguistic anthropology of education, which the chapters in the present volume develop and elaborate with great richness and depth.

What Wortham calls the problem of "chunking," that is, "given a stream of speech and indefinite potentially relevant context, how do speakers and analysts know which chunks cohere and have implications for establishing some recognizable meaning?" has long been present in work in LAE, and has been addressed in various ways. Ethnographers of communication might initially chunk speech events by looking for locally named speech events, boundaries marked by participant change or gaze change, or boundary violations which signal the existence of a boundary (Hymes, 1968, pp.110, 123), while micro-ethnographers might rely heavily on nonlinguistic features such as rhythm, gaze, and posture for initial chunking (Erickson, 1996). The emergence of poetic structure, that is, patterns of indexical cues across segments of language use (and not just in isolated instances) has also been an ongoing concern in linguistic anthropology, certainly in Hymes's ethnopoetics (as acknowledged by Wortham), but also, for example, in ethnographic studies of classroom discourse (Mehan, 1979; Sinclair & Coulthard, 1975).

The strands of linguistic anthropology of education, both the earlier and the new, share a fundamental focus on the situated nature of communicative interaction and a recognition of the multiple and alternative social roles and identities available to participants in communicative interaction. Each one, however, implies a somewhat different route to ensuring that schools allow all learners to participate equally in the interaction, and by extension, the learning that goes on there. The ethnography of communication, by providing clear documentation on alternative ways of speaking and writing, offers the potential for educators to incorporate a range of culturally appropriate/compatible communicative styles in classrooms. Interactional sociolinguistics, by revealing the multiple linguistic means by which we embed social meanings in interaction, provides clues by which educators can increase our sensitivity to communicative success and breakdown. Microethnography, with its emphasis on the importance of situationally emergent social identity and comembership, suggests that, no matter what the social and cultural givens in an interaction, there is always the possibility for communication that builds up rather than breaking down participants' learning. The "new" linguistic anthropology of education, which applies a set of precise and powerful tools and concepts in analysing discourse, thereby providing insights into "the relationship between larger sociocultural patterns and the (re)production of inequity, on the level of person-to-person interaction, inside the classroom" (Rymes, this volume; see also Rymes, 2001), offers hope that attending to the micro-level of interaction in the classroom can in fact contribute to addressing societal inequities. Taken together, these approaches provide educators with a truly powerful set of insights and tools for implementing change in our schools.

LAE INTERNATIONALLY LINKED TO LINGUISTIC ETHNOGRAPHY

In bringing together recent work in the linguistic anthropology of education in a volume by that title, Wortham and Rymes have helpfully focused our attention on the existence of a tradition of such research. Across the Atlantic ocean, UK scholars engaged in ethnographic research on language and literacy have recently begun to gather in a series of meetings (at Leicester in March 2001, at Aberystwyth in April 2002) to talk about the various traditions of work in this area, which they have provisionally dubbed linguistic ethnography, encompassing such topics as the new literacy studies (Street, Barton, and others), institutional discourse (Sarangi, Roberts), urban heteroglossia (Rampton, Harris), multilingualism (Martin-Jones, Arthur, Creese), and classrooms and community (Gregory, Williams, Maybin).

A concern that has arisen in the UK group is that the term *linguistic ethnography* sidelines research on literacies—arguably the best-established strand in the United Kingdom—and the suggestion is made that "ethnography of communication may well prove to the best descriptor" (cf. the Leicester meeting website, www.baal.org.uk/ling_ethno/). Interestingly, the same could be said for linguistic anthropology on this side of the Atlantic; the ethnography of communication explicitly includes written as well as spoken language, both in and out of schools. Just as linguistic anthropological attention to socialization has moved more and more into educational settings, so attention to socialization into literacy and literacy practices has moved more and more out of them. A recent volume edited by Hull and Schultz (2002), entitled *School's Out!* represents this work. Similarly, a session organized and chaired by Schultz and E. Skilton-Sylvester at the 2000 American Anthropological Association meetings, on "Historical, Empirical, and Theoretical Reconsiderations of the Ethnography of Communication in Education," was heavily oriented toward work on literacies in and out of school, including workplace literacies, multilingual literacies, and electronic literacies, among others.

Wortham has also convened a couple of invitational meetings on the linguistic anthropology of education, held at Penn GSE in conjunction with the Ethnography in Education Research Forum in March (2000 and 2002). This year's meeting will include attendance by some of the UK scholars who have particpated in the linguistic ethnography meetings. Jim Collins (contributor to this volume) has participated in both sets of meetings, which clearly have terrain in common.

Though many questions remain unresolved and still more are yet to be raised with regard to the nuances of identifying the exact terrain of LAE and contextualizing it in terms of other interdisciplinary work and relationships, the content of this volume and the wealth of research tradition it springs from are testimony enough to LAE having earned a place as a field of research which has as its central focus the role of language—as indexical to implicit positionings, identities, and ideologies—in learning and teaching, which takes as premise that insights from work in linguistic anthropology and educational research are mutually informing, and which comprises multiple strands of work sharing in common a series of concepts and the tool of systematic discourse analysis. As a field combining linguistics, anthropology, and education, it intersects and overlaps also with similarly interdisciplinary fields such as educational linguistics, educational anthropology, and linguistic ethnography.

Linguistic anthropology of education is, perhaps fundamentally, a field that seeks to understand macro-level societal phenomena, and in particular societal inequities, in terms of micro-level person-to-person interaction, in the hopes of enabling work for change from both the bottom up and the top down. This has certainly been a consistent underlying theme since the earliest days of LAE, one reiterated regularly. Gumperz (1986, p. 45) writes about linguistic anthropologists' perennial concern for why some students learn while others fail to achieve. Hymes reminds us that we are about contributing "to the transformation of linguistic inequality" (Hymes, 1996, p. 101). González and Arnot-Hopffer (this volume) note that "whenever micro-phenomena are examined carefully, implicit ideologies are revealed" and, following Zentella (1997), call LAE an anthropolitical linguistics, "an approach that connects language to complex issues of political economy and social identities" (González & Arnot-Hopffer, this volume). This implies that linguistic anthropologists of education have an obligation to bring their considerable analytical skills to bear on enabling change toward greater equity in our educational policies and practices. At a session on anthropolitical linguistics and language policy at the 2001 American Anthropological Association meetings, Jaffe (contributor to this volume) noted that two arenas where anthropolitical linguists can be active are in clear-cut cases of linguistic discrimination and in less clear-cut issues of language rights, in either case bringing a focus on language as communicative practice, on the ethnographic study of policymaking, and on exposing relationships between linguistic and social hierarchies, all strengths of the linguistic anthropology of education charted here. Placing linguistic anthropology of education in context means, ultimately, allowing and indeed urging its practitioners to put its resources to work to change that context for the better.

NOTES

1. Nancy Hornberger has been on the faculty of the Educational Linguistics program since 1985, and Stanton Wortham in the Education, Culture, and Society program since 1998; earlier linguistic anthropologists at Penn GSE included Shirley Brice Heath, Bambi Schieffelin, Katherine Woolard, Rebecca Freeman, Frederick Erickson and, of course, Dell Hymes. The infusion of interests in language and ethnography extends beyond the Educational Linguistics and Education, Culture, and Society programs as well.

2. The following sections on ethnography of communication, interactional sociolinguistics, and microethnography contain material from Hornberger (1995), reprinted with permission of Multilingual Matters.

REFERENCES

Au, K., & Jordan, C. (1981). Teaching reading to Hawaiian children: Finding a culturally appropriate solution. In H. T. Trueba, G. P. Guthrie, & K. H. Au (Eds.), *Culture and the Bilingual Classroom: Studies in Classroom Ethnography* (pp. 139–152). Rowley, MA: Newbury House.

Basso, K. (1974). The ethnography of writing. In R. Bauman & J. Sherzer (Eds.), *Explorations in the Ethnography of Speaking* (pp. 425–432). Cambridge: Cambridge University Press.

Blom, J. P., & Gumperz, J. (1986 [1972]). Social meaning in linguistic structure: Code-switching in Norway. In J. J. Gumperz, & D. Hymes (Eds.), *Directions in Sociolinguistics* (pp. 407–434). New York: Holt, Rinehart, and Winston.

Boggs, S. T., Watson-Gegeo, K. A., & McMillen, G. (1985). *Speaking, Relating, and Learning: A Study of Hawaiian Children at Home and at School.* Norwood, NJ: Ablex.

Carbaugh, D. (Ed.). (1990). *Cultural Communication and Intercultural Contact.* Hillsdale, NJ: Lawrence Erlbaum.

Cazden, C. B. (1988). *Classroom Discourse: The Language of Teaching and Learning.* Portsmouth, NH: Heinemann.

Cazden, C., John, V., & Hymes, D.H. (Eds.). (1972). *Functions of Language in the Classroom.* New York: Teachers College Press.

Chick, J. K. (1996). Safe-talk: Collusion in apartheid education. In H. Coleman (Ed.), *Society and the Language Classroom* (pp. 21–39). Cambridge: Cambridge University Press.

Chomsky, N. (1965). *Aspects of the Theory of Syntax.* Cambridge, MA: MIT Press.

Edelsky, C. (1986). *Writing in a Bilingual Program: Había una Vez.* Norwood, NJ: Ablex.

Erickson, F. (1996). Ethnographic microanalysis. In S. L. McKay & N. H. Hornberger (Eds.), *Sociolinguistics and Language Teaching* (pp. 283–306). New York: Cambridge University Press.

Erickson, F., Cazden, C., Carrasco, R., & Maldonado-Guzman, A. (1983). *Social and Cultural Organization of Interaction in Classrooms of Bilingual Children.* Final report to the National Institute of Education. (Unpublished report).

Erickson, F., & Mohatt, G. (1982). Cultural organization of participation structures in two classrooms of Indian students. In G. Spindler (Ed.), *Doing the Ethnography of Schooling: Educational Anthropology in Action* (pp. 132–174). New York: Holt, Rinehart, and Winston.

Erickson, F., & Shultz, J. (1982). *Counselor as Gatekeeper: Social Interaction in Interviews*. New York: Academic Press.

Fairclough, N. (1989). *Language and Power*. New York: Longman.

Freeman, R. D. (1998). *Bilingual Education and Social Change*. Clevedon, U.K.: Multilingual Matters.

Garfinkel, H. (1986 [1972]). Remarks on ethnomethodology. In J. Gumperz & D. Hymes (Eds.), *Directions in Sociolinguistics: The Ethnography of Communication* (pp. 301–324). New York: Basil Blackwell.

Gumperz, J. J. (1972). Verbal strategies in multilingual communication. In R. Abrahams & R. C. Troike (Eds.), *Language and Cultural Diversity in American Education* (pp. 184–195). Englewood Cliffs, NJ: Prentice-Hall.

Gumperz, J. J. (1972[1970]). Sociolinguistics and communication in small groups. In J. B. Pride & J. Holmes (Eds.), *Sociolinguistics* (pp. 203–224). New York: Penguin Books.

Gumperz, J. J. (1982). *Discourse Strategies*. Cambridge: Cambridge University Press.

Gumperz, J. J. (1986[1972]). Introduction. In J. J. Gumperz & D. H. Hymes (Eds.), *Directions in Sociolinguistics: The Ethnography of Communication* (pp. 1–25). New York: Basil Blackwell.

Gumperz, J. J. (1986). Interactional sociolinguistics in the study of schooling. In J. Cook-Gumperz (Ed.), *The Social Construction of Literacy* (pp. 45–68). Cambridge: Cambridge University Press.

Gumperz, J. J., & Hymes, D.H. (Eds.). (1972). *Directions in Sociolinguistics: The Ethnography of Communication* (Re-issued in 1986 by Basil Blackwell, New York). New York: Holt, Rinehart, and Winston.

Guthrie, G. P. (1985). *A School Divided: An Ethnography of Bilingual Education in a Chinese Community*. Hillsdale, NJ: Lawrence Erlbaum.

Guthrie, L. F. (1983). Contrasts in teachers' language use in a Chinese-English bilingual classroom. In J. Handscomb, R. Orem, & B. Taylor (Eds.), *On TESOL '83: The Question of Control* (pp. 39–52). Washington: TESOL.

Heath, S. B. (1978). *Outline Guide for the Ethnographic Study of Literacy and Oral Language from Schools to Communities*. Philadelphia: University of Pennsylvania, Graduate School of Education.

Heath, S. B. (1983). *Ways with Words: Language, Life and Work in Communities and Classrooms*. Cambridge: Cambridge University Press.

Hornberger, N. H. (1988). *Bilingual Education and Language Maintenance: A Southern Peruvian Quechua Case*. Berlin: Mouton.

Hornberger, N. H. (1989). Trámites and transportes: The acquisition of second language communicative competence for one speech event in Puno, Peru. *Applied Linguistics, 10*(2), 214–230.

Hornberger, N. H. (1995). Ethnography in linguistic perspective: Understanding school processes. *Language and Education, 9*(4), 233–248.

Hornberger, N. H. (2001). Educational linguistics as a field: A view from Penn's program on the occasion of its 25th anniversary. *Working Papers in Educational Linguistics, 17*(1-2), 1–26.

Hull, G., & Schultz, K. (Eds.). (2002). *School's Out!: Bridging Out-of-School Literacies with Classroom Practice*. New York: Teachers College Press.

Hymes, D. H. (1964). Introduction: Toward ethnographies of communication. *American Anthropologist, 66*(6), 1–34.

Hymes, D. H. (1968). The ethnography of speaking. In J. A. Fishman (Ed.), *Readings in the Sociology of Language* (pp. 99–138). The Hague: Mouton.

Hymes, D. H. (1972a). On communicative competence. In J. B. Pride & J. Holmes (Eds.), *Sociolinguistics: Selected Readings* (pp. 269–293). Harmondsworth, U.K.: Penguin Books.

Hymes, D. H. (1972b). Models of the interaction of language and social life. In J. Gumperz & D. Hymes (Eds.), *Directions in Sociolinguistics: The Ethnography of Communication* (pp. 35–71). New York: Holt, Rinehart, and Winston.

Hymes, D. H. (1974). *Foundations in Sociolinguistics: An Ethnographic Approach.* Philadelphia: University of Pennsylvania Press.

Hymes, D. H. (1990). Epilogue: The things we do with words. In D. Carbaugh (Ed.), *Cultural Communication and Intercultural Contact* (pp. 419–429). Hillsdale, NJ: Lawrence Erlbaum.

Hymes, D.H. (1996). Report from an underdeveloped country: Toward linguistic competence in the United States. *Ethnography, Linguistics, Narrative Inequality: Toward an Understanding of Voice* (pp. 63–105). Bristol, PA: Taylor & Francis.

Hymes, D. H., & Gumperz, J.J. (Eds.). (1964). Toward ethnographies of communication. *American Anthropologist, 66* (6), entire issue.

Jaffe, A. (1999). *Ideologies in Action: Language Politics on Corsica.* Berlin: Mouton.

Jakobson, R., & Halle, M. (1956). *Fundamentals of Language.* Graoenhage, Mounton.

Kochman, T. (1981). *Black and White Styles in Conflict.* Chicago: University of Chicago Press.

Martin-Jones, M. (1995). Code-switching in the classroom: Two decades of research. In L. Milroy & P. Muysken (Eds.), *One Speaker, Two Languages: Cross-Disciplinary Perspectives on Code-Switching* (pp. 90–111). Cambridge: Cambridge University Press.

McKay, S. L., & Hornberger, N. H. (Eds.). (1996). *Sociolinguistics and Language Teaching.* New York: Cambridge University Press.

McLaughlin, D. (1992). *When Literacy Empowers: Navajo Language in Print.* Albuquerque: University of New Mexico Press.

Mehan, H. (1979). *Learning Lessons.* Cambridge, MA: Harvard University Press.

Mehan, H. (1981). Ethnography of bilingual education. In H. Trueba, Guthrie, G. P., & K. Au (Eds.), *Culture and the Bilingual Classroom* (pp. 36–55). Rowley, MA: Newbury House.

Milk, R. D. (1981). Language use in bilingual classrooms: Two case studies. In M. Hines & W. Rutherford (Eds.), *On TESOL '81* (pp. 181–191).

Mohatt, G., & Erickson, F. (1981). Cultural differences in teaching styles in an Odawa school: A sociolinguistic approach. In H. T. Trueba, G. P. Guthrie, & K. Au (Eds.), *Culture and the Bilingual Classroom: Studies in Classroom Ethnography* (pp. 105–119). Rowley, MA: Newbury House.

Paulston, C. B., & Tucker, G. R. (Eds.). (1997). *The Early Days of Sociolinguistics: Memories and Reflections.* Dallas: Summer Institute of Linguistics.

Philips, S. U. (1983). *The Invisible Culture: Communication in Classroom and Community on the Warm Springs Reservation* (reissued 1993, Prospect Heights, IL: Waveland Press ed.). New York: Longman.

Pike, K. (1967 [1954]). Emic and etic standpoints for the description of behavior. In K. Pike (Ed.), *Language in Relation to a Unified Theory of the Structure of Human Behavior* (pp. 37–72). The Hague: Mouton.

Roberts, C., Jupp, T., & Davies, E. (1991). *Language and Discrimination: A Study of Communication in Multiethnic Workplaces.* New York: Longman.

Rymes, B. (2001). *Conversational Borderlands: Language and Identity in an Alternative Urban High School*. New York: Teachers College Press.

Sacks, H., Schegloff, E., & Jefferson, G. (1974). A simplest systematics for the organization of turn-taking in conversation. *Language, 50*, 696–735.

Sapiens, A. (1982). The use of Spanish and English in a high school bilingual civics class. In J. Amastae & L. Elías-Olivares (Eds.), *Spanish in the United States: Sociolinguistic Aspects* (pp. 386–412). Cambridge: Cambridge University Press.

Saville-Troike, M. (1989). *The Ethnography of Communication: An Introduction*. New York: Basil Blackwell.

Shuman, A. (1986). *Storytelling Rights: The Uses of Oral and Written Texts among Urban Adolescents*. Cambridge: Cambridge University Press.

Silverstein, M. (1992). The indeterminacy of contextualization: When is enough enough? In A. DiLuzio, & P. Auer (Eds.), *The Contextualization of Language* (pp. 55–75). Amsterdam: John Benjamins.

Sinclair, J. M., & Coulthard, M. (1975). *Towards an Analysis of Discourse: The English Used by Teachers and Pupils*. London: Oxford University Press.

Spindler, G., & Spindler, L. (2000). *Fifty Years of Anthropology and Education, 1950–2000: A Spindler Anthology*. Mahwah, NJ: Lawrence Erlbaum.

Spolsky, B. (1974). Linguistics and education: An overview. In T. A. Sebeok (Ed.), *Current Trends in Linguistics* (Vol. 12, pp. 2021–2026). The Hague: Mouton.

Spolsky, B. (1975). Linguistics in practice: The Navajo reading study. *Theory into Practice, 14*(5), 347–352.

Szwed, J. F. (1981). The ethnography of literacy. In M. F. Whiteman (Ed.), *Writing: The Nature, Development, and Teaching of Written Communication* (Vol. 1, pp. 13–23). Hillsdale, NJ: Lawrence Erlbaum.

Vogt, L., Jordan, C., & Tharp, R. (1987). Explaining school failure, producing school success: Two cases. *Anthropology and Education Quarterly, 18*(4), 276–286.

Wortham, S. (1994). *Acting out Participant Examples in the Classroom*. Philadelphia: John Benjamins.

Wortham, S. (1995). Experiencing the great books. *Mind, Culture & Activity, 2*, 67–80.

Zentella, A. C. (1982). Code-switching and interaction among Puerto Rican children. In J. Amastae & L. Elías-Olivares (Eds.), *Spanish in the United States: Sociolinguistic Aspects* (pp. 354–385). Cambridge: Cambridge University Press.

Zentella, A. C. (1997). *Growing Up Bilingual: Puerto Rican Children in New York*. Malden, MA: Blackwell Publishers.

Index

About the Editors and Contributors

ELIZABETH ARNOT-HOPFFER is the bilingual curriculum specialist and a Spanish reading teacher at Davis Bilingual Magnet School in Tucson, Arizona. She has worked as a bilingual classroom and resource teacher for Tucson Unified School District and as a teacher educator at the University of Arizona. Ms. Arnot-Hopffer is site coordinator for a longitudinal study of language ideology and biliteracy development sponsored by the Spencer Foundation.

JAMES COLLINS is professor in the Department of Anthropology and Reading at the State University of New York at Albany. There he teaches courses on language and culture and on sociolinguistic perspectives on literacy and advises dissertations in both departments. He has published on social theory and linguistics, critical studies of language and education, and Native American languages, cultures and societies. Among significant publications are *Understanding Tolowa Histories: Western Hegemonies and Native American Responses* (1998) and *Literacy and Literacies: Texts, Power, and Identity* (with Richard Blot), in press.

NORMA GONZÁLEZ is an associate professor in the Department of Education, Culture and Society at the University of Utah. She is the author of a book on language socialization entitled *I Am My Language: Discourses of Women and Children in the Borderlands* and co-editor of a volume entitled *Classroom Diversity: Connecting Curriculum to Students' Lives* (2001). Her research and teaching focus on language use in context, anthropological perspectives on students' funds of knowledge, and teachers as researchers.

AGNES WEIYUN HE has published extensively in the areas of discourse linguistics and educational linguistics. Her research interests are centered around language use and language education. She is the author of *Reconstructing Institutions: Language Use in Academic Counseling Encounters* (1998) and co-editor of *Talking and Testing: Discourse Approaches to the Assessment of Oral Proficiency* (1998). In recent years, she has been focusing on the linguistic and cultural development of Chinese American children. She is currently a lecturer in the Chinese Language Program and an adjunct research associate professor in the Department of Linguistics at the State University of New York at Stony Brook.

NANCY H. HORNBERGER is professor of education and director of educational linguistics at the University of Pennsylvania Graduate School of Education, where she also convenes the annual Ethnography in Education Research Forum. She specializes in sociolinguistics and linguistic anthropology, language planning and policy and practice for indigenous and immigrant language minorities in the United States and internationally.

ALEXANDRA JAFFE has conducted ethnographic fieldwork since 1988 on the island of Corsica. Her focus has been on language ideologies and how they fram Corsican minority language activism and its popular reception. She has written about these issues with reference to the media, literature, public discourse and education. Her book, *Ideologies in Action: Language Politics on Corsica*, was published in 1999. Her most recent fieldwork, in 2000, was an ethnographic study of a bilingual Corsican school. She is current an associate professor in the Linguistics Department at California State, Long Beach.

KEVIN O'CONNOR is a researcher with the National Center on English Learning and Achievement at the University of Wisconsin-Madison, where he is also a lecturer in the Department of Psychology. In his research, he draws on theoretical and methodological developments in linguistic anthropology to study sociocultural aspects of meaning, learning, and identity. Currently, he is conducting an ethnographic study of the development of language and literacy practices in urban middle school classrooms.

BETSY RYMES teaches in the Department of Language Education at the University of Georgia. In both her teaching and her research, she approaches content learning by examining its relationship to social, cultural, and linguistic context. Her current research examines the social foundations of second language learning in multiple contexts in Northeast Georgia. She is the author of *Conversational Borderlands: Language and Identity in an Alternative Urban High School* (2001), as well as numerous articles and essays in such journals as *Language and Society*, *Discourse and Society*, *Linguistics and Education*, and *Anthropology & Education*.

KAREN STOCKER currently researches the mutual effects of schooling and identity for students from an indigenous reservation who attend high school outside the reservation, in a town rife with xenophobia and racism. She has worked in Costa Rica since 1993 on this project and others, including work with the first women voters of Costa Rica, studies on the effects of tourism on small rural towns, and other topics.

STANTON WORTHAM teaches at the University of Pennsylvania Graduate School of Education. His research applies techniques from linguistic anthropology to study interactional positioning and social identity development that go on under the surface of classroom discussion about subject matter. He has also studied discursive mechanisms for moral and political positioning in autobiographical narrative and media discourse. His work has involved action research and service learning, ethnography in urban and rural high schools and their surrounding communities, and discourse analysis. His recent publications include *Acting Out Participant Examples in the Classroom* (1994), *Narratives in Action* (2001) and *Education in the New Latino Diaspora* (2001).